Religious Liberty in Western and Islamic Law

RELIGIOUS LIBERTY IN WESTERN AND ISLAMIC LAW

Toward a World Legal Tradition

Kristine Kalanges

OXFORD
UNIVERSITY PRESS

OXFORD
UNIVERSITY PRESS

Oxford University Press, Inc., publishes works that further Oxford University's objective of excellence
in research, scholarship, and education.

Oxford New York
Auckland Cape Town Dar es Salaam Hong Kong Karachi Kuala Lumpur Madrid Melbourne
Mexico City Nairobi New Delhi Shanghai Taipei Toronto

With offices in
Argentina Austria Brazil Chile Czech Republic France Greece Guatemala Hungary
Italy Japan Poland Portugal Singapore South Korea Switzerland Thailand Turkey
Ukraine Vietnam

Published by Oxford University Press, Inc.
198 Madison Avenue, New York, New York 10016

Oxford is a registered trademark of Oxford University Press
Oxford University Press is a registered trademark of Oxford University Press, Inc.

Library of Congress Cataloging-in-Publication Data

Kalanges, Kristine.
  Religious liberty in Western and Islamic law : toward a world legal tradition /
Kristine Kalanges.
     p. cm.
  Includes bibliographical references and index.
  ISBN 978-0-19-985946-7 ((hardback) : alk. paper)
  1. Freedom of religion—United States 2. Freedom of religion (Islamic law)
  3. Freedom of religion (International law) 4. Religion and law. I. Title.
  K3258.K35 2012
  342.08'52—dc23   2011041067

123456789

Printed in the United States of America on acid-free paper

Note to Readers
This publication is designed to provide accurate and authoritative information in regard to the subject
matter covered. It is based upon sources believed to be accurate and reliable and is intended to be current as of the time it was written. It is sold with the understanding that the publisher is not engaged in
rendering legal, accounting, or other professional services. If legal advice or other expert assistance is
required, the services of a competent professional person should be sought. Also, to confirm that the
information has not been affected or changed by recent developments, traditional legal research techniques should be used, including checking primary sources where appropriate.

(Based on the Declaration of Principles jointly adopted by a Committee of the
American Bar Association and a Committee of Publishers and Associations.)

You may order this or any other Oxford University Press publication by
visiting the Oxford University Press website at www.oup.com

For my parents,
Kris and Denise Kalanges,
in whose home I first learned to love God and my neighbor.

And for my grandparents,
Jay and Marjorie Guthrie,
for their unfailing support.

CONTENTS

Author Biography   *xi*
Preface   *xiii*

1. Introduction   *1*
  I. Religious Liberty in Western and Islamic Law: Two
     Questions   *6*
  II. The Theoretical Challenge   *8*
    A. *The New Haven School*   *10*
    B. *Legal Rules and International Society*   *12*
    C. *World Legal Tradition: Berman's Comparative*
      Integrative Jurisprudence   *14*
    D. *Clarifying the Argument*   *22*
2. Theological and Philosophical Origins of Religious
  Liberty in the U.S. Constitution   *26*
  I. The Protestant Reformation and the Early
     Modern Origins of Freedom of Religion   *27*
    A. *Martin Luther and the Two Kingdoms*   *28*
    B. *John Calvin and Freedom of Conscience*   *32*
    C. *From Theological Doctrine to Democratic Form*   *35*
  II. The Genesis of the American Constitutional
     Experiment in Religious Liberty   *38*
    A. *The "Soul Liberty" of Roger Williams*   *42*
    B. *John Locke's Separation Principle*   *44*
    C. *James Madison and Religious Freedom as an*
      "Inalienable Right"   *46*
  III. Religious Freedom in the First Amendment
     of the U.S. Constitution   *47*
    A. *The Establishment Clause*   *49*
    B. *The Free Exercise Clause*   *51*

3. Religious Liberty in International Human
Rights Law   55
  I. Freedom of Religion in International
    Human Rights Law   56
    A. *Universal Declaration of Human Rights*   59
    B. *International Covenant on Civil and
      Political Rights*   62
    C. *U.N. Declaration on the Elimination of All Forms of
      Intolerance and of Discrimination Based on
      Religion or Belief*   64
    D. *Spotlight on the Issues–Religious Minorities
      and Proselytism*   68
  II. International Religious Rights: Monitoring and
    Enforcement Regimes   71
    A. *The U.S. Commission on International Religious
      Freedom*   71
    B. *The European Court of Human Rights*   73
  III. *Dignitatis Humanae*: The Catholic Church and
    the Moral Case for Religious Freedom   76
4. Religious Liberty and *Shari'a*   82
  I. Principles of Islamic Law–A Brief Overview   84
  II. Freedom of Religion in Islamic Law   90
    A. *The Rights of Religious Minorities*   91
    B. *Apostasy and Islam*   93
  III. Religious Liberty and Islamic Reformation   96
5. Between Religion and Law: Politics as
  an Intervening Variable   102
  I. Middle East Meets West: Political Contestation
    and Islamic Identity   104
    A. *Arab Nationalism and Islamism*   106
    B. *(Re)Constructing Middle Eastern Identity in
      Response to the West*   111
  II. Religious Liberty in the Constitutions of
    Muslim States   114
    A. *Freedom of Religion in Muslim
      States–A Brief Overview*   115
    B. *The Islamic Republic of Iran*   116
    C. *The Republic of Turkey*   123
    D. *The Arab Republic of Egypt*   128
    E. *The Islamic Republic of Pakistan*   134

6. Religious Liberty in Islamic
   International Law   *140*
      I. Islam and Human Rights–Origins of
         the Debate   *141*
      II. Religious Freedom in Islamic Human Rights
         Declarations   *147*
      III. Interpreting the Emergence of Contemporary
         Islamic International Law   *151*
      IV. Some Regional and Strategic Implications of the
         International Debate   *156*
7. Conclusion: Toward a World Legal Tradition   *168*

Index   *183*

AUTHOR BIOGRAPHY

Kristine Kalanges is Assistant Professor of Justice, Law and Society in the School of Public Affairs at American University. She holds a JD from Yale Law School, where she was a John M. Olin Fellow in Law, Economics, and Public Policy, and a PhD from Georgetown University, where she was a Graduate Fellow in International Relations. Previously, she practiced law in the New York office of Cleary Gottlieb Steen & Hamilton LLP and served in Washington, D.C. as a law clerk for the U.S. Department of Justice.

PREFACE

This book argues that differences between Western and Islamic legal formulations of religious freedom are attributable, in substantial part, to variations in their respective religious-intellectual histories. Further, it suggests that while divergence between the two bodies of law challenges the characterization of religious liberty as a uniform, universal human right, the dilemma of religious freedom – the difficult choice between the universality of religious liberty rights and peaceful co-existence of diverse legal cultures – may yet be transformed through the cultivation of a world legal tradition. This argument is advanced through comparative analysis of human rights instruments from the Western and Muslim worlds, with attention to the legal-political processes by which religious and philosophical ideas have been institutionalized.

The first part of the book charts the evolution of religious liberty as a human right in the West, beginning with the influence of Reformation theology (e.g., Luther's separation of church and state and Calvin's theology of limited sovereignty and natural law). Protestant ideas were elaborated and modified in early America, where the religious and philosophical arguments of Roger Williams, John Locke, and James Madison centrally informed the Establishment and Free Exercise Clauses of the First Amendment to the U.S. Constitution.

This historic experiment in religious liberty contributed, in turn, to the Western formulation of religious freedom as a human right, as reflected (albeit incompletely) in the 1948 Universal Declaration of Human Rights, the 1966 International Covenant on Civil and Political Rights, and the 1981 U.N. Declaration on the Elimination of All Forms of Intolerance and of Discrimination Based on Religion or Belief. Against the backdrop of these international treaty debates, a comprehensive rationale for religious freedom and human rights was offered in the teachings and diplomacy of the Catholic Church – a rationale rooted in both reason and Christian revelation.

During roughly the same historical period (i.e., the latter half of the twentieth century), Islamic international law (*as-siyar*) began to emerge as an alternative/oppositional human rights paradigm. Its formulations of religious freedom were, and remain, facially incompatible with global human rights norms. The second part of the book explores the reasons for, and the implications of, this conflict.

From the outset of the tradition, Islam maintained that there should be no compulsion in religion. Yet classical Islamic law also differentiated between the rights of Muslims and non-Muslims, as well as between different types of non-Muslims; the legacy of this *dhimmi* system has persisted, to the detriment of religious freedom for religious minorities. Also, as orthodox Islam has traditionally proclaimed *Shari'a* to be eternal and immutable truth, apostasy has been punishable by serious physical pain or death. At least historically, Islamic law has proven to be inconsistent with accepted international standards of religious freedom. Because Islam is not just a religion of rules, but also one of interpretation (in some though not all schools of thought), Muslim reformers have advocated for changes in the Islamic approach to religious liberty. Their efforts have been complicated, however, by shifts in the political landscape, especially the rise of political Islam.

Beginning in the 1970s, Islamists sought to institutionalize their religious and political power in state constitutions, to the detriment of religious freedom in countries like Iran, Egypt, and Pakistan. Concurrently, and building on the momentum of national and transnational Muslim identification, they started developing Islamic alternatives to Western international law. The resulting agreements, such as the Universal Islamic Declaration of Human Rights and the Cairo Declaration on Human Rights in Islam, challenge the universality of religious human rights. Even in Muslim-majority Turkey, a declared secular state, Islam remains an immediate and powerful force animating legal-political action and debates about the scope and content of religious liberty.

To the extent that contemporary *as-siyar* represents a countermodel of human rights, the dilemma of religious freedom would appear to hold: the universality of religious human rights could not be secured alongside institutional recognition of formulations based on *Shari'a*. However, Muslim reformers offer a different vision of Islam, under which the scope and content of religious liberty could perhaps be universalized, even as diverse religious and philosophical principles were invoked to legitimate the resulting laws and institutions. This appears to be in part what Harold Berman meant by a world legal tradition. Yet, as the Conclusion suggests, religious liberty is threatened not only in the Muslim world but also in the West, where defending it will require remembering and recovering the foundations of Western and international human rights law in, among other things, Judeo-Christianity. Therefore, cultivating sustainable pluralism, while providing for and protecting religious freedom and human rights, will depend upon bringing the faiths of many (including those beyond the Western and Islamic worlds) into conversation with the reason that is accessible to all.

This project was initially conceived during my graduate studies at Yale Law School and Georgetown University. It evolved into a dissertation under the guidance of a distinguished faculty committee to whom I am most grateful: Anthony Clark Arend (Chair) and Christopher Joyner, who co-led the Institute for International Law and Politics, and Thomas Banchoff, who directs the Berkley Center for Religion, Peace, and World Affairs – all at Georgetown. My graduate studies were generously funded by the University's Department of Government.

Additional support was graciously provided by American University, as I conducted further research and revised the manuscript for publication. I have received encouragement and excellent advice from many colleagues in the School of Public Affairs, including Bill Davies, Jon Gould, Mana Zarinejad, Diane Singerman, Ed Maguire, Rita Simon, Mohamed Alaa, Gamze Zeytinci, Meg Weekes, and Bill LeoGrande. Hadar Harris at AU's Washington College of Law provided an opportunity for me to discuss these ideas with legal academic faculty from Pakistan. Helpful research assistance was performed by Stephanie Slade. Anna Castro always made sure I had everything I needed. Allison Comins-Richmond welcomed me when I arrived at AU.

This book was brought to completion by an outstanding team at Oxford University Press, including my editor, Kevin Pendergast, and assistant editors, Jessica Picone and Courtney Thorpe. Jeremy Bernfeld and Zachary Marco provided valuable editing assistance. Two anonymous reviewers prepared very thoughtful comments that were instrumental in clarifying and strengthening the manuscript. When I presented a draft of Chapter 6 at the American Political Science Association, Mahmood Monshipouri similarly offered an insightful reading and instructive guidance. As I was wrapping up this project, Zachary Calo generously connected me to law and religion scholars around the world who are interested in similar issues: my conversations with Zak have been a source of renewed energy and purpose about the important work that remains to be done.

Several other people provided helpful comments on early portions of this work, including Oona Hathaway, Giulia Good Stefani, Michael Gottesman, Chris Mandernach, and Rick Bailey. I received additional insight on various ideas engaged here from Anthony Kronman, Joshua Mitchell,

Daniel Brumberg, Charles Kupchan, James Q. Whitman, and W. Michael Reisman. My thinking about the relationship between law and culture was influenced by time spent working with Roy Godson and Jeff Berman. For conversations that informed my approach to these matters more generally, I thank Sean Strasburg, Sarah Pitlyk, Christian Huebner, Josh Copeland, Fr. Richard Cipolla, Parag Khanna, Vivek Krishnamurthy, Anthony Martinez, and Brian Smith. Kate Desormeau, Meghan Giulino, James Fleming, and Dan Winter were supportive throughout, as were my sisters, Amber Pierce and Jill Kalanges, and my brother-in-law, Sam Pierce.

Also, I would be remiss if I did not take this opportunity to acknowledge the many public school teachers who helped a young girl from humble roots pursue big dreams. While the list is too long to include here, please know that I remember you all with gratitude. Special appreciation goes to Gail Gardner and Judy Robinson, who introduced me to oratory and debate, and Pat Crouser, who refined my writing.

I am particularly thankful for Dave Balaam, my undergraduate mentor and dear friend, who has remained throughout the years a kindred spirit, source of wisdom, and fellow traveler. The same can be said of Ryan Polich and Bob Hemm, who have profoundly affected the way I think, live, and experience the world. Most people are fortunate if they have one such friend; I have been extraordinarily blessed with two.

Finally, I am often asked how it is that I came to study the intersection of law and politics with religion. The roots of this are in my childhood. When I was twelve years old, two things happened that were to shape the course of my intellectual life. First, I read everything I could find in the county library system on the Holocaust, which sparked a deep and lasting concern with justice. Second, my father began introducing me to classic works of theology and philosophy, framed by conversations about the consequences of ideas. While my thinking has certainly developed and evolved over the years, my core interests have remained fundamentally the same. But to this desire to seek truth has been added the foundational call to love and serve others – something I learned from my mother. This book, then, and the larger research agenda of which it is part reflect who I have become under the enduring influence of my first teachers: Kris and Denise Kalanges. It is to them that this work is dedicated; and to my grandparents, Jay and Marjorie Guthrie, who have loved and supported me unfailingly, and from whom I have gotten the feistiness that has helped me to persevere in the face of all obstacles.

Of course, the opinions expressed herein, and any errors, are entirely my own. In writing about an inherently interdisciplinary subject, I have traversed widely over fields in which there are rich literatures and accomplished experts. I welcome their conversation and endeavor to continue deepening my knowledge and understanding.

Washington, DC
2011

CHAPTER 1

Introduction

The formation of a world legal tradition, combining the Western legal tradition with that of other cultures, will inevitably challenge each legal tradition to examine the belief-system that it reflects and to compare that belief-system with the belief-systems underlying the others. All such belief-systems share a common commitment to a spiritual reality that guides the process by which love of neighbor is to be practiced. Such a commitment is necessary if the forces of world integration are to overcome the forces of disintegration, and if the integration is to take place not in the unholy spirit of the Tower of Babel but with full respect for the pluralism of its constituent elements.

—*Harold J. Berman*[1]

It can be easy to perceive within the framework of international human rights law a universalism that transcends religious and political difference. The language of law itself contributes to this impression, framed as it so often is in terms of legitimate authority and neutral principles. However, in an era of globalization, the nature and extent of such legitimacy and neutrality appear as questions in the eyes of ever more diverse beholders, and while those who look with a Western gaze may be satisfied (at least initially), those whose vision has been shaped by the non-Western world sometimes see matters differently.

These differences are salient to debates about human rights, generally, and the right to freedom of religion or belief, in particular. Religious liberty, sometimes referred to as the first freedom, emerged and evolved within a specific historical context—one integrally informed by both sacred and secular intellectual traditions in the West, as well as by their attendant legal-political institutionalization. As international law has developed,

---

1. Harold J. Berman, "The Western Legal Tradition in a Millennial Perspective: Past and Future," *Louisiana Law Review* 60 (2000): 763.

its reach has expanded to include states outside of this originary context. The vast majority of these have demonstrated a strong desire to participate in the constitutive processes by which international law is constructed. Whether they are willing or able to arrive at the same human rights formulations, especially with regard to freedom of religion, is a separate question and one that is the subject of this book.

Before proceeding to a discussion of the specific research project, however, a few preliminary observations are in order: first, on the relationship between religious liberty and human rights; and second, on the global resurgence of religion and its significance for contemporary international law and politics.

As to the first point, religious liberty rights merit special attention in part because they are closely correlated (for reasons that will be conceptually developed in later chapters) with the observance of other human rights. For example, in one comparison of ratings for religious freedom with ratings for political rights and civil liberties in one hundred one countries, the ratings for religious freedom were identical to or within one point of the ratings for civil liberties in eighty-seven of them.[2] This "interdependence of human rights" is further suggested by the fact that violations of religious rights "almost invariably" involve the violation of other rights, including those catalogued by international law scholar Johan D. van der Vyver: "the right to life, liberty and security of the person; the right to freedom from torture or cruel, inhuman, or degrading treatment or punishment; the right to freedom from discrimination; the right to a fair and public hearing by an independent and impartial tribunal; the right to freedom of movement and residence; the right to freedom of opinion and expression; freedom of assembly and association; and the right to privacy."[3] In other words, "[r]eligion not only exists in a transcendent realm but is a fundamental and integral part of all human freedom."[4]

This connection assumes even greater significance in view of the second point, namely, that the world is experiencing a religious resurgence with profound implications for contemporary international relations. To be more precise, it is not so much that greater numbers of people are religious

2. Paul A. Marshall, "The Range of Religious Freedom," in *Religious Freedom in the World*, ed. Paul A. Marshall (Lanham, MD: Rowman & Littlefield, 2008), 8.
3. Johan D. van der Vyver and John Witte, Jr., eds., introduction to *Religious Human Rights in Global Perspective: Legal Perspectives* (Boston: Martinus Nijhoff Publishers, 1996), XLVI.
4. Marshall, "The Range of Religious Freedom," 8. See also Brian J. Grim and Roger Finke, *The Price of Freedom Denied: Religious Persecution and Conflict in the Twenty-First Century* (New York: Cambridge University Press, 2011).

(even though their choice of religion may be changing, as with the spread of Pentecostalism throughout the Global South), but rather that their religiosity has acquired new theoretical and empirical salience for international law and politics.

Even prior to the September 11th terrorist attacks, the "secularization thesis" (i.e., that modernization leads inevitably to a decline in religious experience at both social and individual levels) was being challenged.[5] Leading sociologists observed that while modernization has had some secularizing effects, it has also led to counter-secularization movements; moreover, social secularization does not necessarily imply secularization at the level of individual belief and behavior, and some religious organizations continue to exert social and political influence despite loss of widespread membership.[6] Additionally, the religious communities that have survived and prospered in modern society are precisely those that, contrary to expectation, have refused adaptation strategies, instead maintaining "beliefs and practices dripping with . . . supernaturalism."[7] Some of these are, as shall be seen, the same religious communities whose contributions to the development of religious liberty as a human right provide international law with powerful moral anchors.

Perhaps it should not be surprising, then, that nearly four centuries after the publication of Grotius's *De Jure Belli ac Pacis* (positing law as a means of tempering religious war), religion remains bound up with the cultivation of international law. Indeed, religious teachings and traditions have historically been fertile sources of international legal content, providing inspiration for enthusiasts (e.g., the nineteenth-century movement to promote international arbitration and adjudication), and serving as a legitimating force that, in turn, generates voluntary compliance.[8] As law and religion scholar John Witte, Jr. notes:

> [H]uman rights laws are inherently abstract ideals . . . [that] depend upon the
> visions of human communities and institutions to give them content and

---

5. Barry Rubin, "Religion and International Affairs," in *Religion, the Missing Dimension of Statecraft*, ed. Douglas Johnston and Cynthia Sampson (New York: Oxford University Press, 1994), 21.

6. Peter L. Berger, "The Desecularization of the World: A Global Overview," in *The Desecularization of the World: Resurgent Religion and World Politics*, ed. Peter L. Berger (Grand Rapids, MI: Ethics and Public Policy Center & William B. Eerdmans Publishing Company, 1999), 2–3.

7. Ibid., 4.

8. Scott Thomas, "The Global Resurgence of Religion, International Law and International Society," in *Religion and International Law*, ed. Mark W. Janis and Carolyn Evans (Boston: Martinus Nijhoff Publishers, 1999), 321–22.

coherence, to provide the "scale of values governing the(ir) exercise and concrete manifestation." Religion is an ineradicable condition of human lives and communities. Religions invariably provide . . . "scales of values" by which many persons and communities govern themselves.[9]

Put briefly, an international legal and political system built on democracy and human rights needs religion to survive.[10]

Yet acknowledging the vital role of religion poses new problems even as it solves others. In recent decades, more than one hundred new, mostly non-Western states have joined the international political community, bringing with them a wide variety of religious teachings and traditions.[11] While modernity may not have borne out the secularization thesis, it has undeniably resulted in religious pluralism in social life and at the level of individual consciousness.[12] Globalization and its corresponding patterns of migration have accelerated this process, leaving virtually no corner of the world untouched by the diversity of faith communities.[13]

Importantly, religious pluralism is not solely a result of modernity, but also represents a reaction to it: that is, the global resurgence of religion reflects, in part, "the failure of the modernising, secular state to produce both democracy and development in the Third World," as well as "the search for authenticity" in such countries.[14] This is particularly relevant given legal-political landscapes in which religious plurality is hierarchically ordered—with majority religious traditions and dominant political cultures shaping the coexistence of faith communities.[15]

In sum, if religion is an important source of international legal norms, if globalization means that religious and value homogeneity can no longer be taken for granted, and if the global resurgence of religion in part represents a project of self-definition by non-Western countries, then variation among the religious traditions (and legal-political cultures) that dominate Western and non-Western states suggests a fundamental challenge to the

9. John Witte, Jr., "Law, Religion and Human Rights," *Columbia Human Rights Law Review* 28 (1996): 2.

10. Ibid., 31.

11. Mark W. Janis, introduction to *Religion and International Law*, xi.

12. Peter L. Berger, "Orthodoxy and Global Pluralism," *Demokratizatsiya* (Summer 2005): 438.

13. Ibid., 439.

14. Scott M. Thomas, "Taking Religious and Cultural Pluralism Seriously: The Global Resurgence of Religion and the Transformation of International Society," *Millennium: Journal of International Studies* 29, no. 3 (2000): 817.

15. Thomas Banchoff, introduction to *Democracy and the New Religious Pluralism* (New York: Oxford University Press, 2007), 6.

universalizabilty of the principles upon which international human rights law is based.[16]

This tension is evident both at the meta-level (i.e., human rights broadly conceived) and with regard to specific rights (e.g., freedom of religion). The former is rendered problematic because "(t)he religions disagree among themselves about the nature of human beings, their goal, their good, and their responsibilities, and this disagreement is clearly demonstrated in different approaches to human rights."[17] Similarly, the latter is complicated by the growing religious pluralism in states, which correlates with increases in problems concerning freedom of religion.[18]

Against this backdrop emerges what might be termed "the dilemma of religious freedom," poignantly captured by international relations scholar Daniel Philpott:

> [A]lthough religious freedom is central to the tradition of human rights, expressed in both international and constitutional law and in moral and religious sources, it is also contrary to the principled policies of several contemporary regimes. It is a right that, if valid, ought to limit the sovereignty of states, yet one whose validity is contested. … Relinquishing [sic] an important human rights commitment or provoke conflict over deep values: this is the difficult choice.[19]

A difficult choice indeed—one that echoes across the literature and policy debates, haunted by the specter of Samuel P. Huntington's "clash of civilizations" thesis, and, if unnavigable, one that would bode ill for the prospects of a (relatively) peaceful international order founded on democracy and human rights.[20] This book is not naïve about the nature and stakes of religion and politics, but neither is it prepared to concede the inevitability of a (paradoxical) trade-off between human rights and peaceful coexistence. Thus, it attempts to reframe the debate such that the choice not only becomes traversable, but is itself transformed.

16. W. Michael Reisman, "Aftershocks: Reflections on the Implications of September 11," *Yale Human Rights and Development Law Journal* 6 (2003).

17. Peter Stuart, "A Christian Perspective on Religious Freedom in a Pluralist World," *Stimulus* 15, no. 2 (May 2007): 38.

18. Tage Kurten, "Introduction: Freedom of Religion in a New Millennium," *Studia Theologica* 54 (2000): 2.

19. Daniel Philpott, "Religious Freedom and the Undoing of the Westphalian State," *Michigan Journal of International Law* 25 (2004): 993.

20. Samuel P. Huntington, *The Clash of Civilizations and the Remaking of World Order* (New York: Simon & Schuster, 1998).

To do so requires journeying through the conceptual, legal, and political history of religious liberty in the human rights instruments of the West, as well as in those of the most developed alternative human rights paradigm to date—that which is oriented by Islam.[21] The contours of this journey are as follows.

I. RELIGIOUS LIBERTY IN WESTERN AND ISLAMIC LAW: TWO QUESTIONS

Speaking of his experience as a member of the 1946 UNESCO Committee on the Theoretical Bases of Human Rights, Jacques Maritain famously stated, "We agree on these rights, *provid[ed] we are not asked why*. With the 'why,' the dispute begins."[22] This pithy observation captured the tremendous difficulty in attempting to craft a global consensus around the foundation for human rights, a consensus that was not achieved despite the accomplishment of the 1948 Universal Declaration of Human Rights (UDHR). This lack of underlying agreement acquired new significance in 1981, and again in 1984, when Said Rajaie-Khorassani, Iran's representative to the 36th and 39th sessions of the United Nations General Assembly, declared that the UDHR represented a secular interpretation of Judeo-Christian tradition that could not be implemented by Muslim states.[23] Throughout, this book analyzes that claim, focusing especially on the right to freedom of religion or belief.

The international legal substance of religious liberty rights will be explored at length in proceeding chapters. For now, it is worth noting that debates about this right include not only the boundaries of free thought,

21. Neither the "West" nor "Islamic" (and permutations thereof) are unproblematic terms. There is tremendous diversity within each grouping, not just between them. However, as this book shows, they are analytically and historically meaningful categories that illuminate certain ideational and institutional differences, which are in turn legally and politically salient. This project endeavors to remain true to their complexity and sometimes contradictions, while presenting the important insights that may be gained by their use.

22. Kevin J. Hasson, "Religious Liberty and Human Dignity: A Tale of Two Declarations," *Harvard Journal of Law and Public Policy* 27 (2003): 81, quoting Jacques Maritain, *Man and the State* (Chicago: University of Chicago Press, 1956), 77 (alteration in Hasson, italics in original).

23. David G. Littman, "Human Rights and Human Wrongs," *National Review Online* (January 19, 2003); U.N. GAOR, 36th Sess., 3d Committee, paras. 10–19, U.N. Doc. A/C.3/36/SR.29 (Nov. 4, 1981); U.N. GAOR, 39th Sess., 3d Committee, paras. 91–95, U.N. Doc. A/C.3/39/SR.65 (Dec. 17, 1984).

but also those of free exercise, that is, the extent to which "religious orientations, rationales, and authorities of any kind are permitted a determinative role in the lives of their carriers and in the operation of other social institutions."[24] These controversies are directly relevant to the question of the (in)compatibility of Western and Islamic understandings of freedom of religion. For example, in a study of forty-four predominantly Muslim countries, the U.S. Commission on International Religious Freedom found that despite the ratification by many of them of the UDHR and the International Covenant on Civil and Political Rights (ICCPR), several nonetheless maintain constitutional provisions that limit the freedom to manifest a religion or belief, in contradiction to their treaty obligations.[25] What is striking is not the inconsistency per se, but rather that it is so widespread among countries that claim an Islamic identity.[26]

This fact, in keeping with others to be presented and in view of both the statement made by Iran's representative and the creation of alternative human rights models by Islamic states, raises two primary research questions. First, why are there differences between Western and Islamic human rights instruments as they pertain to freedom of religion or belief? Second, what are the implications of these differences for religious liberty as a human right? These two questions are intended as positive (or descriptive) endeavors. However, insofar as it calls for a response, the second question also contains an explicitly normative dimension.

In reply to the first question, this book demonstrates that variation in the religious-intellectual histories of the Western and Islamic worlds has contributed significantly to divergence in their respective formulations of freedom of religion or belief. Ideas matter, especially religious ones.

24. Peter Beyer, "Constitutional Privilege and Constituting Pluralism: Religious Freedom in National, Global, and Legal Context," *Journal for the Scientific Study of Religion* 42, no. 3 (2003): 334.

25. Tad Stahnke and Robert C. Blitt, "The Religion-State Relationship and the Right to Freedom of Religion or Belief: A Comparative Textual Analysis of the Constitutions of Predominantly Muslim Countries," *Georgetown Journal of International Law* 36 (2005): 947–1078.

26. This also suggests one fundamental problem with the argument, associated with noted human rights scholar Jack Donnelly, that the absence of philosophical consensus on the foundation of human rights is ultimately unimportant in view of the actual/practical consensus that exists. See Jack Donnelly, *Universal Human Rights in Theory and Practice* (Ithaca: Cornell University Press, 1989). International human rights treaties are one obvious measure of this practical consensus. However, insofar as those pertaining to religious liberty are persistently violated by signatories with a common religious-cultural orientation, there is good reason to suspect that the absence of an underlying philosophical consensus does indeed matter and that practical consensus will not suffice.

In response to the second question, this book suggests that while these divergent formulations indeed challenge the characterization of religious liberty as a uniform, universal human right, they do not necessarily result in an intractable "dilemma of religious freedom." Rather, the cultivation of a world legal tradition bears the hope that human rights and religious pluralism can meaningfully coexist.

II. THE THEORETICAL CHALLENGE

This book sits squarely at the intersection of international law and politics. As such, it should draw upon the theoretical insights of both disciplines. While that may sound facile, it is potentially quite complicated: international relations (IR) theory is prone to dismiss international law as epiphenomenal, while international legal scholars often fail to account sufficiently for the realities of political power. There is, too, the additional burden of incorporating religion, for this project claims that religious ideas drive the unfolding of legal-political processes in history. Thus, the search for a coherent theoretical framework is especially challenging, but also very necessary.

In order to understand the framework chosen and its particular appropriateness for the research questions at hand, it is helpful to start with an overview of the main schools of thought at the intersection of international law and politics, including what we might learn from them and what they risk obscuring. A particularly clear picture of the evolution of modern international relations theory and its connection to international law is provided by Christopher C. Joyner, who describes it in terms of the "four intellectual waves" of the twentieth century—idealism, realism, neoliberalism, and constructivism.[27]

Historically, idealism emphasized international law, morality, and multilateral organization, rather than power politics, as the driving forces in international relations; its regard for morality as the source of international political and legal principles is reflected in contemporary human rights law.[28] Under the weight of the incredible destruction and depravity of the Second World War, however, idealism gave way to realism's focus on

27. Christopher C. Joyner, "International Law Is, as International Relations Theory Does?," review of "Foundations of International Law and Politics," by Oona A. Hathaway and Harold Hongju Koh, and "The Politics of International Law," ed. Christian Reus-Smit, *American Journal of International Law* 100 (2006): 249–50.
28. Ibid., 250–51.

politics as the struggle for power—a perspective helpful for understanding the significance of political processes, but less instructive as to why, absent a central enforcing authority, governments nevertheless obey "nearly all international rules nearly all of the time."[29]

The importance of domestic politics and the role of international norms and institutions in fostering this type of cooperation are seemingly better explained by neoliberalism, which emphasizes how international law and organizations can improve society in conjunction with state and non-state actors.[30] For example, stable forms of cooperation include international legal regimes (consisting of principles, norms, rules, and decision-making procedures), which may be especially well-positioned to promote multilateral collaboration on matters of serious concern.[31]

Despite their differences, each of these three schools of thought is relatively static in comparison to the fourth. Through its insistence that legal-political realities result from the mutually-constitutive interaction of agents and structures (e.g., international agreements and laws), constructivism spotlights factors such as legitimacy, narrative, deliberation, and the dynamic character of international order.[32] It also brings the relationship between internal and external morality—mediated by rhetorical knowledge—to the forefront, creating openings for international, intercultural, and interdisciplinary acts of interpretation and change over time.[33]

From these four intellectual waves of IR theory, scholars and decision-makers collectively receive insights relevant to the research questions: from idealism, morality as a source of international principles; from realism, the importance of power and the political process; from neoliberalism, the ability of international law and organizations to secure cooperation; and from constructivism, the formation of meaning and the instantiation of legitimacy at the intersection of ideas and institutions. These perspectives facilitate analysis of the comparative legal, religious, and political traditions in the Western and Islamic worlds from many angles.

Still, they are foremost political theories, which only secondarily pay (varying degrees of) attention to history, religion, and the law. Absent an

---

29. Ibid., 252.
30. Ibid., 253–54.
31. Christopher C. Joyner, "Legal Theory in Ferment: What International Legal Theory Can Learn from International Relations Theory," *American Society of International Law Proceedings* 94 (2000): 213.
32. Joyner, "International Law Is, as International Relations Theory Does?," 255–56.
33. Jutta Brunnee and Stephen J. Toope, "International Law and Constructivism: Elements of an Interactional Theory of International Law," *Columbia Journal of Transnational Law* 39 (2000).

explicitly jurisprudential component, each is ultimately inadequate to the task of explaining precisely why religious liberty rights are different in the two spheres and what scholars, jurists, and political leaders are to make of it. For that, a theoretical framework better tailored to the crossroads of law and politics is needed—one that recognizes the operation of international law in political arenas, as well as the variation of international legal contexts across time, space, and culture.[34] Next, three alternative frameworks are considered in turn, the last of which incorporates religion and is thus preferred.

A. The New Haven School

One possible alternative to mainstream international relations theory is the New Haven School of jurisprudence.[35] Characterized by a policy-science approach, the New Haven School understands law not as a body of rules, but as a social process of decision.[36] Importantly, in focusing on the world constitutive processes by which law is constructed, this jurisprudential tradition reveals the political character of legal formation—especially in the international arena. Because it appreciates the potential importance of a wide variety of actors beyond the unitary sovereign state, it diffuses sovereignty and, some argue, may even facilitate legal pluralism.[37]

The New Haven School's techniques are also helpful for understanding a multiplicity of views. For example, it emphasizes "observational standpoint," such that scholars are called upon to recognize the profound impact of their own cultural categories on cross-cultural observation,[38] as well as "contextual mapping," based on the principle that legal concepts are more accurately understood when the contexts in which they are used are better understood.[39]

34. Christopher C. Joyner, "Stalking the Legal Lexicon of International Relations," review of *International Law: A Dictionary*, by Boleslaw A. Boczek, *International Studies Review* 8 (2006): 473–74.

35. W. Michael Reisman and Aaron M. Schrieber, *Jurisprudence: Understanding and Shaping Law* (New Haven: New Haven Press, 1987), 573–90.

36. Bardo Fassbender, "The United Nations Charter as Constitution of the International Community," *Columbia Journal of Transnational Law* 36 (1998): 544–46.

37. Paul Schiff Berman, "A Pluralist Approach to International Law," *Yale Journal of International Law* 32 (2007): 305–07.

38. W. Michael Reisman, "Autonomy, Interdependence, and Responsibility," *Yale Law Journal* 103 (1993): 403–04.

39. Winston P. Nagan and Craig Hammer, "The Changing Character of Sovereignty in International Law and International Relations," *Columbia Journal of Transnational Law* 43 (2004): 149.

The strengths of this jurisprudence are impressive, and its influence should not be underestimated. Nevertheless, it is also problematic in ways that are relevant to comparative religious and political analyses of law formation and compliance. For instance, critics of the New Haven School contend that:

> [b]y connecting process and context with an overriding set of normative values . . . [it] came to support the notion that "a clear and specific rule of law or treaty obligation may be disregarded if it is not in accord with a fundamental goal of the international community," a goal too often set by reference to U.S. national interest.[40]

Similarly, in addition to defining international law as that which is obeyed, and therefore rendering meaningless the question of whether one has an obligation to obey an unjust law (i.e., defining out a key moral and political inquiry),[41] the normative construct of the New Haven School "virtually dissolves the restraints of rules and opens the way for partisan or subjective policies disguised as law."[42]

Another difficulty warrants special attention here, for it concerns a concept that will make a pivotal appearance later in this book—human dignity.[43] According to the New Haven School, "[a] public order of human dignity is defined as one which approximates the optimum access by all human beings to all things they cherish: power, wealth, enlightenment, skill, well-being, affection, respect, and rectitude."[44] Rectitude, which refers in part to freedom of religion, involves the creation of inner worlds of meaning and value in the individual and collective life: the "rectitude process" is to be

40. Harold Hongju Koh, "Why Do Nations Obey International Law?," review of *The New Sovereignty: Compliance with International Regulatory Agreements*, by Abram Chayes and Antonia Handler Chayes, and *Fairness in International Law and Institutions*, by Thomas M. Franck, *Yale Law Journal* 106 (1997): 2623, quoting Oscar Schacter, "Symposium: McDougal's Jurisprudence: Utility, Influence, Controversy," *American Society of International Law Proceedings* 79 (1985): 271.

41. Eduardo Moises Penalver, "The Persistent Problem of Obligation in International Law," *Stanford Journal of International Law* 36 (2000): 277–78.

42. Melissa A. Waters, "Normativity in the 'New' Schools: Assessing the Legitimacy of International Legal Norms Created by Domestic Courts," *Yale Journal of International Law* 32 (2007): 457.

43. For an analysis of the ways in which the U.S. Supreme Court and constitutional courts the world over employ diverse concepts of human dignity, and how those concepts can and often do conflict, see Neomi Rao, "Three Concepts of Dignity in Constitutional Law," *Notre Dame Law Review* 86 (2011).

44. W. Michael Reisman, Siegfried Wiessner, and Andrew R. Willard, "The New Haven School: A Brief Introduction," *Yale Journal of International Law* 32 (2007): 576.

universally protected by international human rights law, even though the actual content of various rectitude processes differs across cultures.[45]

This combination of purportedly objective structure and subjective content may be understood as representing "the modernist attempt to retain human access to unconditional truth by supplanting religion with science, in this instance social science."[46] Unfortunately, by failing to recognize that religious teachings and traditions contribute not only to the content of law and morality but also to the very processes by which that content is determined, the New Haven School cannot adequately engage questions about the (in)commensurability of human rights formulations insofar as they derive from (different) religious foundations.

Moreover, by rendering the specific content of rectitude (and thus freedom of religion) almost entirely relative, it becomes considerably more awkward to assert that anything short of violent atrocity definitively violates the principle of human dignity. Thus, while the strengths of the New Haven School are instructive and certainly worth keeping in mind as this project proceeds, the School's limitations preclude its full application here.

B. Legal Rules and International Society

A second and related alternative to mainstream international relations theory is Anthony Clark Arend's model, explicated most fully in *Legal Rules and International Society*.[47] One trouble many international law scholars confront as they attempt to build bridges with international relations theorists is their own relative lack of methodological rigor; they tend to favor normative argument to the exclusion of positive empirical analysis.[48] Arend's work is a noteworthy exception—a genuinely interdisciplinary framework grounded in a methodology appropriate to scholars, practitioners, and policymakers alike.

45. W. Michael Reisman, "International Law and the Inner Worlds of Others," *Saint Thomas Law Review* 9 (1996): 25–26.
46. Richard A. Falk, "Casting the Spell: The New Haven School of International Law," review of *Jurisprudence for a Free Society: Studies in Law, Science and Policy*, by Harold D. Lasswell and Myres S. McDougal, *Yale Law Journal* 104 (1995): 2002.
47. Anthony Clark Arend, *Legal Rules and International Society* (New York: Oxford University Press, 1999).
48. Jack Goldsmith, "Sovereignty, International Relations Theory, and International Law," *Stanford Law Review* 52 (2000): 979–87.

He highlights "the distinctiveness of international *legal* rules and the role they play in international relations," exploring their function in structuring the international system, influencing state behavior, and regulating the activity of some non-state actors.[49] Arend's unique contribution is his synthesis of the insights of traditional positivism with those of the New Haven School—building on their individual strengths and attempting to avoid their weaknesses—all in service of a new method for identifying rules of international law.[50]

Reflecting his training as a scholar of international relations, Arend's model assumes that the international system is anarchic, that sovereign unitary states are the central actors, and that states consent to the creation of international law via treaties, custom, and general principles.[51] Then, reflecting his legal background, Arend draws upon the New Haven School to construct a basic authority-control test by which international rules may be identified: a rule of international law exists if it is authoritative and controlling (determined empirically with the aid of an index). To preserve methodological rigor, he qualifies the New Haven School by emphasizing identifiable decision-making elites (whose perceptions determine the existence of authority), the use of *opinio juris* as a concrete marker of the authoritativeness of a rule, and a separation of legal and moral rules (which also makes possible the examination of moral deficiencies in the law).[52]

There are several advantages to Arend's model. It coherently and compellingly interweaves constructivist international relations theory with two jurisprudential traditions, while providing international law with a method based on empirical data. Taken together, these features facilitate the rehabilitation of international law within the political science community (one main goal of the text). Moreover, it theoretically elucidates and empirically identifies distinct rules of international law, thereby demonstrating the relevance of international legal rules to interactions on the world stage. As a result, Arend reveals what might be termed the mutual constitution of international law and politics, which renders interdisciplinary research not only productive, but also necessary.[53]

49. Robert J. Beck, Anthony Clark Arend, and Robert D. Vander Lugt, *International Rules: Approaches from International Law and International Relations* (New York: Oxford University Press, 1996), 289–307.
50. Arend, *Legal Rules and International Society*, 86.
51. Ibid., 86–87.
52. Ibid., 87–88.
53. David J. Bederman, "Constructivism, Positivism, and Empiricism in International Law," *Georgetown Law Journal* 89 (2001).

With this in mind, the primary disadvantage of Arend's model for the research questions at hand is basically one of emphasis. His theory is primarily (though not exclusively) concerned with the identification of international legal rules—a crucial task, to be sure, but not one that is the focus of this book. Rather, this project begins with rules of international law and then asks from whence they came, with a view to understanding why different (religious) traditions generate different rules.

Admittedly, Arend's model suggests a potential weakness in this research design. Though the first half of the book is oriented by what he would presumably agree are legal rules (e.g., domestic rules in the case of the U.S. Constitution and international rules in the form of United Nations treaties), the second half centers on agreements (e.g., the Universal Islamic Declaration of Human Rights and the Cairo Declaration on Human Rights in Islam) that may not rise to the level of international legal rules as Arend defines them. There might be some debate on this point, and what determination would result is uncertain.

Nevertheless, even assuming that the Islamic human rights instruments were deemed insufficient as international legal rules, such would not prove especially harmful to this project for two reasons. First, while Islamic human rights law is nascent relative to its Western counterpart, this quality does not necessarily diminish either its present or its potential significance. Second, this book is at least as much concerned with the conceptual foundations of international legal rules (their legitimacy) as it is with the rules themselves (their authority and control). As will become evident, the conceptual development of Islamic human rights may be observed and analyzed well prior to their codification in binding rules of international law. Therefore, although Arend's model represents a considerable interdisciplinary achievement, it is not the one best suited to address this research problem.

C. World Legal Tradition: Berman's Comparative Integrative Jurisprudence

A third approach thus warrants consideration—one that incorporates law, religion and politics, provides for an understanding of change over time, and is explicitly global in scope and comparative in method. With more time to explore and cultivate this theory's tremendous potential, Harold J. Berman—the twentieth-century's leading scholar of law and religion—may have once again redefined the field. He died before he could fully articulate his vision for a world legal tradition (the latest instantiation of his integrative jurisprudence).[54] Fortunately, the general shape and elements of his theory are preserved, and, contextualized by his life's work, its foresight and creative genius are readily discernible.

Accordingly, in what is perhaps best understood as a project of theory development,[55] this book utilizes "world legal tradition" as the theoretical framework within which to explore the comparative development of religious liberty in Western and Islamic human rights instruments.[56] It employs Berman's theory as a guide to answering the research questions, seeking also to demonstrate the analytical leverage and practical power of his ideas.

Explaining Berman's contribution to the field of law and religion provides a good introduction to his thought. This is aptly done by Witte, who characterizes his mentor's work in the following way:

> [Berman] has demonstrated that law has a religious dimension, that religion has a legal dimension, and that legal and religious ideas and institutions are intimately tied. He has shown that there can be no divorce between jurisprudence and theology, legal history and church history, legal ethics and theological

54. Douglas Martin, Obituary, "Harold J. Berman, 89, Who Altered Beliefs About Origins of Western Law, Dies," *The New York Times*, November 18, 2007. See also Howard O. Hunter, ed., *The Integrative Jurisprudence of Harold J. Berman* (Boulder, CO: WestviewPress, 1996).

55. This book uses the term development, as distinct from construction, to signify the nascent state of world legal tradition as a theory. While Berman's "integrative jurisprudence" evolved over many years and is widely known and studied, world legal tradition is a relatively recent instantiation of it. All of its constitutive elements are identified by him, so this project certainly cannot claim to be constructing it. At the same time, I am unaware of its systematic application to questions at the intersection of international law and politics by any other scholars to date. Even Berman's own published writings do little more than sketch the possibilities in broad, rather abstract language. Hence, since one learns what a theory is in part by what it does, use of world legal tradition as a theoretical frame for the book (and the resulting application to the research questions) contributes to the development of the theory itself. For an earlier attempt to grapple with law and world culture, see Adda B. Bozeman, *The Future of Law in a Multicultural World* (Princeton, NJ: Princeton University Press, 1971). For a recent, albeit brief, mention of a world legal tradition in a somewhat different context, see David B. Goldman, *Globalisation and the Western Legal Tradition: Recurring Patterns of Law and Authority*, Law in Context (Cambridge, UK; New York: Cambridge University Press, 2007).

56. With rare exceptions, this book will refer to the theory as "world legal tradition," since that name distinguishes it from the broader intellectual endeavor to which it is related (i.e., "integrative jurisprudence"), while serving as a simpler, more accessible and relevant descriptor than possible alternatives (e.g., "ecumenical jurisprudence of the Holy Spirit"—another of Berman's designations).

ethics. He has argued that law and religion need each other—law to give religion its social form and function, religion to give law its spirit and vision.[57]

Yet, as Berman articulated in his *Law and Revolution* series, politics must also be considered as a third party to the intimate relationship between law and religion.[58] He had already planned a third volume in this series and, at the time of his death, was in the midst of planning a fourth.[59] Some of Berman's more recent work suggests that the development of a world legal tradition may have been a primary focus.

For example, in October 1999, Berman delivered two lectures on "The Western Legal Tradition in a Millennial Perspective: Past and Future," as part of Louisiana State University's Edward Douglass White Lectures on Citizenship.[60] The first lecture, on history, concerned the development of the Western legal tradition from its origins in the late eleventh and twelfth centuries through the national revolutions in Germany, England, France, and the United States (i.e., the subjects of his first two books in the *Law and Revolution* series).[61] The second lecture, on prophecy, concerned the crisis of the Western legal tradition in the twentieth century (e.g., the Russian Revolution and the World Wars), and also the future of the Western legal tradition as it enters a multicultural millennium and encounters an evolving tradition of world law.[62] These themes from the second lecture may have been the subjects of the planned third and fourth volumes of his *Law and Revolution* series, respectively. Indeed, Berman's discussion of world law provides the contours of an insightful new theory.

57. Martin E. Marty, "The Religious Foundations of Law," *Emory Law Journal* 54 (2005): 294, quoting John Witte, Jr., "A New Concordance of Discordant Canons: Harold J. Berman on Law and Religion," in Hunter, *Integrative Jurisprudence* 99 (alteration in Marty).

58. In *Law and Revolution: The Formation of the Western Legal Tradition* (Cambridge, MA: Harvard University Press, 1983), Berman discusses the roots of modern Western legal institutions and concepts in the papal revolution, when political lines were drawn between the Church and secular rulers. In *Law and Revolution II: The Impact of the Protestant Reformations on the Western Legal Tradition* (Cambridge, MA: Belknap Press of Harvard University Press, 2003), Berman explores how the sixteenth-century German Reformation and the seventeenth-century English Revolution gave birth to a civil order distinct from religion.

59. Martin, Obituary, "Harold J. Berman, 89, Who Altered Beliefs About Origins of Western Law, Dies."

60. Berman, "The Western Legal Tradition in a Millennial Perspective: Past and Future," 739.

61. Ibid., 739–52.

62. Ibid., 752–63.

Berman observes that community formation and the evolution of a common legal tradition require a common set of spiritual values, common concepts of human nature, and a shared understanding of the relation of persons to society; in short, a common language and a common belief system.[63] The great cultures of the world are distinguished, in part, by their different languages and different belief systems. Nonetheless, Berman notes:

> [I]n the twentieth century the diverse cultures of the world have been joined together in a world economy and in an emerging world society, with branches of a common world law and the beginnings of a world legal tradition. And that is the great challenge to humanity . . . to transform the world society into a world community and to transform the branches of world law into an evolving world legal tradition.[64]

On its own, his observation sounds optimistic to the point of naïveté and risks conjuring a false—and therefore dangerous—universalist utopia, not unlike that of the idealists during the interwar period. But Berman is well-steeped in history, and, shortly after this, he sets forth a more specific framework for the encounter between the Western and world legal traditions.

Berman's theory is relational: each tradition has something to learn from the other.[65] The contribution of the West is the very concept of a legal tradition itself, which includes "the conscious historical evolution of law . . . its conscious balancing of continuity and change, its concept of an ongoing autonomous legal tradition that can even survive great revolutions and be renewed by them."[66] According to Berman, this Western concept rests upon the integration of three main schools of legal philosophy: positivism (rooted in political will), natural law theory (rooted in moral reason and conscience), and historical jurisprudence (rooted in historical experience).[67]

---

63. Ibid., 761.
64. Ibid.
65. As a theory, world legal tradition is simultaneously descriptive, predictive, and normative. Berman believed in the accuracy and rightness of his historical sociological jurisprudence, its contemporary application, and his prediction that the third millennium would witness the transformation of the emerging world society into a world community—a transformation in which the gradual creation of a world legal tradition could and should play a pivotal role. Ibid., 763. A spiritual sense of hope, cautious but genuine, suffuses his remarks on the subject.
66. Ibid., 762.
67. These are the jurisprudential traditions that Berman long sought to combine in his "integrative jurisprudence." See Harold J. Berman, *Faith and Order: The Reconciliation of Law and Religion*, Emory University Studies in Law and Religion (Atlanta, GA:

Not until the twentieth century was natural law theory "almost wholly subordinated to positivism" and the historical school "almost entirely eliminated"—developments that Berman laments.[68]

Thus, the reciprocal contribution that an evolving world legal tradition can make to its Western counterpart is "to challenge it to rediscover its religious roots and its threefold source in . . . politics, morality, and history," to illuminate the untenability of separating the "is" of political will from the "ought" of moral reason and the "was and is becoming" of historical memory.[69] Elsewhere, Berman refers to this as part of a broader "integrative jurisprudence" and deems it necessary to the recognition, interpretation, and support of world law.[70] In summarizing what the West may learn from its encounter with the world legal tradition, Berman eloquently captures one theoretical ambition of this book: "the moral and historical basis of law in other cultures challenges the West to re-examine the moral and historical basis of its own legal tradition and to reconcile the various religious influences that in the past have played significant roles in the formation of that tradition."[71]

By bringing these two traditions—one established, one emergent, both evolving—into conversation with each other, Berman seeks peaceful integration defined by love of neighbor and meaningful respect for difference in the form of religious pluralism. This pluralism should recognize and integrate the Christian traditions of the West, including Roman Catholic, Lutheran, and Calvinist conceptions of law (which he correlates with natural law, positivism, and historical tradition, respectively); non-Christian faiths, including but not limited to Judaism and Islam, that "recognize the God-given character of the human qualities of will, reason, and memory;" and even secular belief systems (or civil religions) that privilege spiritual over material values in pursuit of order and justice.[72]

These traditions intersect not only in the West, but also in "world law," which Berman defines to include public international law, contractual and

Scholars Press, 1993). All of the relevant disciplines are there—law, politics, religion, and history. One way of understanding world legal tradition is as a consciously comparative integrative jurisprudence.

68. Berman, "The Western Legal Tradition in a Millennial Perspective: Past and Future," 762.

69. Ibid.

70. Harold J. Berman, "World Law: An Ecumenical Jurisprudence of the Holy Spirit," Emory University School of Law Public Law and Legal Theory Research Paper Series 05–4 (February 2005).

71. Berman, "The Western Legal Tradition in a Millennial Perspective: Past and Future," 763.

72. Berman, "World Law: An Ecumenical Jurisprudence of the Holy Spirit," 11.

customary legal norms governing cross-border relations among persons and enterprises—in short, "what was once called *jus gentium*, the law of nations, the common law of mankind, embracing common features of the various legal systems of the peoples of the world."[73] The vision thus seems to be one in which the great religions emphasize their tendency to be universalistic and tolerant (rather than their competing tendency to be exclusivist) in pursuit of a humane global governance—governance supported crucially, though not exclusively, by a comparative integrative jurisprudence of international law.[74]

Before exploring how world legal tradition as a theory informs the research method here, a clarifying theological observation is in order. Berman's analysis could be interpreted as attempting to reconcile the problem of the many and the one in the "world in time," and, by implication, as "immanentizing the eschaton."[75] In other words, world legal tradition might be understood as underestimating the extent of human brokenness and overestimating the capacity of human institutions—legal and political—to perfect an imperfect world.[76] If such were the case, it would, in the view of this project, represent a grave mistake: theologically speaking, it would flirt with pride; in the political arena, it would fundamentally misconstrue the dilemma and risk walking the road shared by all false universalisms in history—a pathway marked by ever more (not less) violence and injustice.[77]

This book cannot claim definitively that such an interpretation would be inaccurate. However, Berman, citing the influence of Christian historian and philosopher Eugen Rosenstock-Huessy, writes of the Holy Spirit as inspiring diverse peoples to listen to and learn from each other in the hope of overcoming divisive forces and discovering their common humanity.[78] The location of the unifying impulse in a transcendent source signals a

---

73. Ibid., 13.

74. Richard A. Falk, "A Worldwide Religious Resurgence in an Era of Globalization and Apocalyptic Terrorism," in *Religion in International Relations: The Return from Exile*, ed. Fabio Petito and Pavlos Hatzopoulos (New York: Palgrave, 2003), 184–85.

75. James V. Schall, "The Encyclical on Hope: On the 'De-Immanentizing' of the Christian Eschaton," *Ignatius Insight* (December 3, 2007).

76. William J. Wagner, "The Just and the Holy Are One: The Role of Eschatology in Harold Berman's Vision of Normative Jurisprudence," *Emory Law Journal* 42 (1993): 1075–77.

77. See, for example, Howard Caygill, *Levinas and the Political* (New York: Routledge, 2002).

78. Berman, "World Law: An Ecumenical Jurisprudence of the Holy Spirit," 4–5. Berman notes the following works by Rosenstock-Huessy: *The Christian Future: Or the Modern Mind Outrun* (New York, 1946), reprinted with Introduction by Harold Stahmer (New York, 1966), pp. 113–31; *Heilkraft und Wahrheit: Konkordanz der politischen und der kosmischen Zeit* (1952, reprinted 1991), p. 35ff.

certain theological humility that speaks to the above concerns, but does not entirely resolve them.

Therefore, because it implicates both how the theory is here developed and deployed (to answer the positive/descriptive research questions), as well as how the results are interpreted (to address the normative element), this project's assumptions should be rendered explicit: it maintains that religious differences are real, that they are significant, and that they will neither disappear nor cease to be relevant in world history. Religious beliefs and practices are sources of deep meaning for the vast majority of the world's people; hence, religious difference inherently bears the potential for conflict—legal, cultural, and political.

Even still, while this book does not advance a vision of human institutions as capable of eliminating this potential for discord generally and permanently, it does not follow that specific disputes cannot be mediated or diffused, or even that common ground cannot be established where once enmity reigned. Recalling the "dilemma of religious freedom," the immediate challenge is to transform the "difficult choice" between religious liberty as a universal human right and peaceful coexistence of diverse legal-political cultures. The cultivation of a world legal tradition is an important component of that transformation. This is the spirit in which Berman's theory is here understood, and this is the spirit in which it will be applied. A discussion of this book's methodology further illuminates this theoretical orientation.

World legal tradition focuses attention on the comparative moral and historical bases of law in the subject spheres of study—here, the Western and Islamic worlds. Within these two areas, its integrative jurisprudence requires consideration of the contributions made by religion, politics, and historical circumstance to the evolution of law. Berman's integration of these three is not syncretic. In particular, Berman emphasizes history (too often overlooked by legal scholars, in his opinion) both because its tendency toward synthesis imbues jurisprudence with coherence,[79] and also because it serves as a normative source of law.[80] Professor of law and philosophy William Wagner explains:

> Berman . . . holds the apprehension of value to originate historically and to be mediated through changing historical circumstances by means of subjective and objective human structures. It follows that the elements of an adequate

79. Wagner, "The Just and the Holy Are One," 1053.
80. Paula G. Shakelton, "Remembering What Cannot Be Forgotten: Using History as a Source of Law in Interpreting the Religion Clauses of the Connecticut Constitution," *Emory Law Journal* 52 (2003): 998.

normative jurisprudence should be found "piecemeal" in the record of historical reflection, awaiting the creative insight that can transform them into a synthesis capable of meeting the challenges at the moment.[81]

This recourse to historical record serves this book well, for it facilitates careful examination of the development and institutional processing of ideas over time.

In that light, this project proceeds as a comparative analysis of religious liberty in human rights instruments from the West and the Muslim world. It is comprised of two main parts. The first part (Chapters 2 and 3) charts the historical evolution of religious liberty as a human right in the West, noting especially: the significance of Reformation theology; early American constitutionalism; the development of modern human rights law; and the integration of religious freedom with human dignity in the teachings and diplomacy of the Catholic Church.[82]

The second part (Chapters 4, 5, and 6) probes the emergence of Islamic international law as an alternative/oppositional paradigm of human rights.[83] It discusses: religious freedom in Islamic law and thought from the classical through the modern periods; the resurgence of Islamic law and politics and the cultivation of Islamic identity in reaction to the secularism of Western imperial power; religious liberty laws and practices in four Muslim states; and contemporary Islamic international law.[84] The inclusion of political factors here is essential, as this problem cannot be adequately engaged from an exclusively legal or religious point of view.

Throughout, this book emphasizes the relationship between comparative religious context and the specific content of religious liberty in human rights provisions. Further, it analyzes the legal and political processes by which this relationship comes to be institutionalized. To that end, each chapter considers one or a series of legal texts (e.g., constitutions,

81. Wagner, "The Just and the Holy Are One," 1053–54.
82. Primary legal texts considered in the first part include: the U.S. Constitution; the 1948 Universal Declaration of Human Rights; the 1966 International Covenant on Civil and Political Rights; and the 1981 UN Declaration on the Elimination of All Forms of Intolerance and of Discrimination Based on Religion or Belief.
83. The term "alternative/oppositional" is used throughout this book to signify the different ways in which these documents can be interpreted. As Chapters 5 and 6 discuss, their nature and significance are contested.
84. Primary legal texts considered in the second part include: the constitutions of Iran, Turkey, Egypt, and Pakistan; the Universal Islamic Declaration of Human Rights; and the Cairo Declaration on Human Rights in Islam.

declarations, and treaties), exploring the conceptual progression and legal-political institutionalization of religious freedom that they represent.[85]

Collectively, this project seeks to break new theoretical ground by reframing the debate as one that must account for comparative religious context (i.e., not just the contributions of Islamic law to Muslim states, but also Judeo-Christian contributions to the Western legal tradition), and also by suggesting how a world legal tradition might be forged so as to constitute a new type of foundational consensus—one that could make practical consensus on religious liberty, and possibly other human rights issues, both achievable and lasting. It closes by discussing the legal, religious, and political implications of the research findings for the present historical moment. Specifically, it highlights the role of religion in constructing legal and political institutions capable not just of protecting religious liberty, but also more broadly of sustaining pluralism in the West.

D. Clarifying the Argument

As a subject, the encounter between the West and Islam is invariably controversial.[86] It would be neither possible nor helpful to address all of the related debates in a single book; therefore, defining the research questions and approach necessarily incorporates some issues to the exclusion of others. Moreover, discussions of foundational principles within and across religious-cultural systems can generate concerns about relativism, with

---

85. In order to trace the interaction of religious and secular arguments in policy debates effectively, comparative politics scholar Thomas Banchoff proposes a method for distinguishing between them. A policy argument counts as religious when it meets two conditions: first, it must (directly or indirectly) reference a particular religious tradition; and second, it must be articulated from within a particular religious tradition (by those who either identify with or authoritatively represent it). Banchoff defines religious tradition as "beliefs, practices, or institutions linked back to divine revelation or claims about the transcendent." Thomas Banchoff, "Stem Cell Politics, Religious and Secular: The United States and France Compared," in *Democracy and the New Religious Pluralism*, ed. Thomas Banchoff (New York: Oxford University Press, 2007), 304. Unless otherwise specified, the legal and political policy arguments that this book identifies as "religious" meet Banchoff's criteria.

86. Religion has made and will continue to make vital contributions to legal and political institutions. At times, it conditions the content and perceived legitimacy of law. The fact that certain religious beliefs and practices cause great harm is a matter of utmost concern and one that this book confronts directly. Informed criticism of religious claims can be a healthy and necessary element of robust legal and political debate; indeed, this project engages in such criticism at various points. The central issue is not "religion or no religion;" rather, it is one of specific religious claims and modalities.

significant descriptive and normative implications. Thus, before turning to the task at hand, a few thoughts on the choices made and philosophical approach adopted here.

1. Islamic Extremism

This book does not undertake a thorough examination of Islamic extremism. That may lead some to wonder whether its ability to treat the issue of Islam and human rights is thereby limited. Yet the general exclusion of Islamic extremism is intentional. As a preliminary matter, it distracts from the arguably more difficult question engaged in this project. No one is arguing that honor killings or terrorism represent a counter-model of human rights. Rather, insofar as those practices are defended, it is by appeal to a *particular* interpretation of Islam. Whether such represents a legitimate interpretation (and, by extension, whether such legitimacy if ascribed/conferred would render moot the question of compatibility between Islam and human rights) is indeed an important issue that merits careful scrutiny, but it is not the subject of this book.[87]

Instead, it begins not from an area of contestation, but from an area of *seeming* agreement: treaties signed by Western and Muslim-majority countries alike that determine international standards of religious liberty—a human right of special significance insofar as its protection/violation correlates with the protection/violation of many other human rights. The fact that said treaties are routinely, indeed, systematically violated by signatory countries that are predominantly Muslim raises the question of whether *any* interpretation of Islam is compatible with religious liberty. This is

87. For a provocative discussion of the relationship between religious extremism and terrorism, see Amos N. Guiora, *Freedom from Religion: Rights and National Security* (New York: Oxford University Press, 2009). Paul Cliteur argues that the roots of religious terrorism are to be found in religion itself, focusing his criticisms upon the Abrahamic faiths and advocating instead a particular form of moral and political secularism (characterized by atheism, criticism of religion, free speech, and moral autonomy). Paul Cliteur, *The Secular Outlook: In Defense of Moral and Political Secularism* (Hoboken, NJ: Wiley-Blackwell, 2010); Paul Cliteur, "Religion and Violence or the Reluctance to Study This Relationship," *Forum Philosophicum* 15 (2010). See also J. Caleb Clanton, review of *The Secular Outlook: In Defense of Moral and Political Secularism*, by Paul Cliteur, *Notre Dame Philosophical Reviews* (2011). Legal scholar Silvio Ferrari rejects this general proposition, arguing that it is important to distinguish religion and religious freedom from religious violence and extremism: the latter is unacceptable, while the former must be protected. Silvio Ferrari, "Individual Religious Freedom and National Security in Europe after September 11," *Brigham Young University Law Review* 2004 (2004).

compounded by the creation of documents such as the Universal Islamic Declaration of Human Rights and the Cairo Declaration on Human Rights in Islam, both of which diverge from international legal standards of religious freedom and both of which have been offered as an alternative/ oppositional paradigm of human rights.

Put differently, it is common to focus the debate on whether or not the Taliban and al-Qaeda represent "authentic Islam." It is less common and possibly more challenging to ask whether even the non-extreme forms of Islam are compatible with international human rights law. This bears centrally on the question of whose rights are to be protected, while also engaging the prior question of whether there is sustainable consensus as to the scope and content of those rights. The focus on religious liberty is therefore intended to illuminate issues that are fundamental but all too often lost when the whole of Islam and human rights, not to mention terrorism and Islamic extremism, are thrown into the mix. That said, to the extent that it bears directly on the research questions, Islamic extremism (including its internal effect upon the Muslim community, e.g., the persecution of non-dominant Muslim groups) is discussed in later chapters.

2. Cultural Relativism vs. World Legal Tradition

This book should in no way be construed as a defense of moral, philosophical, or cultural relativism—positions it deems to be ultimately indefensible. Nevertheless, it recognizes two empirical realities that make debates about Western and Islamic law incredibly difficult: first, there is no universal agreement as to the scope and content of international human rights provisions, particularly those concerned with religious liberty; and second, at least part of this disagreement stems from disputes that are religious and philosophical in character. This book documents those realities, considers their implications, and contemplates a way forward.

In so doing, it makes three core arguments, which should also be understood as contributions to the development of a world legal tradition. First, even accounting for the manipulation of religion by some politicians and factions in Muslim societies, certain interpretations of Islam are absolutely and undeniably incompatible with international legal standards of religious liberty.[88] Against such interpretations, religious freedom must be

---

88. Here, this book agrees with Bassam Tibi that the battle over human rights standards has a definite religious-cultural component. See Bassam Tibi, "Islamic Law/

unequivocally defended. The second argument concerns Islamic scholars who appear to offer a means of reconciling Islam with human rights law, which is highly relevant for those Muslim leaders and communities that embrace Islam as a significant criterion by which to evaluate legal and political institutions.[89] These interpretations of *Shari'a* may prove compatible with religious liberty, and if they gain support among a significant portion of the global Muslim population, the "dilemma of religious freedom" may become less intractable with time. The practical outcome of these scholars' work is by no means guaranteed, but both the Western and Muslim worlds should hope that they succeed.

Third, this book argues that an integral part of any discussion of Western or international human rights law is serious consideration of its historical rootedness in Judeo-Christianity—a fact that becomes even more relevant when it is compared to law rooted in a different religious tradition. The first and most robust arguments for religious freedom have historically come from Judeo-Christian contributions to the Western legal tradition. Where that tradition has developed and persisted, religious liberty rights have enjoyed the most consistent protection; where it has arguably begun to falter, the religious freedom of Jews, Christians, Muslims, and others is increasingly jeopardized. Therefore, the Western encounter with Islam should provoke reflection in both directions, for in both cases, it appears that certain religious resources are essential to the protection of religious liberty.

Shari'a, Human Rights, Universal Morality and International Relations," *Human Rights Quarterly* 16 (1994).

89. Differentiating between Muslim scholars and schools of Islamic thought is consistent with Banchoff and Wuthnow's argument that discussion of religion and human rights must take as a point of departure the existence of pluralism within religions and not just between them or between the religious and the secular. Thomas Banchoff and Robert Wuthnow, eds., *Religion and the Global Politics of Human Rights* (New York: Oxford University Press, 2011).

CHAPTER 2

Theological and Philosophical Origins of Religious Liberty in the U.S. Constitution

Years ago, at a notable dinner in London, that world-famed statesman, John Bright, asked an American statesman, himself a Baptist, the noble Dr. J. L. M. Curry, "What distinct contribution has your America made to the science of government?" To that question Dr. Curry replied: "The doctrine of religious liberty." After a moment's reflection, Mr. Bright made the worthy reply: "It was a tremendous contribution."
        —*George W. Truett*[1]

Amer.ca was the first nation in history to assemble a constitutional framework that institutionalized the separation of church and state in order to secure religious liberty.[2] Its innovative approach was dual in nature: the First Amendment of the U.S. Constitution provides for separation through disestablishment, alongside the free exercise of religion. The conceptual origins of these legal constructions can be found in the Judeo-Christian thought and Enlightenment philosophy of the Western world.[3]

1. George W. Truett, "Baptists and Religious Liberty," *The Reformed Reader* (May 16, 1920).
2. Derek H. Davis, "The Evolution of Religious Freedom as a Universal Human Right," *Brigham Young University Law Review* 2002 (2002): 222.
3. The theological portion of this chapter's account, necessarily limited by space, focuses on the Protestant Reformation because it provided crucial formulations of and justifications for separation and freedom of conscience—ones instrumental to the evolution of the early modern state. However, the Christian origins of religious freedom can be traced as far back as the Gospels, with significant precursors in Judaism and the Hebrew Bible. These are well-documented by many scholars,

This chapter discusses the early modern origins of freedom of religion in the Protestant Reformation (including the contributions of Martin Luther and John Calvin), the genesis of the "American constitutional experiment in religious liberty"[4] (noting, especially, the influence of Roger Williams, John Locke, and James Madison), and the formulation of religious freedom in and subsequent jurisprudence of the First Amendment (e.g., the Establishment and Free Exercise Clauses). The historical priority of America's institutionalization of religious liberty and its subsequent influence upon international law means that no examination of religious freedom in the West is complete without it.[5]

I. THE PROTESTANT REFORMATION AND THE EARLY MODERN ORIGINS OF FREEDOM OF RELIGION

This story begins with the essential contribution made by Martin Luther's theological separation of religious and political spheres of governance, particularly his exclusive assignment of legal authority to the state. This epochal move supported the separation of church and state in nascent Western liberal democracies. Luther's ideas were simultaneously developed and challenged by John Calvin's theology of limited sovereignty and natural law, contributing to the ever-present cultural-institutional tension between more and less vigorous visions of disestablishment and free exercise. The translation of these theological doctrines into forms of social and

including Rabbi David Novak and E. Gregory Wallace. See David Novak, *In Defense of Religious Liberty* (Wilmington, DE: Intercollegiate Studies Institute, 2009); E. Gregory Wallace, "Justifying Religious Freedom: The Western Tradition," *Penn State Law Review* 114 (2009). Rex Ahdar and Ian Leigh distill the contemporary Christian defense of religious freedom into eight core principles: the principle of voluntariness; the Christological injunction; the persecution injunction; the fallibility principle; the eschatological or providential confidence; the ecumenical or universal principle; the principle of the unrestricted conscience; and the dual authority principle. Rex Ahdar and Ian Leigh, *Religious Freedom in the Liberal State* (New York: Oxford, 2005), 36–37.

4. This phrase is borrowed from John Witte, Jr. and appears in many of his writings on the subject.

5. This book's account of religious liberty emphasizes the history and consequences of ideas, especially theological ones. For a narrative that focuses on political and interest-based considerations underlying religious liberty (e.g., the desire of political leaders to stay in power and/or promote the economic well-being of their countries), see Anthony Gill, *The Political Origins of Religious Liberty* (New York: Cambridge University Press, 2008). For the alternative argument that spiritual concerns, rather than material interests, propelled religious toleration, see Perez Zagorin, *How the Idea of Religious Toleration Came to the West* (Princeton, NJ: Princeton University Press, 2003).

political order was at times democratic and at others oppressive. Then as now, religious liberty in the West was not unambiguous.

A. Martin Luther and the Two Kingdoms

Reformation theology contributed significantly to the transformations in law and politics characterizing the early modern state.[6] Historically, its doctrines provided crucial justifications for what would eventually become separation of church and state and, in some cases, disestablishment. Protestant Reformers understood their movement, in part, as a reaction against corrupt central authority in favor of individual judgment (exemplified by Martin Luther)[7] and local rule (exemplified by the English King Henry VIII).[8]

The Reformation's legal, religious, and political manifestations, while complex, exhibited certain common features: an emphasized division of spiritual and temporal realms, the principle of individual responsibility, and the dignity of the common person.[9] Law thus emerged variously in Protestant theology as a means of impeding the corruption of humanity and society's degeneration into chaos, as an instrument for convincing

6. The beginning of the Reformation is commonly marked at October 31, 1517—the date on which Luther nailed his 95 theses to the Castle Church door at Wittenberg. From the mid-nineteenth century onward, Reformation historians have tended to focus their analyses on the period in between that event and the 1555 Peace of Augsburg. More recently, however, a very different periodization has developed. Specifically, some contemporary legal historians divide the Reformation era into three overlapping segments, each characterized by a unique sociopolitical thrust: first, a diffuse evangelical movement centered by calls for Gospel-centered religious reform (ca. 1517–1525); second, a structural reformation in which civil authorities compelled liturgical and ecclesiastical reforms (ca. 1520–1545); and third, a confessional age throughout which the construction of national or otherwise territorial churches and creedal wars propelled religious, legal and political evolution. C. Scott Pryor and Glenn M. Hoshauer, "Puritan Revolution and the Law of Contracts," *Texas Wesleyan Law Review* 11 *Symposium: The Common Law of Contracts as a World Force in Two Ages of Revolution: A Conference Celebrating the 150th Anniversary of* Hadley v. Baxendale (2005): 296–97. Much of the theology informing the Reformation was produced and published during the first two of these periods, first by Luther and approximately two decades later by Calvin.

7. See generally John Dillenberger, ed., *Martin Luther: Selections from His Writings* (New York: Anchor, 1958).

8. John W. Danford, *Roots of Freedom: A Primer on Modern Liberty* (Wilmington, DE: ISI Books, 2000), 39.

9. Ibid., 40–44.

individuals internally of their own sinfulness, and as a call to new life for believers by providing indicators of salvation.[10]

Luther's emphasis upon the singular importance of faith (*sola fide*) forthwith deprived the visible church of its traditional intermediary role, thereby challenging the fundamental legitimacy of its medieval legal and political preeminence.[11] In other words, by asserting that the Church was constituted by the priesthood of all believers, rather than the clerical hierarchy, Luther effectively relegated its earthly existence to the corrupt temporal realm.[12]

Laws were essential to the governance of the secular world. Political theorist Joshua Mitchell writes: "While the government that *does* rule over human souls is an invisible Christian government where 'all are alike subject to each other,' because the great majority of human beings will never be Christian, the invisible government that ministers to Christian souls must be supplemented by a visible government that produces peace among the unrighteous."[13] Luther thus acknowledged the necessity and appropriateness of legal and political forms of authority that were entirely separate from those ecclesiastical in nature. However, he cautioned that the jurisdiction of temporal authority was limited to the legislation of laws governing life, property and external affairs on earth, extending not to "laws for the soul."[14]

---

10. Eugenio Corecco, *The Theology of Canon Law: A Methodological Question* (Pittsburgh, PA: Duquesne University Press, 1992), 80–81.

11. J.A. Fernandez-Santamaria, *Natural Law, Constitutionalism, Reason of State, and War* (New York: Peter Lang, 2005), 36. Beginning with Luther, the Protestants rejected the two dominant paradigms informing sixteenth-century Europe—Thomism and humanism. As a monk deeply steeped in the Augustinian tradition, Luther believed that no corner of the human mind or soul was untouched by the corruption of the Fall. Therefore, he rejected the Thomistic optimism that, despite humanity's failings, people remained capable of reasoning and then following God's laws. Further, Luther renounced humanism's precepts that individuals could employ their rational powers to understand God's will and that they retained the freedom to do what was necessary to earn their salvation. The basis for these rejections was two-fold: first, Luther perceived God not as a rational legislator accessible to human reason, but as a magisterial, omnipotent authority inscrutable to human reason; and second, the fallen state of humanity was such that it had nothing to offer God, but rather was fully dependent upon the Almighty's merciful offering of grace. Ibid., 36–37.

12. Chris Brown, Terry Nardin, and Nicholas Rengger, eds., *International Relations in Political Thought* (New York: Cambridge University Press, 2002), 204.

13. Joshua Mitchell, *Not by Reason Alone: Religion, History, and Identity in Early Modern Political Thought* (Chicago: University of Chicago Press, 1996), 37 (italics in original), quoting Martin Luther, "Temporal Authority: To What Extent It Should Be Obeyed (1523)," in *Luther's Works, Volume 45* (St. Louis, MO: Fortress Press and Concordia Publishing House, 1966): 131–32.

14. Fernandez-Santamaria, *Natural Law, Constitutionalism, Reason of State, and War*, 38, note 32.

In his sophisticated analysis of law and theology in the Lutheran Reformation, John Witte, Jr. articulates the significance of this "two kingdoms" framework: "The earthly kingdom is the realm of creation, of natural and civil life, where a person operates primarily by reason and law," whereas "[t]he heavenly kingdom is the realm of redemption, of spiritual and eternal life, where a person operates primarily by faith and love."[15] The former is distorted by sin and so must be governed by Law, whereas the latter is renewed by grace and may thus be guided by the Gospel. This classic formulation of Law and Gospel prominently informed Luther's teachings on legal and political life, fostering transformation in early modern notions of hierarchy, spheres of governance, and the role of princely authority.

For example, throughout the Middle Ages, the natural world was understood in terms of a great chain of being (*scala naturae*), according to which each of God's creatures and human societies were strictly ordered in a hierarchical system. Those nearer to the top of this pyramid were closer to God, while those nearer to the bottom required priestly mediation to relate to the divine. Such a schema was used to justify traditional Roman Catholic arguments for the superiority of the pope to the emperor, the clergy to the laity, canon law to civil law, and the Church to the state.[16] Luther's theory of the two kingdoms collapsed this hierarchy, privileging instead the horizontal relationship of all human beings and institutions under a Creator; by implication, each individual had a proper place and a corresponding vocation or divine calling, but all were equal before God and, as such, could communicate directly with Him.

This reconceptualization of hierarchy facilitated Luther's doctrine of the three estates—family, Church, and state. "In Luther's view," Witte notes, "God has ordained three basic forms and forums of authority for governance of the earthly life: the domestic, ecclesiastical, and political authorities... . Not only were these three natural estates of family, Church, and state created equally, rather than hierarchically: only the state, in Luther's view, held legal authority."[17] The power of the sword was to be used for enforcing positive laws designed to preserve order in the corrupted earthly kingdom. Accordingly, Luther distinguished between the spiritual authority of the Church to teach the laws of God and the formal legal authority of

15. John Witte, Jr., *Law and Protestantism: The Legal Teachings of the Lutheran Reformation* (New York: Cambridge University Press, 2002), 5.
16. Ibid., 6.
17. Ibid., 7.

the state to impose the laws of men.[18] The seeds of modern church-state separation were thus sown.[19]

18. Ibid., 8. Further, insofar as these realms were to be bridged, such duty fell to the Christian monarch—God's vice-regent—who was to elaborate divine law and reflect divine justice on earth, while serving as the "father of the community." Political authority was therefore divine in origin, but temporal in operation. These twin visions of princely rule served, according to Luther, to check the abusive potential of either operating independently. Together, they provided "the core ingredients of a robust Christian republicanism and budding Christian welfare state." Ibid., 9.

19. A central dilemma confronting legal and political thinkers during and immediately following the Reformation was whether and how individual and communal interests in "usable rights" could be negotiated vis-à-vis duties owed to specific authorities, particularly those identified with emerging "states." A. G. Roeber, "The Law, Religion, and State Making in the Early Modern World: Protestant Revolutions in the Works of Berman, Gorski, and Witte," *Law and Social Inquiry* 31 (2006): 199, 202. Responses to this dilemma differed in form and content depending upon the adopted confessional paradigm and the region at issue. For example, in Germany, a large group of jurists and moralists utilized Luther's core insights to construct complex new theories of law and politics. Witte, *Law and Protestantism*, 9, note 37.

Berman develops an interesting portrait of these individuals in *Law and Revolution II* by incorporating contributions to the discourse from leading jurists, including Phillip Melanchthon and Johann Oldendorp. To summarize Berman, Melanchthon taught passionately on ethics and social justice, and his views on these subjects combined with the new Reformation vision of natural and positive law to replace the Thomistic tradition in those parts of Europe where Lutheranism came to dominate. Melanchthon's work on legal philosophy interwove his teachings on moral and political philosophy, as he crafted a Lutheran-inspired systematic philosophy of law anchored by three pillars: first, the relationship of natural law to divine law; second, the uses of natural law in civil society; and third, the relationship of natural law to positive law. Oldendorp was authorized by the University of Marburg to introduce a basic reform of legal education—one that brought the entire corpus of law into a philosophical and historical relationship with the word of God. Like Melanchthon, Oldendorp developed a tri-partite legal philosophy emphasizing Biblical teachings, faith, and conscience. However, his philosophy was differently systematized and focused on the following: first, a theory of the interrelationships of divine, natural, and positive law; second, a theory of equity; and third, a theory of politics and the state. Regarding the third, Oldendorp acknowledged a tension between his belief in the supremacy of the natural law of conscience over civil law, on the one hand, and his understanding of the civil polity as ordained by God and commanding unconditional obedience, on the other. He attempted to reconcile this tension by allowing for a substantial list of "exceptions" (i.e., instances in which a citizen's conscience might compel his disobedience to civil authorities). Additionally, Oldendorp believed that the state had a moral and legislative duty to enact laws that conformed to God's will. As with other Lutheran-inspired jurists, however, these latter efforts brought German jurisprudence uneasily close to the charges Protestant theologians had first laid at the feet of the Catholic Church and the Holy Roman Empire. This was a line that, for a variety of reasons, Reformers in England were less likely to cross. Harold J. Berman, *Law and Revolution II: The Impact of the Protestant Reformations on the Western Legal Tradition* (Cambridge, MA: Belknap Press of Harvard University Press, 2003), 78, 88, 93–94.

B. John Calvin and Freedom of Conscience

Trained as a lawyer, John Calvin's writings spanned more than three decades, and while he maintained a strong theological orientation, he commented often and significantly on legal and political matters.[20] Generally, Calvinism (or Reformed Protestantism) asserts the seeming paradox that human will is corrupt by nature, yet is also capable of doing good in the world.[21] According to Calvinist doctrine, those who are measured against the law by their sinfulness fall short and are condemned. Still, there is hope for them because "one's inability to live up to the law forces one to look beyond the law for salvation, happiness, and reward."[22]

Law and religion scholar Marci Hamilton observes that, from an institutional perspective, this means that human motives and actions are to be distrusted. Additionally, though individuals ought to be diligently self-reflective, the law must nonetheless guide them away from their natural predispositions toward error.[23] Calvin's emphasis on distrust led him, like Luther, to disavow any hierarchy of individuals in the eyes of God, and to focus his pragmatic efforts on structuring institutions so as to avoid the secular and clerical abuses of the past.[24]

However, when compared with Luther and his followers, Calvinists were characterized by extraordinary religious and social discipline. In his persuasive account of Calvin's influence on early modern state power, comparative historical sociologist Philip Gorski elaborates the groundwork for this phenomenon.[25] Specifically, Calvin taught that the church was the spiritual arm of the Christian community within the broader context of a

20. John Calvin, *Institutes of the Christian Religion*, ed. John T. McNeil (Louisville, KY: Westminster John Knox Press, 1960) [hereinafter Calvin, *Institutes*].

21. Marci A. Hamilton, "The Calvinist Paradox of Distrust and Hope at the Constitutional Convention," in *Christian Perspectives on Legal Thought*, ed. Michael W McConnell, Robert F. Cochran, Jr., and Angela C. Carmella (New Haven, CT: Yale University Press, 2001), 293–94, citing Calvin, *Institutes*, bk. II, ch. II, s. 26 at 86; bk. II, ch. III, s. 5 at 295; bk. II, ch. VII, s. 8 at 356.

22. Hamilton, "The Calvinist Paradox of Distrust and Hope at the Constitutional Convention," 294, citing Calvin, *Institutes*, bk. II, ch. VII, s. 7 at 356; bk. II, ch. VIII, s. 4 at 370.

23. Hamilton, "The Calvinist Paradox of Distrust and Hope at the Constitutional Convention," 295, citing Calvin, *Institutes*, bk. II, ch. II, s. 26–27 at 286–89; bk. II, ch. III, s. 1–14 at 289–309; bk. II, ch. I, s. 2 at 242; bk. II, ch. V, s. 19 at 340; bk. II, ch. VII, s. 13 at 361–62; bk. II, ch. VII, s. 8 at 356–57.

24. Hamilton, "The Calvinist Paradox of Distrust and Hope at the Constitutional Convention," 295–96, citing Calvin, *Institutes*, bk. II, ch. V, s. 17 at 338; bk. IV, ch. II, 1040–53; bk. IV, ch. XX, s. 4 at 1490; bk. IV, ch. VII, s. 19 at 1138–39.

25. Philip S. Gorski, *The Disciplinary Revolution: Calvinism and the Rise of the State in Early Modern Europe* (Chicago: University of Chicago Press, 2003), 19–22.

Christian polity—a polity to be guided by a civil magistrate who would compel the community as a whole to obey Biblical law, while advocating social improvement through reform programs, including popular education and poor-relief.[26]

Calvin also made vital contributions to constitutional theory, notably in his so-called doctrine of limited sovereignty and in his interpretation of natural law, both of which turn heavily on the role of conscience. Broadly, the Calvinist political state is connected directly with religion. As the esteemed editor of Calvin's *Institutes of the Christian Religion*, John T. McNeill, observes, the Reformed Protestant state "protects and supports the worship of God, promotes justice and peace, and is a necessary aid in our earthly pilgrimage toward heaven—as necessary as bread and water, light and air, and more excellent in that it makes possible the use of these, and secures higher blessings to men."[27]

Political power is nevertheless strictly demarcated under Calvinist theology. Thus, while Luther sought political support for the organization of the church and counseled respect for government, Calvin cautioned that the power of monarchs should be as limited as possible.[28] Legal historian John Sap provides an unusually clear exposition of this political theology, the relevant sections of which are summarized in this paragraph and the next: Calvin supported obedience to the state, which derived its power from God, but his support extended only insofar as the government was led by a benevolent and righteous authority. Public magistrates might act to check the power of kings. The right of resistance could be exercised, indeed, *must* be exercised by magistrates on behalf of the liberty of the people, when such a right was recognized by the constitution. This would later be extended by Calvinist monarchomachs (originally only Huguenots, but later including pro-democracy forces more generally) into a right to depose kings and queens who violated their contracts with the people. Even Calvin's limited original formulation was revolutionary. His teaching, drawn from the Book of Acts, that individuals had to obey God rather than men, that God's laws were supreme to human laws, translated into both a right and a duty to refuse to obey the government when matters of religion and conscience were at stake.[29]

26. Ibid., 21–22.
27. John Calvin, *On God and Political Duty*, ed. John T. McNeill, 2nd ed. (Indianapolis, IN: Bobbs-Merrill Co., Inc., 1977), xii.
28. John W. Sap, *Paving the Way for Revolution: Calvinism and the Struggle for a Democratic Constitutional State* (Amsterdam: VU University Press, 2001), 64.
29. Ibid., 64–66.

Moreover, as Sap elucidates, Calvin developed particular ideas about natural law and legal authority. First depicted in his 1532 commentary on Seneca's *DeClementia*, Calvin held that while the king was neither formally nor legally bound to comply with the positive law, he was nonetheless morally obliged to do so by both divine and natural law.[30] Yet Calvin's understanding of natural law must be distinguished from the universal metaphysical principles accessible to general reason found in the tradition of Cicero and Aquinas. Consistent with Reformation theology's inward turn, Calvin's natural law was doubly embodied—first, as moral law inscribed on the hearts of individuals and accessible to them via conscience, and second, as legal principles derived from this moral law that required concrete implementation in positive law.[31]

Historically, Elizabethan Puritans grounded their political radicalism and disciplinary emphasis in the reforming zeal and clerical legalism of Calvinism.[32] Indeed, the Calvinist Puritan belief system significantly informed the legal philosophy of many of England's prominent seventeenth-century jurists, especially Matthew Hale. Trained in its central tenets as a youth, Hale incorporated the Reformed Protestant outlook directly into his historical jurisprudence, resulting in an integrated and theologically informed philosophy of law. For example, Berman notes that the Puritans taught that God was a god of law whose divine will was to be translated into legal precepts and institutions. By contrast, Hale and his colleagues found a secular equivalent to biblical law in the pre-sixteenth century heritage of English common law—a narrative they invoked to delegitimize the Tudor-Stuart dynasty's royal prerogative and provoke reformation of the common law itself.[33] Calvin's teachings thus contributed to

30. The latter derived its existence from the natural order in the world, which correspondingly resulted from its authorship by the Creator God.

31. Ibid., 81–82.

32. Joan Lockwood O'Donovan, *Theology of Law and Authority in the English Reformation* (Grand Rapids, MI: William B. Eerdman's Publishing Co., 1991), 7–8.

33. Berman, *Law and Revolution II*, 264–65. See also Matthew Hale, *Historia Placitorum Coronae: The History of the Pleas of the Crown, Volume 1*, ed. Sollom Emlyn (Philadelphia: R.H. Small, 1847). Puritan theology (including its emphasis on the fallen nature of all human beings) also contributed to Hale's philosophy of judging and to his theories of criminal law and contracts. For example, the presumption of innocence was justified in religious terms: while God requires a judge to convict the guilty and acquit the innocent, in the absence of conclusive evidence, acquittal should follow. Henry Cohen, review of *Law and Revolution II: The Impact of the Protestant Reformations on the Western Legal Tradition*, by Harold J. Berman, *The Federal Lawyer* 51 (2004). This would preserve God's role as the final judge, while allowing a guilty person mistakenly acquitted to repent and mend his ways. Similarly, Puritan freedom of conscience demanded that one honor one's commitments—a belief that influenced the default rule of

the transformation not only of religion, but of law and politics as well, first in Europe and later in America.[34]

C. From Theological Doctrine to Democratic Form

A full discussion of the legal and political consequences of the Reformation is beyond the scope of this project. However, a few observations pertaining to religious freedom are instructive. Once unleashed, Protestantism spread quickly throughout the West, splitting into its most basic branches: Lutheranism, Calvinism, and the Anabaptists. As law and religion scholar Douglas Laycock documents, the Lutherans spread throughout much of Germany and all of Scandinavia. The Calvinists spread from their roots in Geneva to France (Huguenots), Holland (Dutch Reformers), England (Puritans), Scotland (Presbyterians), and even as far as the American colonies. The Anabaptists dominated nowhere, but played noteworthy roles in the American colonies, and included Mennonites, the Amish and Quakers, among other groups.[35] In Europe, the Reformation generated parties who contested a uniform Catholic order, some of whom wanted (ironically) to establish their own religions as uniform and public.[36] For instance, where princes succeeded in making Protestantism official, they tended also to make it uniform—requiring worship in a single designated church, outlawing dissent, and making Protestantism "constitutive of their order's legitimacy."[37]

The problem then, not unlike now, was one of religious pluralism, and although Protestants won tolerance in the 1648 Treaty of Westphalia, individual religious freedom was not yet on the horizon.[38] By affirming the

absolute liability in the common law of contracts. Pryor and Hoshauer, "Puritan Revolution and the Law of Contract," 315–16, 349–50.

34. Daniel F. Piar, "Keepers of the New Covenant: The Puritan Legacy in American Constitutional Law," *Journal of Catholic Legal Studies* 49 (2010).

35. Douglas Laycock, "Continuity and Change in the Threat to Religious Liberty: The Reformation Era and the Late Twentieth Century," *Minnesota Law Review* 80 (1996): 1051. Laycock also notes that Anglicanism is considered by some to be a distinct fourth branch, combining Lutheran, Calvinist, Catholic, and institutional elements.

36. Daniel Philpott, "Religious Freedom and the Undoing of the Westphalian State," *Michigan Journal of International Law* 25 (2004): 984. For an interesting collection of essays on differences among Christian denominations with regard to church-state relations and political activity, see Sandra F. Joireman, ed., *Church, State, and Citizen* (New York: Oxford University Press, 2009).

37. Daniel Philpott, "The Religious Roots of Modern International Relations," *World Politics* 55, no. 2 (2000): 231.

38. Ibid., 984.

1555 Peace of Augsburg formulation of *cuius regio eius religio*,[39] Westphalia codified European confessional diversity; however, while this led to greater religious toleration, the general trend was still toward the formation of polities in which territory, political power, and religious confession were closely linked.[40] Perhaps counterintuitively, such arrangements sometimes fostered improvements in religious liberty.

For example, Lutheran princes believed that the laws, though made by them, were subject to divine law; hence, citizens retained the freedom to disobey a secular law if their Christian consciences told them it was contradicted by divine law as revealed in Scripture.[41] Berman notes that the freedom to disobey "was given practical effect by the confederate character of the wider German polity: its multiplicity of principalities made it possible for a conscientious citizen of one German state to move across a very near border to another German state with the same language and culture and historical background."[42]

More broadly, Protestant groups in both Europe and America transformed theological doctrines into democratic forms designed to secure human rights.[43] For example, as Witte illustrates, doctrines of the person and society were cast into democratic social forms (e.g., political equality; civil liberties; freedom to speak, preach and lead in the community; and state promotion of social institutions, such as the church and family). Likewise, doctrines of sin were cast into democratic political forms (e.g., the distribution of political power through a system of checks and balances; limited terms in office; rule of law; and civil disobedience in response to, or impeachment of, officials who abuse power).[44]

Religious intolerance did not disappear, however, even as it evolved to accommodate new social realities. Theologian Reinhold Niebuhr notes that

39. Under this principle ("whose region, his religion"), "princes or city councils were authorized to prescribe the appropriate forms of Evangelical or Catholic doctrine, liturgy, and education for their polities. Religious dissenters were granted the right to worship privately in their homes or to emigrate peaceably from the polity. After decades of bitter civil war, the Peace of Westphalia in 1648 extended this privilege to Reformed Calvinists as well." John Witte, Jr., "A Dickensian Era of Religious Rights: An Update on Religious Human Rights in Global Perspective," *William and Mary Law Review* 42 (2001): 733.

40. Daniel Nexon, "Religion, European Identity, and Political Contention in Historical Perspective," in *Religion in an Expanding Europe*, ed. Timothy A. Byrnes and Peter J. Katzenstein (New York: Cambridge University Press, 2006), 277.

41. Harold J. Berman, "The Spiritualization of Secular Law: The Impact of the Lutheran Reformation," *Journal of Law and Religion* 14 (1999–2000): 345.

42. Ibid.

43. Witte, "Law, Religion and Human Rights," 23.

44. Ibid., 24.

Luther and Calvin "ignored the demands for humility implicit in their own religious insights and pushed for dissenters to be persecuted."[45] Similarly, he argues, seventeenth-century English Puritanism "pled for liberty of conscience when it was itself in danger of persecution; and threatened all other denominations with suppression when it had the authority [in America] to do so."[46]

A similar tension is at work in Hugo Grotius's classic text of international law *De Jure Belli ac Pacis* (The Law of War and Peace), first published in 1625. As a liberal Arminian,[47] Grotius was acutely aware of religious intolerance (he was imprisoned at one point by Dutch Calvinists), and he relied heavily on proofs and evidence from the Bible to demonstrate the true value of and need for international toleration.[48] Yet his propositions, while progressive in some respects, are not conducive to religious freedom for the person. Grotius "supports both the new order of international toleration and a system of intranational absolutism and strict public restrictions on religious belief and practice."[49] He favors international norms that secure freedom and respect among different confessions, but condemns resistance against a sovereign's policies and laws because there is no earthly authority above the king (i.e., no popular sovereignty).[50] Religious freedom therefore developed variably and was neither consistent nor uncontested.

In sum, Luther's division of religious and political spheres, as well as his relegation of legal authority exclusively to the latter, was an institutional break of historic proportions that directly opened up the possibility of

---

45. Thomas C. Berg, "Church-State Relations and the Social Ethics of Reinhold Niebuhr," *North Carolina Law Review* 73 (1995): 1612, quoting Reinhold Niebuhr, *The Nature and Destiny of Man: Human Destiny* (Scribner Library ed. 1964 (1943)), 226–31. Volume 1 of Niebuhr's work, subtitled *Human Nature*, was published in 1941.

46. Berg, "Church-State Relations and the Social Ethics of Reinhold Niebuhr."

47. Arminianism is closely related to Dutch Calvinism, but the two differ as to the exact nature of predestination and salvation. After the death of Jacob Arminius, his followers (who came to be known as the Remonstrants) were initially condemned as heretics and persecuted. Eventually, however, they were granted toleration, and when the Remonstrant Theological Seminary was founded in Amsterdam, Grotius was among its first professors. Robert Picirilli, *Faith, and Free Will: Contrasting Views of Salvation— Calvinism and Arminianism* (Nashville, TN: Randall House, 2002): 9–17.

48. Mark W. Janis, "Religion and the Literature of International Law: Some Standard Texts," in *Religion and International Law*, ed. Mark W. Janis and Carolyn Evans (Boston, MA: Martinus Nijhoff Publishers, 2004), 123. See Hugo Grotius, *De Jure Belli Ac Pacis Libri Tres* (Carnegie Classics of International Law, 1925, No. 3, Vol. 2, Kelse trans. 1646 ed.), Book II, Chapters XI–XV; Book III, Ch. XXV.

49. David Little, "Religion—Catalyst or Impediment to International Law? The Case of Hugo Grotius," *American Society of International Law Proceedings* 87 (1993): 325.

50. Ibid., 322–27.

separation of church and state.[51] Calvin's doctrines of limited sovereignty and natural law concurrently created a meaningful space for freedom of conscience (understood here, in part, as a right to rebellion) and privileged the religious domain in the event of conflict with the political. Separation of church and state and freedom of conscience in the modern West were thus born upon a Christian field, one in which the connections between human failings (sin and corruption) and legal structures (e.g., limited government, religious liberty) are "vital to an understanding of the necessary structures and balances built into modern liberal democracies."[52]

To anticipate the second half of this book, where, on matters relevant to legal and political organization, Islamic thought diverges from Christian doctrine(s), dissonance (however manifested) is to be expected. This is even less surprising given two factors. First, Reformation theology itself points to somewhat different understandings of religious liberty—differences that are far from resolved in Western law and culture. Second, the early institutionalization of Protestant ideas was not without its own patterns of intolerance and oppression—a tension present in Luther, Calvin, and even Grotius. These historical realities caution against on oversimplified narrative of the evolution of religious liberty in the West. That said, Protestant theology and its institutional embodiments profoundly affected early American constitutionalism—the next historical stage in the growth of religious freedom.

II. THE GENESIS OF THE AMERICAN CONSTITUTIONAL EXPERIMENT IN RELIGIOUS LIBERTY

Writing on "the genesis of the American constitutional experiment," John Witte, Jr. explains that the religion clauses of the state constitutions and of the First Amendment (drafted between 1776 and 1791) give expression to sentiments both theological and practical.[53] Further, drawing upon available eighteenth-century sources, Witte sifts through the multiplicity

51. Randy Beck, "The City of God and the Cities of Men: A Response to Jason Carter," *Georgia Law Review* 41 (2006): 124.

52. Paul J. Zwier, "Looking to 'Ground Motives' for a Religious Foundation for Law," *Emory Law Journal* 54 (2005): 361–62.

53. John Witte, Jr. and M. Christian Green, "The American Constitutional Experiment in Religious Human Rights: The Perennial Search for Principles," in *Religious Human Rights in Global Perspective: Legal Perspectives*, ed. Johan D. van der Vyver and John Witte, Jr. (Boston: Martinus Nijhoff Publishers, 1966), 501. See also John F. Wilson, "The Founding Era (1774–1797) and the Constitutional Provision for

of viewpoints to arrive at a useful heuristic. The first pairing, theological perspectives, derives much of its essential content from two religious groups—congregational Puritans and free church evangelicals. The second pairing, political perspectives, incorporates the speeches and writings of both Enlightenment thinkers and civic republicans.[54] Witte's claim is that the "original intent" of the constitution's framers respecting government and religion cannot be reduced to any one of these four groups, but rather, stems from the tensions between them and the principles that emerged from their interaction.[55] Though this chapter will briefly focus on select thinkers who were especially influential (elaborating the link to Reformation theology), a brief overview based on Witte's classification is instructive. The paragraphs that follow summarize some of his key findings.

The Puritans, representing a significant percentage of American citizens at the time of the Revolution, were the New World heirs to European Calvinism.[56] Beginning in the early seventeenth century, they dominated the New England colonies and were therefore able to institutionalize the core principles of their political theology. Conceiving of the church and the state as separate covenantal associations, the Puritans adopted safeguards to ensure basic separation of church and state (e.g., prohibitions against church officials holding political office and political officials holding ministerial office). Yet because both church and state were instruments of God's authority, and because they were linked in nature and function, Witte notes that the Puritans supported the coordination and cooperation of church and state: for example, state provision of material aid and donation of public properties to churches; tax exemptions for religious—and related charitable and educational—organizations; church accommodation of town assemblies, political rallies, and public auctions in their meeting houses; use of parsonages to house orphans, widows, the sick and aged, and victims of abuse or disaster; and the like. Importantly, the Puritans did not tolerate individual religious experimentation, and immigration

Religion," in *The Oxford Handbook of Church and State in the United States*, ed. Derek H. Davis (New York: Oxford University Press, 2010).

54. This is a far more nuanced and historically illuminating scheme than the pop culture alternative pitting disembodied Enlightenment deists against hyperemotional evangelicals. For an example of the latter, see Patrick Allitt, "City on a Hill," *The New York Times*, December 9, 2007.

55. Witte and Green, "The American Constitutional Experiment," 502–03.

56. On the Puritan views, see generally ibid., 505–06. See also Barry Alan Shain, "Eighteenth-Century Religious Liberty: The Founding Generation's Protestant-Derived Understanding," in Davis, *The Oxford Handbook of Church and State in the United States*, 42–74.

restrictions in Massachusetts Bay kept Quakers, Catholics, Jews, Enthusiasts, and other groups almost entirely out.

While the free church evangelicals had fewer opportunities than the Puritans to institutionalize their ideas, their influence upon constitutional ideas was profound. Unlike the Puritans' early progress, the free church evangelicals only emerged as a powerful political force in the colonies after the Great Awakening (c. 1720–1780).[57] Evangelicals, too, supported the separation of church and state, but they agitated for a fuller separation of the two at both individual and institutional levels. Baptist preacher John Leland, for example, proposed amending the Massachusetts Constitution to forbid religious tests for political office, and later even argued that "[t]he notion of a Christian commonwealth should be exploded forever."[58] The religious voluntarism of the evangelicals demanded liberty of conscience to choose or change faith in the quest for God, and they rallied against the forced collection of tithes and the withholding of civil rights from religious minorities (a persecuted category to which they had historically belonged). This, then, was the evangelicals' primary focus—the constitutional freeing of the church from the bonds of law and state, thereby to secure religious pluralism.

Enlightenment thinkers in America were, not surprisingly, more political than theological in orientation (though their views were analogous in many respects to those of the evangelicals).[59] They were guided by a desire

---

57. On the Evangelical views, see generally Witte and Green, "The American Constitutional Experiment," 506–08. See also Steven Waldman, *Founding Faith: Providence, Politics, and the Birth of Religious Freedom in America* (New York: Random House, 2008). Moreover, as Daniel L. Dreisbach illustrates, Williams advocated separation not "to protect the outside world (including the civil polity or society at large) from religious influences, but to preserve the religious purity of the separated church from corrupting external influences." Daniel L. Dreisbach, "The Meaning of the Separation of Church and State: Competing Views," in Davis, *The Oxford Handbook on Church and State in the United States*, 213.

58. Witte and Green, "The American Constitutional Experiment," 507, quoting L.F. Greene, ed., *The Writings of the Late Elder John Leland* (New York: G.W. Wood, 1845), 107. For Leland's further writings on "religious explosion," see Greene, ed., *Writings*, 117–19.

59. On the Enlightenment views, see generally Witte and Green, "The American Constitutional Experiment," 508–11. Although this book primarily emphasizes the contribution of religious ideas, consideration of the Enlightenment and civic republican views are relevant for several reasons. First, some Enlightenment and civic republican thinkers, including John Locke, were not exclusively secular in orientation or argument. Second, secular thought importantly influenced the form and content of religious liberty in the U.S. Constitution, which in turn influenced international law. Finally, to the extent that Western international law reflects secular principles alongside religious principles, this, too, is a point of contention for Islamic countries, especially when those principles appear to be what is elsewhere called "religiously

to free the church from the influence of the state, but also and especially to free the state from the influence of the church. Rejecting political aid, support, privilege, and protection of religion, they argued against the predication of state laws on religious principles. Such views reflected "a profound skepticism about organized religion and a profound fear of an autocratic state."[60] Additionally, these views were grounded by a notion of the person as an individual human being for whom religion is and must be primarily a matter of private reason and conscience; community and corporate religiosity are likewise secondary. Under the particular influence of James Madison and Thomas Jefferson, this vision of religious liberty took hold in post-revolutionary Virginia (e.g., Article 16 of the 1776 Virginia Bill of Rights protected the free exercise of religion; also, the Virginia Statute on Religious Freedom, drafted by Jefferson in 1777 and passed in 1786, began by observing that "almighty God hath created the mind free").[61]

Finally, the civic republicans, who included George Washington among their numbers, advocated liberty of conscience for all, believed in state support for religious pluralism, and opposed both political theocracy and religious establishment.[62] However, in keeping with the Puritans, they desired a public square suffused with a common religious ethic and ethos. Washington himself held that religion and morality were central to civil society,[63] while John Adams argued that government could not function absent a citizenry moderated by religious character.[64] Civic republicans maintained that society needs what might now be called "civil religion"— a corpus of civic ideas and ideals intertwined with religious values and

secular" (that is, not merely "neutral" with respect to various religions, but secular to the point of being atheistic).

60. Ibid., 509.

61. Ibid., 510. On the ways in which phrases like "separation of church and state" and Jefferson's own "wall of separation" have both informed and confused American legal and policy debates, see Daniel L. Dreisbach, *Thomas Jefferson and the Wall of Separation between Church and State* (New York: New York University Press, 2002). See also Christopher L. and Lawrence G. Sager Eisgruber, *Religious Freedom and the Constitution* (Cambridge: Harvard University Press, 2007).

62. On the civic republican views, see generally Witte and Green, "The American Constitutional Experiment," 511–14.

63. See Vincent Phillip Muñoz, "Religion and the Common Good: George Washington on Church and State," in *The Founders on God and Government*, ed. Daniel L. Dreisbach, Mark D. Hall and Jeffry H. Morrison (Lanham, MD: Rowman & Littlefield, 2004), 1–22.

64. See John Witte, Jr., "One Public Religion, Many Private Religions: John Adams and the 1780 Massachusetts Constitution," in Dreisbach, Hall, and Morrison, *The Founders on God and Government*, 23–52.

beliefs, offered up in public spiritedness.[65] "Religion and liberty are the meat and drink of the body politic," penned Yale President Timothy Dwight.[66] It followed that some state support of churches was acceptable, for religion was essential to good government. Hence, the 1780 Constitution of Massachusetts insisted that all persons—especially public leaders—maintain rigorous standards of morality and religion. Civic republican views were also highly influential in the Continental Congress (which, among other things, authorized diplomatic ties to the Vatican—a bold move given the anti-Catholic culture of the period).

Witte concludes that each of these four groups—Puritan, evangelical, Enlightenment, and civic republican—contributed to the development and evolution of religious liberty in early American constitutionalism. Moreover, they did so with respect to six distinct themes: liberty of conscience; free exercise of religion; religious pluralism; religious equality; separation of church and state; and disestablishment of religion.[67] These themes echo many of the principle ideas of Protestant theology, and they intersect in different ways and to varying degrees with the key theological and political views discussed immediately above. However, to appreciate their full significance and subsequent effect upon the framers of the U.S. Constitution, it is worth exploring the work of three individuals in greater detail: namely, Roger Williams, John Locke, and James Madison.

A. The "Soul Liberty" of Roger Williams

Roger Williams was a provocative and spirited individual, competent in five languages, whose friends included John Milton and Oliver Cromwell and whose subjects of inquiry ranged from social contract theory to the separation of church and state.[68] He is best remembered, however, for his arguments about conscience and religious freedom; indeed, Williams was

65. See generally Dreisbach, Hall and Morrison, eds., *The Founders on God and Government.*

66. Witte and Green, "The American Constitutional Experiment," 512, quoting Tomothy Dwight, *The Duty of Americans at the Present Crisis, Illustrated in a Discourse Preached on the Fourth of July, 1798* (New Haven, CT, 1798), reprinted in Ellis Sandoz, ed., *Political Sermons of the American Founding Era: 1730–1805* (Liberty Fund, 1991), 1365, 1380.

67. Edward McGlynn Gaffney, Jr., review of "Religion and the American Constitutional Experiment, Essential Rights and Liberties," by John Witte, Jr., *Journal of Law and Religion* 16 (2001).

68. For an extended discussion of Williams, see William Lee Miller, *The First Liberty: Religion and the American Republic* (New York: Knopf, 2003).

America's first thinker on religious liberty.[69] Banished from Massachusetts Bay in the winter of 1635 based on a policy disagreement (he later accused the colony of spiritually raping the conscience of Christians), Williams had serious occasion to contemplate the nature of religious liberty.[70]

What began as an argument for the cause of conscience evolved into a theory of religious freedom, inspired by the Protestant Reformation and by discussions of church-state relations during the time of the English Civil War.[71] Although some suggest that Williams's justifications for the special treatment of conscience now falter in an era marked by the erosion of moral objectivism,[72] and others attempt to shore up conscience by pairing moral objectivism with moral authenticity,[73] Williams's ideas remain essential to a proper understanding of American thought on freedom of religion—past and present.

In 1644, Williams published his most famous work on the subject, "The Bloody Tenent, of Persecution, for Cause of Conscience."[74] His writings were not merely academic: six years prior, Williams had founded the colony of Providence, affording him ample opportunity to test his ideas about religion, civil society, and the social contract. The fruit of Williams's lifelong experiment may be seen in the enduring power of his ideas about religious freedom and their deep connection to American understandings of constitutional democracy. To Williams, conscience is inviolable because it is the path by which we discover God and do His will (i.e., freedom properly understood is freedom to do what God requires, hence "soul liberty"); in addition, conscience is sacred because it is an inalienable and universal aspect of being human (and thus resides in people of any race, ethnicity, or sex—a truly radical idea at the time).[75] "Since conscience is the core of religion, a way must be found to safeguard conscience within society," legal scholar Edward Eberle explains. "For Williams, the way was law. Law is

69. Edward J. Eberle, "Introduction," *Roger Williams University Law Review* 10 *Symposium: Religious Liberty in America and Beyond: Celebrating the Legacy of Roger Williams on the 400th Anniversary of His Birth* (2005) [hereinafter *Roger Williams Symposium* (2005)]: 279.

70. Edward J. Eberle, "Roger Williams on Liberty of Conscience," *Roger Williams Symposium* (2005): 301.

71. Eberle, "Introduction," 280.

72. Steven D. Smith, "The Tenuous Case for Conscience," *Roger Williams Symposium* (2005).

73. Kathleen A. Brady, "Foundations for Freedom of Conscience: Stronger Than You Might Think," *Roger Williams Symposium* (2005).

74. Edward J. Eberle, "Roger Williams on Liberty of Conscience," *Roger Williams Symposium* (2005): 289.

75. Ibid., 290–96.

needed to tame man's natural instinct to control. Thus, Williams set out to erect legal structures to protect religious freedom."[76]

These included toleration of contrary beliefs and opinions, equal rights for all citizens, separation of church and state, advocacy and delineation of different jurisdictions of church and state, the absence of a national church, and the treatment of churches as equal in standing to other organizations in society.[77] Theologically, Williams drew upon Christian tradition, generally, but specifically that of Luther and (especially) Calvin. However, he also moved beyond them, and his principle of non-coercion—along with the other components and legal structures enumerated above—form the core of what America and the Western world now understand as a *right* to religious freedom.[78]

B. John Locke's Separation Principle

Raised in a Puritan household, John Locke grew to be a very religious man. Perhaps that is why he did not shy from using religious claims to advance his philosophy; in fact, his first volume on civil government (upon which the better known second one builds) cites Scripture as a basis of argument.[79] Nevertheless, Locke advocated the separation of religion and politics in order to prevent an alliance between the authorities of each, for it was such separation that he believed made religious freedom and a peaceable civil society possible.[80] He was influenced in this opinion by a diplomatic mission to Brandenburg in 1665, during which he observed Catholics, Calvinists, and Lutherans living "in toleration" alongside each other.[81] Locke held that precluding the establishment of an official religion was

76. Ibid., 297.
77. Ibid., 303. Legal philosopher Martha Nussbaum links the emphasis Williams placed on equality and toleration with the contemporary political philosophy of John Rawls (particularly his "Original Position"). Martha C. Nussbaum, *Liberty of Conscience: In Defense of America's Tradition of Religious Equality* (New York: Basic Books, 2008).
78. Eberle, "Roger Williams on Liberty of Conscience," 317.
79. H. Wayne House, "A Tale of Two Kingdoms: Can There Be Peaceful Coexistence of Religion with the Secular State?," *BYU Journal of Public Law* 13 (1999): 226–27.
80. J. Paul Martin, "Religions, Human Rights, and Civil Society: Lessons from the Seventeenth Century for the Twenty-First Century," *Brigham Young University Law Review* 2000 (2000): 938.
81. Frederick W. Guyette, "A Dream Dialogue on Religious Liberty," *Journal of Law and Religion* 20 (2004–05): 463.

essential to such peaceful coexistence,[82] and that the lack of an official religion would have the further effect of encouraging public discourse about religious doctrine. He reasoned that allowing individuals to exchange ideas without eliminating the basic theological and epistemological categories of truth and error would prevent a descent into relativism and indifferentism.[83]

The originality of Locke's contribution derives in part from his "persistent theoretical defense of freedom of conscience and religion as a basis from which natural rights, popular sovereignty, limitations on political power and separation of church and state are derived."[84] For example, his principal arguments for individual freedom rest upon the notions that true faith requires sincerity and that coercion in matters of conscience and religion betray the letter and spirit of Christian love.[85] Moreover, religious freedom is necessary because, according to Locke, a church is a "voluntary society of men, joining themselves together of their own accord in order to the public worshipping of God, in such manner as they judge acceptable to Him, and effectual to the salvation of their souls."[86]

An additional consequence of religion as a matter of personal conviction (rather than coercion) is that state sovereignty must be limited; that is, according to Locke, the state should be separate from the church.[87] These, along with Locke's other writings, many of which similarly integrate religious and political argument, exerted enormous influence upon eighteenth-century American leaders.[88] "Most Americans had absorbed Locke's works as a kind of political gospel; and the Declaration, in its forms, in its phraseology, follows closely certain sentences in Locke's second treatise on

82. Locke's theory of toleration, while historically progressive, was limited too. For example, because Locke (and his contemporaries) thought that Catholics owed their primary allegiance to a foreign power, he considered their beliefs destructive to all human society. Thus, Locke "endorsed the application of force to Catholics as a means by which they might be 'converted' to the truth of Protestantism." Martin, "Religions, Human Rights, and Civil Society," 938, quoting Richard Ashcroft, "Religion and Lockean Natural Rights," in *Religious Diversity and Human Rights*, ed. Irene Bloom, J. Paul Martin, and Wayne Proudfoot (New York: Columbia University Press, 1996), 207.

83. Jónatas E. M. Machado, "Freedom of Conscience and the Rights of Non-TOFTers," *Roger Williams Symposium* (2005): 445.

84. Jónatas E. M. Machado, "Freedom of Religion: A View from Europe," *Roger Williams Symposium* (2005): 458.

85. Ibid., 458.

86. John Locke, *A Letter Concerning Toleration* (Amherst, NY: Prometheus Books, 1990), 22.

87. Machado, "Freedom of Religion: A View from Europe," 459.

88. They also continue to influence Supreme Court jurisprudence today. See Stanley Fish, "Monkey Business," *The New York Times*, December 2, 2007.

government."[89] One such founder who knew and reflected upon Locke's ideas was James Madison.

C. James Madison and Religious Freedom as an "Inalienable Right"

James Madison, author of the most important document setting forth the founders' conception of religious freedom, maintained that religious liberty can only be secure if it is undergirded by religious faith.[90] In his "Memorial and Remonstrance Against Religious Assessments," Madison remarks that religious freedom derives not from the personal autonomy of the individual, but as "an inference from the sovereignty of God and the duty of human beings to obey God as they understand Him. Religious exercise . . . is an inalienable right because it follows from the duties owed to God by His creatures."[91] Hence, in keeping with Luther's view of the two kingdoms,[92] individuals have no right to consent to any civil government that stands in the way of their duties to the Ultimate Sovereign.[93] Put differently, while citizens have duties to both God and civil society, the duties to God always take precedence.[94]

This vision is entirely consistent with four affirmations articulated years earlier in the Virginia Declaration of Religious Liberty of 1776 (Jefferson's bill that Madison pushed through the Virginia legislature[95]): namely, "the *greatness* of the Creator; the *duty* of the creature to recognize, be grateful to, and adore that Creator; the *freedom* of soul that the Creator endowed in humans for such acts; and the *friendship* with humans that God desired."[96]

---

89. House, "A Tale of Two Kingdoms," 227, quoting Carl Lotus Becker, *The Declaration of Independence: A Study on the History of Political Ideas* (New York: Harcourt, Brace and Co., 1922, 1942).

90. Harold J. Berman, "Religious Freedom and the Challenge of the Modern State," *Emory Law Journal* 39 (1990): 164. For greater elaboration of Madison's views, see Miller, *The First Liberty: Religion and the American Republic*.

91. Michael W. McConnell, "Why Is Religious Liberty the 'First Freedom'?," *Cardozo Law Review* 21 *Symposium: A Roundtable on Constitutionalism, Constitutional Rights & Changing Civil Society* (2000): 1247.

92. Ibid., 1246.

93. Ibid., 1247.

94. Michael W. McConnell, "'God Is Dead and We Have Killed Him!': Freedom of Religion in the Post-modern Age," *Brigham Young University Law Review* 1993 (1993): 169.

95. See Steven D. Smith, "Blooming Confusion: Madison's Mixed Legacy," *Indiana Law Journal* 75 (2000): 61.

96. Michael Novak, "The Truth About Religious Freedom," *First Things* (March 2006): 17.

It is also consonant with the "unapologetically religious character of eighteenth-century Enlightenment discourse" and "its persistent reliance on the premise of a providential order," for at the time of America's founding, nearly everyone "shared a belief in a divine Author or Architect who created the universe according to an intelligent and benevolent plan."[97]

As a matter of public policy, Madison denied that the health of religion was in any way dependent upon governmental support, rejected both religious tests for public office and established colonial religions, and asserted the importance of strict separation of church and state.[98] He also expressed deep and persistent concern about the ability of government to influence or control individual liberty.[99] In sum, Madison believed that religious freedom is dependent for its security upon religious faith, explicitly rejected governmental support at any level for any religious sect, and refused any abridgment of religious liberty.[100] These three stances correlate well with the First Amendment, with, respectively, its religious foundation and its two prongs of religious liberty—the Establishment and Free Exercise Clauses. Such correlation is perhaps to be expected, as Madison was instrumental in drafting it.[101]

III. RELIGIOUS FREEDOM IN THE FIRST AMENDMENT OF THE U.S. CONSTITUTION

The First Amendment of the U.S. Constitution was preceded by many colonial laws supporting religious freedom. For example, the Maryland Act Concerning Religion (1649) recognized freedom of worship, while the Charter of Rhode Island and Providence Plantations (1663) and the Concessions and Agreements of West New Jersey (1677) offered explicit

97. Steven D. Smith, "Recovering (From) Enlightenment?," *San Diego Law Review* 41 (2004): 1276–77.

98. Mark G. Valencia, "Take Care of Me When I Am Dead: An Examination of American Church-State Development and the Future of American Religious Liberty," *SMU Law Review* 49 (1996): 1590.

99. Ibid., 1591.

100. Ibid., 1593. See also Garrett Ward Sheldon, "Religion and Politics in the Thought of James Madison," in Dreisbach, Hall, and Morrison, *The Founders on God and Government*, 83–116.

101. For an extended discussion of Madison's role at the time of drafting, see Michael W. McConnell, John H. Garvey, and Thomas C. Berg, *Religion and the Constitution* (New York: Aspen Publishers, 2002), 71–79.

protection of religious liberty.[102] These documents and others, especially given their historical context discussed above, help illustrate the extent to which religious liberty was understood to be a right of the people prior to the drafting of the Constitution. Indeed, when it was presented to the states for ratification, a significant portion of the population was dissatisfied by the lack of an explicit guarantee as to the limitations on federal government power.[103]

The subsequent movement for a Bill of Rights (with direct demands for the right to religious liberty) was successful, yet these original ten amendments should be understood not as alterations to the Constitution, but as fundamentally continuous extensions of it. The First Amendment, for example, changed nothing: "it simply specified an existing reality—that religious liberty was a natural right retained by the people and that the government had no jurisdiction over it." It was enacted "to reassure the people of the government's understanding" of that fact.[104]

This right to freedom of religion is announced in the opening line of the First Amendment, which reads, in pertinent part: "Congress shall make no law respecting an establishment of religion, or prohibiting the free exercise thereof."[105] The first prong, the Establishment Clause, proscribes the government from establishing a state religion, while the second prong, the Free Exercise Clause, guarantees the free exercise of conscience.[106] Contrary to those who argue that the two are inherently inconsistent,[107] the Religion

---

102. Fernando Rey Martinez, "The Religious Character of the American Constitution: Puritanism and Constitutionalism in the United States," *Kansas Journal of Law and Public Policy* 12 (2003): 479.

103. Thomas Curry, "Interpreting the First Amendment: Has Ideology Triumphed over History?," *DePaul Law Review* 53 (2003): 5.

104. Ibid., 5. See also Bruce T. Murray, *Religious Liberty in America: The First Amendment in Historical and Contemporary Perspective* (Amherst: University of Massachusetts Press, 2008).

105. For a comprehensive treatment of American jurisprudence as it pertains to religious freedom, see Douglas Laycock, *Religious Liberty: Volume One (Overviews & History)* (Grand Rapids, MI: Wm. B. Eerdmans Publishing Co., 2010); Douglas Laycock, *Religious Liberty: Volume Two (The Free Exercise Clause)* (Grand Rapids, MI: Wm. B. Eerdmans Publishing Co., 2010). See also Davis, ed., *The Oxford Handbook of Church and State in the United States*; Donald L. Drakeman, *Church, State, and Original Intent* (New York: Cambridge University Press, 2010); Kent Greenawalt, "Secularism, Religion and Liberal Democracy in the United States," *Cardozo Law Review* 30 *Symposium: Constitutionalism and Secularism in an Age of Religious Revival: The Challenge of Global and Local Fundamentalism* (2009); McConnell, Garvey and Berg, eds., *Religion and the Constitution*.

106. Thomas M. Franck, "Is Personal Freedom a Western Value?," *American Journal of International Law* 91 (1997): 596.

107. For an examination of how this tension plays out in contemporary Free Exercise Clause jurisprudence, see Philip C. Aka, "The Supreme Court and the Challenge

Clauses represented not a compromise but, rather, "the unified demand of the most vigorous advocates of religious liberty," designed to enable people with divergent religious views to live peacefully together as political equals, free from coercion or oppression.[108]

On a related note, although subsequent jurisprudence has applied the First Amendment to protect non-religious belief,[109] the original meaning of religion almost certainly meant a system of beliefs with a theistic view of the supernatural and likely encompassed only monotheistic belief systems.[110] This interpretation is not uncontested,[111] as evidenced most recently by public debate in America about "the faithful vs. the secularists."[112] Still, even those who argue that, in a pluralistic and skeptical age, there are legitimate grounds for questioning whether it is reasonable to interpret the Religion Clauses as proceeding from religious foundations nevertheless concede that "the government has favored religion" and "this favoritism has not been regarded as unconstitutional."[113] A brief inspection of early arguments—religious and political—in favor of the respective clauses helps elucidate why.

A. The Establishment Clause

Though scholars disagree as to the exact number, it is widely accepted that most colonies exhibited some degree of church-state establishment by the time of the Revolution.[114] It may seem odd, then, that it was the

of Protecting Minority Religions in the United States: Review of Garrett Epps, to an Unknown God: Religious Freedom on Trial," *Scholar* 9 (2007).

108. Laycock, "Continuity and Change in the Threat to Religious Liberty," 1088.

109. On the American jurisprudence of religious liberty as a dynamic tradition, rather than a uniform principle or the result of shifts in political interests, see Steven D. Smith, "Separation as a Tradition," *Journal of Law and Politics* 18 (2002): 215–70.

110. Lee J. Strang, "The Meaning of 'Religion' in the First Amendment," *Duquesne Law Review* 40 (2002).

111. On the difficulty of defining "religion" coherently for purposes of American law, as well as the impossibility of protecting religious freedom so long as "religion" is narrowly defined, see Winnifred Fallers Sullivan, *The Impossibility of Religious Freedom* (Princeton, NJ: Princeton University Press, 2005); Christopher Caldwell, "Sacred Cow of Religious Rights," *Financial Times* (London), July 15, 2005.

112. David Brooks, "Faith vs. The Faithless," *The New York Times*, December 7, 2007.

113. Steven H. Shiffrin, "The Pluralistic Foundations of the Religion Clauses," *Cornell Law Review* 90 (2004): 61–62.

114. Richard Albert, "American Separationism and Liberal Democracy: The Establishment Clause in Historical and Comparative Perspective," *Marquette Law Review* 88 (2005): 883–94.

proponents of disestablishment who were more likely to offer religious arguments or theological justifications for their position.[115] To complicate matters, there was significant diversity of opinion among the religious communities themselves. For example, while Congregationalists and Presbyterians each traced their theologies to Calvin, they advanced different principles in the establishment debates, driven not "solely by theology but also by historical incidents that placed them in relative positions of power or weakness."[116]

Partly as a result, no single religious group can take sole credit for the Establishment Clause, though several have made important contributions to the following core disestablishment principles: church and state are functionally distinct (Congregationalists); government may not prefer any religion over any other (Presbyterians); government may not coerce believers into any religious belief (Baptists); government must be tolerant of all beliefs (Quakers); and the believer may believe in a church order that is not like the civil order, but still be able to embrace the principles of democratic republicanism in the civil sphere (Roman Catholics).[117]

These core principles were complemented by at least five different understandings of separation that emerged during the early American republic: first, the church must be protected from the state; second, the religious believer's liberty of conscience must be protected from intrusions of both church and state; third, the state should be protected from the church; fourth, individual governments should be protected from interference by the federal government in their local religious affairs; and fifth, society should be protected from unwelcome participation in and support for religion.[118] Underlying all of this, of course, was the fight between Protestants and Catholics—over separation of church and state generally, but about the place and role of the state's law vis-à-vis religion particularly.[119]

115. Michael W. McConnell, "Establishment and Disestablishment at the Founding, Part I: Establishment of Religion," *William and Mary Law Review* 44 (2003): 2206.

116. Marci A. Hamilton and Rachel Steamer, "The Religious Origins of Disestablishment Principles," *Notre Dame Law Review* 81 (2006): 1768.

117. Ibid., 1788–89.

118. John Witte, Jr., "That Serpentine Wall of Separation," *Michigan Law Review* 101 (2003): 1889–91.

119. Marci A. Hamilton, "'Separation': From Epithet to Constitutional Norm," *Virginia Law Review* 88 (2002): 1448. For an extended discussion of these issues and "The Catholic Question in America," see Walter J. Walsh, "The First Free Exercise Case," *George Washington Law Review* 73 (2004). Relatedly, historian David Sehat argues that throughout most of its history, American Protestant elites curtailed or denied altogether the religious freedom of Roman Catholics, Mormons, and freethinkers.

Interestingly, the separation of church and state neither culminated with the adoption of the Establishment Clause in 1791, nor was hastened by it; rather, in the early republic, the Establishment Clause was known (and appreciated) for acting as a bar to federal government interference in state treatment of religion.[120] The actual work of disestablishment took place at the state level, driven largely by religious people working for biblical reasons,[121] many of whom were attempting to protect the independence of their churches and promote religious flourishing—not to eliminate all connection between religion and government. Thus, in response to twentieth-century Supreme Court jurisprudence erecting a "high and impregnable" wall between church and state, the spiritual heirs of those early religious advocates are returning to the historical record with the hope of "reclaiming" the true meaning of the Establishment Clause and the First Amendment.[122]

B. The Free Exercise Clause

Questions about the nature and forms of religious organization and practice are closely related to questions of political order.[123] Religious liberty results from "the appropriate adjustment between government and religion, the religious and the secular, and the people and their government."[124] As constitutional expert and former appellate judge Michael W. McConnell observes, during the 150 years prior to the 1789 drafting and 1791 ratification of the First Amendment, Americans experienced a higher degree of religious diversity than had previously existed anywhere else in the world.[125] This pluralism made such questions about the relationship of religious

David Sehat, *The Myth of American Religious Freedom* (New York: Oxford University Press, 2011).

120. Carl H. Esbeck, "Dissent and Disestablishment: The Church-State Settlement in the Early American Republic," *Brigham Young University Law Review* 2004 (2004): 1590.

121. Ibid. See also Kent Greenawalt, "History as Ideology: Philip Hamberger's Separation of Church and State," *California Law Review* 93 (2005).

122. Robert L. Cord, *Separation of Church and State: Historical Fact and Current Fiction* (Grand Rapids, MI: Baker Book House, 1988).

123. William Johnson Everett, "Ecclesial Freedom and Federal Order: Reflections on the Pacific Homes Case," *Journal of Law and Religion* 12 (1995–96): 372.

124. Marci A. Hamilton, "Slouching toward Globalization: Charting the Pitfalls in the Drive to Internationalize Religious Human Rights," *Emory Law Journal* 46 (1997).

125. Michael W. McConnell, "The Origins and Historical Understanding of Free Exercise of Religion," *Harvard Law Review* 103 (1990): 1421.

experience to political order uniquely challenging, and their resolution developed incrementally.

"Free exercise" first appears as a term in an American legal document in Lord Baltimore's 1648 direction to his new Protestant governor in Maryland that Christians, and in particular Roman Catholics, were not to be disturbed in the "free exercise" of their religion.[126] This was followed in 1663 by the Rhode Island Charter's use of the formulation "liberty of conscience," and though its influence was likely limited (Rhode Island was at that time "the pariah among colonies, with a reputation for disorder and instability"), its language appeared shortly thereafter in Agreements with prospective settlers in Carolina and New Jersey.[127] These latter Agreements are especially instructive, since they contained language effectively encompassing both belief and conduct—limiting the free exercise of religion solely for the prevention of either "Lycentiousnesse" or injury to others.[128]

Five years later, in 1669, the proprietors of Carolina issued the Fundamental Constitutions. Though they never took full effect, the Fundamental Constitutions are noteworthy for two reasons. First, John Locke, principal adviser and assistant to Lord Ashley, drew upon his theories of religious toleration to help draft it; and second, it provided exceptionally broad freedom for Christians—but also, radically, for "Jews, heathens, and other dissenters from the purity of Christian religion," Native Americans, and even slaves—to choose among religions (though freedom of non-religion and individualistic non-institutionalized belief were strictly excluded).[129] This was, for the historical period, a very expansive understanding of religious freedom, generally, and free exercise, specifically.

Such privileging of religious exercise persisted (albeit differentially) throughout the seventeenth and eighteenth centuries to the time of the First Congress. As mentioned earlier, religion occupied a special place in prevailing religious and philosophical understandings of human judgment. The existence of God (a natural and nearly universal belief in the early republic) meant that His will (expressed in the consciences of the faithful)

---

126. Ibid., 1425. Reflecting upon the Reformation, America's founding period, the drafting of the Constitution and the jurisprudence of U.S. courts, it is possible to perceive the early development of religious freedom not just as an outgrowth of Christian teachings and Enlightenment philosophy, but also as the historical record of bitter contestation between Protestants and Catholics over several centuries.

127. Ibid., 1426.

128. Ibid., 1427.

129. Ibid., 1428–29.

was superior to other forms of individual or social judgment.[130] Thus, the right to free exercise of religion was, fundamentally, an institutional protection of a transcendent duty.

There were, of course, exceptions to this prevailing sensibility. Jefferson found the more intense varieties of religious expression that were widespread in America (e.g., Enthusiasm) to be absurd and hoped that religious freedom would lead all citizens on a rational march toward Unitarianism— a position with which aggressive interpretation of the Free Exercise Clause was incompatible.[131] But many founders recognized that Enlightenment solutions were misplaced in the United States. Madison, in a letter to Jefferson, wrote: "However erroneous or ridiculous these grounds of dissention and faction may appear to the enlightened Statesman or the benevolent philosopher, the bulk of mankind, who are neither Statesmen nor philosophers, will continue to view them in a different light."[132] Free exercise thus answered the question of the relationship of religion to political order with pluralism, limited sovereignty, and the right—if not the *duty*—of people to follow their consciences on their own paths to God.[133]

In summary, the U.S. Constitution was the first national framework to institutionalize the separation of church and state in order to secure religious liberty. Its innovative approach, providing for both disestablishment and free exercise, was rooted in a long religious and political history— one stemming historically from the theology of the Protestant Reformation (especially Luther's doctrine of the two kingdoms and Calvin's theology of conscience) and, more proximately, from the religious arguments of Puritans and evangelicals (including Roger Williams) and the theologically informed political arguments of Enlightenment thinkers and civic

130. Ibid., 1497–98.
131. Ibid., 1514–15. For a sustained treatment of Jefferson's views, see Dreisbach, *Thomas Jefferson and the Wall of Separation between Church and State*.
132. McConnell, "The Origins and Historical Understanding of Free Exercise of Religion," 1515.
133. But see Marci A. Hamilton, "The Belief/Conduct Paradigm in the Supreme Court's Free Exercise Jurisprudence: A Theological Account of the Failure to Protect Religious Conduct," *Ohio State Law Journal* 54 (1993). Hamilton observes that the Supreme Court's Free Exercise jurisprudence has shifted markedly from this vision, especially in recent times. The Court's threshold inquiry is now whether the contested religious interest is belief or conduct—the former is protected absolutely, while the latter is subject to state law. She argues that this belief/conduct paradigm manifests a distinctly Protestant worldview, namely, the Protestant Pauline theology of the relationship between faith and works under the law. In this article, Hamilton advocates for a larger Pauline vision, one in which religious life is viewed as a dialectical relationship between faith and works of love, such that Free Exercise jurisprudence is revitalized.

republicans (such as John Locke and James Madison). In shaping a nation, the American constitutional experiment also influenced other liberal democracies, as well as the development of international human rights law.[134] Consequently, it was vital to the evolution of religious freedom in the West.

134. Richard W. Garnett, "Francis Bacon Takes on the Ghouls: The 'First Principles' of Religious Freedom," review of "Religion and the American Constitutional Experiment: Essential Rights and Liberties," by John Witte, Jr., *Green Bag* 3 (2000).

CHAPTER 3
Religious Liberty in International Human Rights Law

It is in accordance with their dignity as persons—that is, beings endowed with reason and free will and therefore privileged to bear personal responsibility—that all men should be at once impelled by nature and also bound by a moral obligation to seek the truth, especially religious truth. They are also bound to adhere to the truth, once it is known, and to order their whole lives in accord with the demands of truth. However, men cannot discharge these obligations in a manner in keeping with their own nature unless they enjoy immunity from external coercion as well as psychological freedom. Therefore the right to religious freedom has its foundation not in the subjective disposition of the person, but in his very nature.

—*Dignitatis Humanae*[1]

Freedom of religion, long desired by individuals and religious dissenters in particular, did not become a legal reality until the modern era (e.g., through the First Amendment), and even as late as the Second World War, one global study declared a total absence of "a generally accepted postulate of international law that every State is under legal obligation to accord religious liberty within its jurisdiction."[2] However, in the relatively brief historical period since, freedom of religion or belief has become just such an accepted postulate of international law.

1. Vatican Ecumenical Council II, "*Dignitatis Humanae (Declaration of Religious Freedom),* On the Right of the Person and Communities to Social and Civil Liberty in Religious Matters" (December 7, 1965).
2. James E. Wood, Jr., "The Relationship of Religious Liberty to Civil Liberty and a Democratic State," *Brigham Young University Law Review* 1998 (1998): 492–93, quoting Norman J. Padelford, *International Guarantees of Religious Liberty* (New York: International Missionary Council, 1942).

This chapter explores key elements of that development, beginning with an examination of religious liberty provisions in international human rights law—the major documents and treaties, as well as issues of special concern. Next, it briefly considers two additional sources of international rights monitoring and enforcement: the U.S. Commission on International Religious Freedom and the European Court of Human Rights. Finally, it discusses the twentieth-century contributions of religious institutions to religious liberty, focusing on the role of the Catholic Church in elaborating a moral foundation for religious freedom and championing it as a pathway to peace. The resulting portrait of religious liberty as an international human right, when combined with the historical evolution of religious freedom presented in Chapter 2, provides a backdrop against which to analyze the emergence of Islamic law as an alternative/oppositional paradigm of human rights.

I. FREEDOM OF RELIGION IN INTERNATIONAL HUMAN RIGHTS LAW

Depending upon one's perspective, the international law of human rights may be understood as either creating or resting upon a universal morality of human rights. This morality is said to consist of the fundamental assertion that every human being has dignity, the ability to claim that particular acts violate human beings, and a belief that those who affirm the inherent dignity of humanity are obligated to mitigate human suffering.[3] These basic claims do not by themselves provoke much controversy. They are also quite consistent with "the transnational diffusion of ideas of human rights in the post-war period and their institutionalization in international organizations," which has "firmly established a charismatic status of 'universal personhood' to which rights are, at least in principle, attached independently from formal state membership or nationality."[4] As with many issues in international law, differences of opinion arise not at the level of generalities, but with regard to specific principles and rights. Religious liberty

3. Michael J. Perry, "A Right to Religious Freedom? The Universality of Human Rights, the Relativity of Culture," *Roger Williams University Law Review* 10 *Symposium: Religious Liberty in America and Beyond: Celebrating the Legacy of Roger Williams on the 400th Anniversary of His Birth* (2005) [hereinafter *Roger Williams Symposium* (2005)]: 414–15.
4. Matthias Koenig, "Religion and Public Order in Modern Nation-States: Institutional Varieties and Contemporary Transformations," in *Religion in the Public Sphere: A Comparative Analysis of German, Israeli, American and International Law*, ed. Winfried Brugger and Michael Karayanni (Berlin: Springer, 2007), 14.

rights are an excellent example of this, as shall be addressed below and in later chapters on Islamic international law.

By way of orientation, the international framework of religious freedom consists of four major documents: the 1948 Universal Declaration of Human Rights (UDHR),[5] the 1966 International Covenant on Civil and Political Rights (ICCPR),[6] the 1981 United Nations Declaration on the Elimination of All Forms of Intolerance and of Discrimination Based on Religion or Belief (1981 Declaration),[7] and the 1989 Vienna Concluding Document (extending the 1981 Declaration's religious liberty norms, especially to religious groups).[8]

5. Universal Declaration of Human Rights, G.A. Res. 217A (III), U.N. GAOR, 3d Sess., at 71, U.N. Doc. A/810 (Dec. 10, 1948).

6. International Covenant on Civil and Political Rights, G.A. Res. 2200A (XXI), 21 U.N. GAOR Supp. (No. 16) at 52, U.N. Doc. A/6316 (1966), Mar. 23, 1976, 999 U.N.T.S. 171.

7. Declaration on the Elimination of All Forms of Intolerance and of Discrimination Based on Religion or Belief, G.A. Res. 36/55, U.N. Doc. A/RES/36/55 (Nov. 25, 1981).

8. OSCE Office for Democratic Institutions and Human Rights (ODIHR), *OSCE Human Dimension Commitments*, vol. 2, *Chronological Compilation*, 3rd ed. (Warsaw: 2011): 39–55. Though the 1989 Vienna Concluding Document is not treated separately here, Principles 16 and 17 are worth noting.

Principle 16:

(16) In order to ensure the freedom of the individual to profess and practise religion or belief, the participating States will, inter alia,

(16.1) take effective measures to prevent and eliminate discrimination against individuals or communities on the grounds of religion or belief in the recognition, exercise and enjoyment of human rights and fundamental freedoms in all fields of civil, political, economic, social and cultural life, and to ensure the effective equality between believers and non-believers;

(16.2) foster a climate of mutual tolerance and respect between believers of different communities as well as between believers and non-believers;

(16.3) grant upon their request to communities of believers, practising or prepared to practise their faith within the constitutional framework of their States, recognition of the status provided for them in their respective countries;

(16.4) respect the right of these religious communities to

- establish and maintain freely accessible places of worship or assembly,

- organize themselves according to their own hierarchical and institutional structure,

- select, appoint and replace their personnel in accordance with their respective requirements and standards as well as with any freely accepted arrangement between them and their State,

- solicit and receive voluntary financial and other contributions;

(16.5) engage in consultations with religious faiths, institutions and organizations in order to achieve a better understanding of the requirements of religious freedom;

(16.6) respect the right of everyone to give and receive religious education in the language of his choice, whether individually or in association with others;

For reasons of space, the first three texts will be the focus of attention here, though it is worth mentioning two other international documents relevant to religious freedom: the 1989 United Nations Convention on the Rights of the Child (e.g., on the rights of parents with regard to a child's religious upbringing),[9] and the 1992 Declaration on the Rights of the Persons Belonging to National or Ethnic, Religious, and Linguistic Minorities.[10] Collectively, these documents reflect the twentieth-century

(16.7) in this context respect, inter alia, the liberty of parents to ensure the religious and moral education of their children in conformity with their own convictions;

(16.8) allow the training of religious personnel in appropriate institutions;

(16.9) respect the right of individual believers and communities of believers to acquire, possess, and use sacred books, religious publications in the language of their choice and other articles and materials related to the practice of religion or belief;

(16.10) allow religious faiths, institutions and organizations to produce, import and disseminate religious publications and materials;

(16.11) favourably consider the interest of religious communities to participate in public dialogue, including through the mass media.

Principle 17:

(17) The participating States recognize that the exercise of the above-mentioned rights relating to the freedom of religion or belief may be subject only to such limitations as are provided by law and consistent with their obligations under international law and with their international commitments. They will ensure in their laws and regulations and in their application the full and effective exercise of the freedom of thought, conscience, religion or belief.

Ibid., 42–43. For a more in-depth discussion of Principles 16 and 17, see W. Cole Durham, Jr., "Perspectives on Religious Liberty: A Comparative Framework," in *Religious Human Rights in Global Perspective: Legal Perspectives,* ed. Johan van der Vyver and John Witte, Jr. (Boston: Martinus Nijhoff Publishers, 1996), 37–44.

9. Convention on the Rights of the Child, G.A. Res. 44/25, U.N. Doc. A/RES/44/25 (Nov. 20, 1989).

For example, see Article 14:

1. States Parties shall respect the right of the child to freedom of thought, conscience and religion.

2. States Parties shall respect the rights and duties of the parents and, when applicable, legal guardians, to provide direction to the child in the exercise of his or her right in a manner consistent with the evolving capacities of the child.

3. Freedom to manifest one's religion or beliefs may be subject only to such limitations as are prescribed by law and are necessary to protect public safety, order, health or morals, or the fundamental rights and freedoms of others.

10. Declaration on the Rights of the Persons Belonging to National or Ethnic, Religious, and Linguistic Minorities, G.A. Res. 47/135, U.N. Doc. A/RES/47/135 (Dec. 18, 1992).

movement toward the internationalization of religious human rights.[11] After discussing the noted texts, two additional areas of special difficulty—the rights of religious minorities and proselytism—are briefly explored.

A. Universal Declaration of Human Rights

Article 18

Everyone has the right to freedom of thought, conscience and religion; this right includes freedom to change his religion or belief, and freedom, either alone or in community with others and in public or private, to manifest his religion or belief in teaching, practice, worship and observance.

The United Nations Charter only cursorily addresses the protection of rights.[12] Article 1(3) identifies international cooperation in promoting respect for human rights as one of the U.N.'s purposes. Article 55(c) commits the U.N. to the promotion of universal respect for and observation of human rights and fundamental freedoms. Article 56 pledges members to jointly and separately assist the U.N. in achieving the goals of Article 55. Thus, while the Charter envisioned the U.N. playing a significant role in the international protection of rights, it was not yet clear what those rights would be (apart, relevantly, from specific reference to non-discrimination on the basis of religion).[13]

The formulation of a comprehensive list of basic human rights and freedoms was instead the goal of the UDHR's drafters—a goal considered so important that, in order to achieve agreement on its provisions, Eleanor Roosevelt (the drafting committee's chair) assured participating states of its legal impotence.[14] Despite the Declaration's lack of binding status, it is significant both for recognizing religious liberty as a human right and for imposing a moral obligation on signatory states to uphold it.[15]

11. For additional discussion of these treaties, see Natan Lerner, *Religion, Secular Beliefs and Human Rights: 25 Years after the 1981 Declaration*, Studies in Religion, Secular Beliefs, and Human Rights, vol. 2 (Boston: Martinus Nijhoff Publishers, 2006); Natan Lerner, *Religion, Beliefs, and International Human Rights*, Religion and Human Rights Series (Maryknoll, NY: Orbis Books, 2000).
12. Carolyn Evans, "Time for a Treaty? The Legal Insufficiency of the Declaration on the Elimination of All Forms of Intolerance and Discrimination," *Brigham Young University Law Review* 2007 (2007).
13. Ibid., 621.
14. Ibid., 622.
15. Derek H. Davis, "The Evolution of Religious Freedom as a Universal Human Right," *Brigham Young University Law Review* 2002 (2002): 226.

To contemporary readers, Article 18's guarantee of "the right to freedom of thought, conscience, and religion" may seem redundant. However, at the time of drafting, freedom of conscience was not universally considered a consolidated legal concept. Incorporated despite some opposition, "freedom of conscience" refers to "pacifism, obedience to superior orders, the power of the state to impose obligations in areas such as taxation, and other controversial problems regarding matters of principle for the individual."[16]

Article 18 also addresses issues that became more problematic when the ICCPR and the 1981 Declaration were drafted—conversion and religious proselytizing.[17] Several religions were uncomfortable with the language, including Orthodox and Catholic Christians, but, then as now, it was most troubling for Muslims.

Charles Malik, Lebanese Ambassador to the U.N. and the United States, was a leading voice in establishing the U.N. Commission on Human Rights. A philosopher and outspoken Arab Christian, Malik insisted that the UDHR include Article 18 (providing for the right to freedom of thought, conscience and religion, including the right to change one's beliefs).[18] Unless the Declaration could "create conditions which [would] allow man to develop ultimate loyalties . . . over and above his loyalty to the State," he cautioned, "we shall have legislated not for man's freedom but for his enslavement."[19] Malik's proposal stemmed from his experiences in Lebanon, a country then known for the relatively harmonious coexistence of its many ethnic and religious groups, which had served as a haven for people fleeing religious persecution.[20]

As human rights scholar Mary Ann Glendon recounts, Malik's amendment "touched a nerve in other states with large Muslim populations," because of both the Qur'anic prohibition of apostasy and deep resentment of Christian missionary activity.[21] The coupling of the freedom to change religion or belief with the freedom of religious expression "appeared to endorse a conception of religious freedom that protected the freedom both

16. Natan Lerner, "The Nature and Minimum Standards of Freedom of Religion or Belief," *Brigham Young University Law Review* 2000 (2000): 911.

17. Ibid., 911–12.

18. Perry, "A Right to Religious Freedom?," 385.

19. Ibid., 385, quoting Charles Malik, "What are Human Rights?," *The Rotarian* (August 1948).

20. Mary Ann Glendon, *A World Made New* (New York: Random House, 2001), 70.

21. Ibid., 70. See also Daveed Gartenstein-Ross, "No Other Gods before Me: Spheres of Influence in the Relationship between Christianity and Islam," *Denver Journal of International Law and Policy* 33 (2005).

of the individual to convert to another religion and for the right of persons of that other religion to seek by argument and example to convert the individual to their faith."[22] Muslim countries, affected by the legacies of colonial occupation and the Islamic prohibition against rejection of Islamic beliefs, were deeply troubled by this aspect of Article 18.

The Saudi Arabian representative, al-Barudi, was especially persistent in his dissent. Objecting generally to the dominance of Western cultural patterns in the text, rejecting the idea that all human beings are endowed with reason and conscience, and challenging the phrase "dignity and rights" as ambiguous, al-Barudi nevertheless reserved his harshest criticism for Article 18.[23] Concerned by the construal of freedom of conscience to include the right to change one's religion, he argued that it was against Islamic law and would open the door to proselytism, political unrest, and perhaps even war; he thus requested that it be amended.[24]

Throughout the committee hearings, the Islamic countries appeared to agree with the Saudi position.[25] However, when the Declaration came before the General Assembly for a final vote, Muhammad Zafrullah Khan of Pakistan presented an Islamic defense of freedom of conscience, citing the Qur'anic prescription against compulsion in religion and the missionary character of Islam itself.[26] The Declaration passed by a vote of forty-eight to zero, with eight abstentions: Saudi Arabia abstained, but all other states with large Muslim populations voted in favor of the Declaration.

Despite these difficulties, the UDHR is widely considered to be the single most important legal document in modern international human rights law, and much of its content is now incorporated into customary international law.[27] Contemporary understandings of religious liberty as a human right are indelibly marked by it. Even so, because of the overriding priority

22. Kevin Boyle, "Freedom of Religion in International Law," in *Religion, Human Rights and International Law: A Critical Examination of Islamic State Practices*, ed. Javaid Rehman and Susan C. Breau (Boston: Martinùs Nijhoff Publishers, 2007), 36.

23. 3 U.N. GAOR, C.3, 127th mtg., U.N. Doc. A/C.3/SR. 127 (1948); David Little, John Kelsay, and Abdulaziz A. Sachedina, *Human Rights and the Conflict of Cultures: Western and Islamic Perspectives on Religious Liberty* (Columbia: University of South Carolina Press, 1988), 35.

24. Little, Kelsay, and Sachedina, *Human Rights and the Conflict of Cultures*, 35–36.

25. Ibid., 36; 3 U.N. GAOR, C.3, 127th mtg., U.N. Doc. A/C.3/SR. 127 (1948).

26. Little, Kelsay, and Sachedina, *Human Rights and the Conflict of Cultures*, 36; 3 U.N. GAOR, 182d Plenary mtg., U.N. Doc. A/PV. 182 (1948). See also Muhammad Zafrullah Khan, *Islam and Human Rights* (Islamabad: Islam International Publications Ltd., 1999).

27. Natan Lerner, "Religious Human Rights under the United Nations," in van der Vyver and Witte, *Legal Perspectives*, 88.

given to its passage, the UDHR could not specify in greater detail the substance of freedom of religion as a right in international law.[28] That task fell to the drafters of the International Covenants nearly two decades later.

B. International Covenant on Civil and Political Rights

Article 18

1. Everyone shall have the right to freedom of thought, conscience and religion. This right shall include freedom to have or to adopt a religion or belief of his choice, and freedom, either individually or in community with others and in public or private, to manifest his religion or belief in worship, observance, practice and teaching.

2. No one shall be subject to coercion which would impair his freedom to have or to adopt a religion or belief of his choice.

3. Freedom to manifest one's religion or beliefs may be subject only to such limitations as are prescribed by law and are necessary to protect public safety, order, health, or morals or the fundamental rights and freedoms of others.

4. The States Parties to the present Covenant undertake to have respect for the liberty of parents and, when applicable, legal guardians to ensure the religious and moral education of their children in conformity with their own convictions.

The International Covenant on Civil and Political Rights (ICCPR) and the International Covenant on Economic, Social and Cultural Rights (ICESCR) were originally intended to be a single treaty. This unified vision was shattered by the politics of the Cold War, but the ICCPR nevertheless succeeded in elaborating upon the specific scope and content of religious liberty rights in international law.[29] Moreover, it remains the only binding treaty that contains a coherent articulation of such rights.[30]

Articles 18 of the UDHR and the ICCPR capture a cornerstone of modern Western political thought, namely, the necessity of freedom of thought, conscience, and religion for pluralistic and democratic society.[31] But just as they sparked controversy in 1948, attempts to define similar provisions in

28. Boyle, "Freedom of Religion in International Law," 38.
29. Evans, "Time for a Treaty?," 622.
30. Lerner, "The Nature and Minimum Standards of Freedom of Religion or Belief," 914.
31. Mashood A. Baderin, *International Human Rights and Islamic Law* (New York: Oxford University Press, 2003), 118.

Article 18 of the ICCPR were met with opposition from Muslim-majority countries (e.g., Egypt, Saudi Arabia, Yemen, and Afghanistan), which agitated for its deletion.[32]

The Saudi Arabian delegate expressed concerns about missionary work, proselytism, the protection of individuals from errors and heresies, conversion born of weakness or credulity, and diverse cultural situations.[33] Islamic law scholar Mashood Baderin notes that rather than completely deleting the controversial clause, a compromise based on submissions from Brazil, the Philippines, and the United Kingdom was achieved.[34] The phrasing, "This right includes freedom to change his religion or belief," was replaced by "This right shall include freedom to have or to adopt a religion or belief of his choice."[35] The Article was then adopted unanimously without reservations, and the ICCPR entered into force in March 1976.

As adopted, Article 18 of the ICCPR guarantees generally the same religious rights as the UDHR, with some important caveats. The ICCPR adds certain rights (e.g., the right of parents to direct the religious education of their children) and, at a broader level, it defines religion so as to encompass both theistic and non-theistic religions.[36] Also, Article 18(2) prohibits coercion, which is generally understood to include not only the use of force or threats, but also "subtle forms of illegitimate influence, such as moral pressure or material enticement."[37]

However, the ICCPR does not explicitly refer to the right to change one's religion. As Natan Lerner notes, "[m]ost specialists interpret the Covenant's Article 18 as fully recognizing the right to change religion, as proclaimed by the Universal Declaration. But its failure to explicitly protect the right to change religion began a downward trend, which became more pronounced and very problematic during the preparation and adoption of the 1981 Declaration."[38] Of particular relevance, the Human Rights Committee

32. Ibid., 118–19; Karl Josef Partsch, "Freedom of Conscience and Expression, and Political Freedoms," in *The International Bill of Rights: The Covenant on Civil and Political Rights*, ed. Louis Henkin (New York: Columbia University Press, 1981), 209–45.

33. 15 U.N. GAOR, C.3, 1021st, 1023d, 1025th mtg., U.N. Docs A/C.3/SR. 1021, 1023, 1025 (1960).

34. Baderin, *International Human Rights and Islamic Law*, 118; 15 U.N. GAOR, C.3, 1026th mtg., U.N. Doc. A/C.3/SR. 1026 (1960).

35. Baderin, *International Human Rights and Islamic Law*, 119; 15 U.N. GAOR, C.3, 1027th mtg., U.N. Doc. A/C.3/SR. 1027 (1960).

36. Davis, "The Evolution of Religious Freedom as a Universal Human Right," 225–26.

37. Lerner, "Religious Human Rights under the United Nations," 91.

38. Lerner, "The Nature and Minimum Standards of Freedom of Religion or Belief," 914–15.

states in its General Comment 22 that "the freedom to 'have or to adopt' a religion or belief necessarily entails the freedom to choose a religion or belief including, *inter alia*, the right to replace one's current religion or belief with another or to adopt atheistic views as well as the right to retain one's religion or belief."[39]

Signatory Islamic states have not formally accepted this understanding of their obligations under the Covenant and uniformly remain outside of the international consensus on this central feature of religious liberty rights.[40] Similar difficulties arise over the definition of "religion or belief," for while the Committee makes clear in its General Comment that Article 18 protects non-theistic and atheistic beliefs (as well as the right not to profess any religion or belief), the Islamic tradition of tolerance extends only to "People of the Book." To date, these issues remain unresolved.

C. U.N. Declaration on the Elimination of All Forms of Intolerance and of Discrimination Based on Religion or Belief

Article 1

1. Everyone shall have the right to freedom of thought, conscience and religion. This right shall include freedom to have a religion or whatever belief of his choice, and freedom, either individually or in community with others and in public or private, to manifest his religion or belief in worship, observance, practice and teaching.

2. No one shall be subject to coercion which would impair his freedom to have a religion or belief of his choice.

3. Freedom to manifest one's religion or belief may be subject only to such limitations as are prescribed by law and are necessary to protect public safety, order, health or morals or the fundamental rights and freedoms of others.

All of the human rights instruments presented here are important, but each is significant for different reasons.[41] The UDHR was revolutionary and, in many respects, gave birth to the modern understanding of international human rights. The ICCPR, while not especially innovative, is critical

---

39. U.N. Human Rights Committee, *General Comment Adopted by the Human Rights Committee under Article 40, Paragraph 4, of the International Covenant on Civil and Political Rights*, para. 5, U.N. Doc. CCPR/C/21/Rev.1/Add.4 (Sept. 27, 1993). See also Boyle, "Freedom of Religion in International Law," 40.

40. Boyle, "Freedom of Religion in International Law," 40–41.

41. Davis, "The Evolution of Religious Freedom as a Universal Human Right," 228.

because it is a binding treaty and, as such, is enforceable in courts. The U.N. Declaration on the Elimination of All Forms of Intolerance and of Discrimination Based on Religion or Belief (1981 Declaration) brings a new degree of rights comprehensiveness to the international law of religious freedom: more than any other document, the international community turns to it in order to determine and define which religious rights should be respected.[42]

Although not binding, the 1981 Declaration allows for certain measures of implementation. For instance, Special Rapporteurs have already been appointed and have begun producing a highly valuable body of information.[43] "Religion" is defined to include "beliefs," which are themselves now understood to include non-theistic convictions, such as atheism, rationalism, and agnosticism.[44] In this way, the 1981 Declaration is expansive. Similarly, Article 6 gives extensive content to liberty of conscience and free exercise of religion, incorporating a list of nine specific freedoms.[45]

However, not all additions have been equally well-received. For example, Article 5 deals specifically with the religious rights of children and their parents.[46] The net effect of its provisions is to juxtapose "the parents' right to rear and educate their children in accordance with their own religion and

42. Ibid., 228.
43. Lerner, "The Nature and Minimum Standards of Freedom of Religion or Belief," 918.
44. Ibid., 919.
45. Declaration on the Elimination of All Forms of Intolerance and of Discrimination Based on Religion or Belief, G.A. Res. 36/55, U.N. Doc. A/RES/36/55 (Nov. 25, 1981).
Article 6: In accordance with article I of the present Declaration, and subject to the provisions of article 1, paragraph 3, the right to freedom of thought, conscience, religion or belief shall include, inter alia, the following freedoms:
    (a) To worship or assemble in connection with a religion or belief, and to establish and maintain places for these purposes;
    (b) To establish and maintain appropriate charitable or humanitarian institutions;
    (c) To make, acquire and use to an adequate extent the necessary articles and materials related to the rites or customs of a religion or belief;
    (d) To write, issue and disseminate relevant publications in these areas;
    (e) To teach a religion or belief in places suitable for these purposes;
    (f) To solicit and receive voluntary financial and other contributions from individuals and institutions;
    (g) To train, appoint, elect or designate by succession appropriate leaders called for by the requirements and standards of any religion or belief;
    (h) To observe days of rest and to celebrate holidays and ceremonies in accordance with the precepts of one's religion or belief;
    (i) To establish and maintain communications with individuals and communities in matters of religion and belief at the national and international levels.
46. Ibid.

beliefs with the state's power to protect the best interests of the child, including the lofty aspirations for the child's upbringing."[47] The Declaration's drafters would not yield to the debates on this matter and refused to offer any principles for the resolution of disputes.

Another controversy surrounding the 1981 Declaration concerns conversion. In response to Muslim objections, references to the right to change one's religion were deleted from the text of both the preamble and Article 1 (therefore departing from both the UDHR and the ICCPR).[48] To satisfy those who objected to the deletion, a new Article 8 was added, providing that nothing in the 1981 Declaration should be construed as detracting from the previous two agreements.[49] One potential result is both absurd and troubling: nations that do not ratify the ICCPR can claim that the right to change one's religion cannot be afforded the status of international law.[50] Though others conclude that the right to change one's religion is implicit in the concept of liberty of conscience and free exercise, the issue persists as a point of contestation.

Article 5:
1. The parents or, as the case may be, the legal guardians of the child have the right to organize the life within the family in accordance with their religion or belief and bearing in mind the moral education in which they believe the child should be brought up.
2. Every child shall enjoy the right to have access to education in the matter of religion or belief in accordance with the wishes of his parents or, as the case may be, legal guardians, and shall not be compelled to receive teaching on religion or belief against the wishes of his parents or legal guardians, the best interests of the child being the guiding principle.
3. The child shall be protected from any form of discrimination on the ground of religion or belief. He shall be brought up in a spirit of understanding, tolerance, friendship among peoples, peace and universal brotherhood, respect for freedom of religion or belief of others, and in full consciousness that his energy and talents should be devoted to the service of his fellow men.
4. In the case of a child who is not under the care either of his parents or of legal guardians, due account shall be taken of their expressed wishes or of any other proof of their wishes in the matter of religion or belief, the best interests of the child being the guiding principle.
5. Practices of a religion or belief in which a child is brought up must not be injurious to his physical or mental health or to his full development, taking into account article 1, paragraph 3, of the present Declaration.
47. John Witte, Jr., "Introduction: The Foundations and Frontiers of Religious Liberty," *Emory International Law Review* 21 *Symposium: The Foundations and Frontiers of Religious Liberty* (2007): 7.
48. Davis, "The Evolution of Religious Freedom as a Universal Human Right," 229.
49. G.A. Res. 36/55.
Article 8: Nothing in the present Declaration shall be construed as restricting or derogating from any right defined in the Universal Declaration of Human Rights and the International Covenants on Human Rights.
50. Davis, "The Evolution of Religious Freedom as a Universal Human Right," 220.

As American lawyer Donna Sullivan observes, the norms in the Declaration "hold a striking potential for conflict with other rights; consequently, the task of applying the Declaration to concrete situations will challenge human rights advocates to devise interpretive approaches that will maximize the protection afforded to all the rights implicated."[51] She continues by noting two general features of the Declaration that are likely to affect the resolution of such conflicts. First, it is directed primarily toward actions taken by governments or individuals who do not subscribe to a given religion or belief against individuals who do. Second, Sullivan notes that "application of the Declaration is most straightforward *when the belief or practice under consideration corresponds to a typically Western model of religion, in which religious institutions and authority are structurally separable from political and other social institutions.*"[52] This observation is consistent with the plethora of controversies surrounding the Declaration's drafting—conflicts animated by differences in the legal philosophies, moral traditions, and political cultures of Western and Islamic constituents.

On the twenty-fifth anniversary of the adoption of the 1981 Declaration, government representatives from fifty countries gathered to discuss its merits and challenges. Four workshops were convened, one of which focused on "Freedom of Religion or Belief vis-à-vis Freedom of Expression."[53] Among other recommendations, workshop members stated that "[t]he debate should be seen in historical context, including the relevant geo-political, ideological and theological frameworks."[54] The importance of dialogue across religious faiths appeared elsewhere in the workshop reports and recommendations, too.[55] To commemorate the occasion, representatives drafted the "Prague Declaration on Freedom of Religion or Belief." In addition to affirming the UDHR, the ICCPR, and the 1981 Declaration, the Prague Declaration presents a robust list of religious freedoms, including the extension of rights to non-theistic and atheistic beliefs, the right

51. Donna J. Sullivan, "Advancing the Freedom of Religion or Belief through the UN Declaration on the Elimination of All Forms of Intolerance and Discrimination," *American Journal of International Law* 82 (1988): 490.
52. Ibid., 490 (emphasis added).
53. Widney Brown and Malik Imtiaz Sarwar, "Workshop 1: Freedom of Religion or Belief vis-à-vis Freedom of Expression," *Religion and Human Rights: An International Journal* 2 (2007): 55–59.
54. Jeroen Temperman, "25th Anniversary Commemoration of the Adoption of the 1981 UN Declaration on the Elimination of Intolerance and Discrimination Based on Religion or Belief: a Report," *Religion and Human Rights: An International Journal* 2 (2007): 25.
55. "Workshop Recommendations," *Religion and Human Rights: An International Journal* 2 (2007): 85–89.

not to believe, the right to manifest religion publicly (usually associated with proselytism), and a condemnation of religious violence.[56] The drafters of the Prague Declaration also included at its end a parenthetical note informing readers that it is not a consensus document.[57]

D. Spotlight on the Issues—Religious Minorities and Proselytism

As previously illustrated, the international law of religious rights, while providing resources for the protection of religious freedom, is not without conflict or inconsistency. Difficult questions remain, among them the place of minority religions in countries where church and state are joined because it is believed that the majority religion represents the only true faith.[58] In such cases, the dominant religion has every incentive to marginalize religious minorities, particularly when they represent "foreign" faiths (note that the issues of religious minorities and proselytism are related).[59] These challenges are exacerbated by the predominance of individualism in international human rights law, as well as by institutional difficulties.[60]

For example, under the European Convention on Human Rights, states are accorded a significant "margin of appreciation" when they choose to legitimate one particular version of a religion over others.[61] Likewise, under the ICCPR, religious minorities are defined so narrowly as to make the invocation of group religious status difficult to achieve and, consequently, likely to produce future discrimination against emergent, less populous groups.[62] National law can similarly be used to discriminate against religious minorities: a study of Russian, Belgian, French, and German law revealed that many countries violate the international treaties to which

56. "Prague Declaration on Freedom of Religion or Belief," *Religion and Human Rights: An International Journal* 2 (2007): 91–92.

57. Ibid., 92.

58. Mark W. Janis, "Faith, the State, and the Humility of International Law," *Journal of Catholic Legal Studies* 45 (2006): 71.

59. Ibid., 71.

60. For the argument that "religious freedom can and should be interpreted as an individual right, and as a group right only if derived from individual rights and not overriding them," see Anat Scolnicov, *The Right to Religious Freedom in International Law: Between Group Rights and Individual Rights* (New York: Routledge, 2011).

61. Bernadette Meyler, "The Limits of Group Rights: Religious Institutions and Religious Minorities in International Law," *St. John's Journal of Legal Commentary* 22 (2007): 537.

62. Ibid., 537–38.

they are signatories by defining disfavored religious groups as "sects," "cults," or groups otherwise ineligible for the treaty protection that comes with religious status.[63] Even more grave, religious minorities are especially vulnerable to slavery, genocide, and other crimes against humanity.[64]

Proposals for improving the status of religious minorities vary. Based on the strong positive correlation between the specific right to religious expression and state human rights practices generally, one scholar-practitioner argues that the right to choose and change one's religion should be recognized as a non-derogable liberty, with other religious liberties (e.g., association and education) subject to a compelling government interest test.[65] Other scholars suggest greater legal accommodation of designated "sacred spaces" for religious minority groups,[66] and the incorporation of international religious rights law into domestic law as part of a comprehensive package of legislative and administrative measures.[67] While they differ on solutions, however, all agree that the situation of religious minorities is not improving, even as the international law of religious freedom continues to develop and advance.

A second issue of concern, alluded to throughout this chapter, is that of proselytism. The clearest and most consistent objections to proselytism are based on the link between extreme forms of the practice and coercion to change one's religion.[68] These were the objections raised, for example, during the drafting of the UDHR, the ICCPR, and the 1981 Declaration. However, while this fear is at times legitimate, it can also be used as a smokescreen to hide other considerations (e.g., the protection of majority religions or established faiths).

At present, there are three rules governing proselytism that are widely accepted in the international community: first, the freedom to change

63. Nathaniel Stinnett, "Defining Away Religious Freedom in Europe: How Four Democracies Get Away with Discriminating against Religious Minorities," *Boston College International and Comparative Law Review* 28 (2005).

64. Nathan A. Adams, IV, "A Human Rights Imperative: Extending Religious Liberty Beyond the Border," *Cornell International Law Journal* 33 (2000).

65. Ibid., 60–63.

66. Alice Diver and John Thompson, "Prayers, Planners and Pluralism: Protecting the Rights of Minority Religious Groups," in *Religion, Human Rights and International Law*, ed. Javaid Rehman and Susan C. Breau (New York: Martinus Nijhoff Publishers, 2007), 465–88.

67. Javaid Rehman, "Religion, Minority Rights and Muslims of the United Kingdom," in Rehman and Breau, *Religion, Human Rights and International Law*, 521–50.

68. Paul M. Taylor, "The Questionable Grounds of Objections to Proselytism and Certain Other Forms of Religious Expression," *Brigham Young University Law Review* 2006 (2006).

religion, which renders laws prohibiting or punishing apostasy unlawful; second, the inclusion of proselytism in the freedom to manifest a religion for some (but not all) religions (therefore, national laws prohibiting all proselytism are inconsistent with international human rights law); and third, proselytism of the kind that utilizes coercive measures impairing free choice is illegal.[69] Although these rules find general support, controversy persists. Perhaps the most contentious issue involves the difficult balance between the freedom to maintain a religion without interference and the freedom to proselytize.[70] This debate has assumed new significance in recent decades, as democratization continues to open up countries previously closed to outsiders. For example, in parts of Russia, Eastern Europe, Africa, and Latin America, "the human rights revolution has brought on something of a new war for souls between indigenous and foreign religious groups."[71]

In view of both the urgency of the issue and the relative silence of international instruments on it, various proposals exist. They emphasize such factors as the connection between proselytism and the recognized right to change one's religion, the need for regulation and protection of the freedom to manifest religious views, the necessity of balancing free expression and privacy rights in a democratic society, and the relationship between religious rights and education.[72]

Others take a stronger view, asserting that "the freedom to engage in proselytism must be protected irrespective of the content of the views asserted by the source, the manner in which those views are asserted, and whether the interference stems from state or private action."[73] While it is not yet clear whether and how the questions raised by proselytism will be resolved, it seems likely to remain a contested issue in international religious rights law, especially given the steadfast differences of opinion expressed by religious groups around the world.

69. Moshe Hirsch, "The Freedom of Proselytism under the International Agreement and International Law," *Catholic University Law Review* 47 (1998): 424–25.
70. Ibid., 425.
71. John Witte, Jr., "A Primer on the Rights and Wrongs of Proselytism," *Cumberland Law Review* 31 (2000–2001): 620.
72. Natan Lerner, "Proselytism, Change of Religion, and International Human Rights," *Emory International Law Review* 12 (1998): 558–59.
73. Tad Stahnke, "Proselytism and the Freedom to Change Religion in International Human Rights Law," *Brigham Young University Law Review* 1999 (1999): 339.

II. INTERNATIONAL RELIGIOUS RIGHTS: MONITORING AND ENFORCEMENT REGIMES

Effective enforcement of international religious rights is hampered by many of the legal and definitional issues presented above. However, two regimes have developed at least some consistency of interpretation, albeit with varying degrees and types of enforcement power.[74] As with the U.N. treaties and declarations, tensions relating to Islam are present in both the U.S. Commission on International Religious Freedom and the European Court of Human Rights.

A. The U.S. Commission on International Religious Freedom

In 1998, the U.S. Congress unanimously passed the International Religious Freedom Act (IRFA) and created the U.S. Commission on International Religious Freedom.[75] This move represented Washington's resolve to take unilateral action, if necessary, to promote the cause of religious freedom around the world (although, paradoxically, this democratic initiative was undertaken with minimal public debate on the floor and little or no public examination of the bill).[76] The Commission is charged with reporting annually on the state of religious freedom around the world, and it serves as an important source of public information on the subject. Interestingly, all data is carefully screened prior to disclosure, and anything that might aggravate the situation of those suffering from religious persecution is classified and withheld.[77] When a country is found in breach of religious freedom, the President may exercise one of fifteen putative options provided for in the Act itself.[78]

74. Adam M. Smith, "The Perplexities of Promoting Religious Freedom through International Law," review of *Can God and Caesar Coexist?*, by Robert Drinan, *North Carolina Journal of International Law and Commercial Regulation* 30 (2005): 749.

75. Orrin G. Hatch, "Religious Liberty at Home and Abroad: Reflections on Protecting This Fundamental Freedom," *Brigham Young University Law Review* 2001 (2001): 416. See also Allen D. Hertzke, *Freeing God's Children: The Unlikely Alliance for Global Human Rights* (Lanham, MD: Rowman & Littlefield Publishers, 2004).

76. J. Paul Martin, "Religions, Human Rights, and Civil Society: Lessons from the Seventeenth Century for the Twenty-First Century," *Brigham Young University Law Review* 2000 (2000): 941.

77. Hatch, "Religious Liberty at Home and Abroad," 419.

78. The International Religious Freedom Act of 1998, Pub. L. No. 105–292, 112 Stat. 2787 (1998); Smith, "The Perplexities of Promoting Religious Freedom through International Law," 751.

One major criticism of IRFA is that while its language expresses an intention to motivate multinational efforts to enforce international religious freedom, enforcement to date has been primarily unilateral.[79] Yet unilateral and multilateral actions are not mutually exclusive. In those instances in which actions taken by the United States under IRFA are consistent and principled and where multilateral or regional mechanisms are weak, it represents a viable and valuable policy tool.[80] That said, multilateral regimes may ultimately be more effective, but developing them requires greater agreement on international standards (especially on the rights of religious minorities), as well as remedying institutional and bureaucratic deficiencies in treaty supervisory bodies.[81]

Critics from the Muslim world object to IRFA on different grounds. They contend that it is an instrument of Western imperialism. More specifically, they contend that IRFA exports American concepts of religious freedom and intrudes upon state sovereignty.[82] Such Islamic critics maintain that IRFA "seeks to foster an Americanized system in which the church and state are kept separate. By doing so," they argue, "IRFA intrudes upon Muslim values because in much of the Muslim world, the Qur'an or Islamic law must control sovereign laws."[83] Moreover, in support of the state sovereignty argument, Muslims assert that religion is central both in the impulse toward nationhood and in reinforcing a country's cultural self-identity.[84] Consistently, Western emphasis upon the separation of church and state and freedom of religion is perceived, at least by some populations, as an existential threat to Islamic law and Muslim identity.[85]

79. Eugenia Relano Pastor, "The Flawed Implementation of the International Religious Freedom Act of 1998: A European Perspective," *Brigham Young University Law Review* 2005 (2005): 744–45.

80. Peter G. Danchin, "U.S. Unilateralism and the International Protection of Religious Freedom: The Multilateral Alternative," *Columbia Journal of Transnational Law* 41 (2002): 128.

81. Ibid., 128–29.

82. Matthew L. Fore, Note, "Shall Weigh Your God and You: Assessing the Imperialistic Implications of the International Religious Freedom Act in Muslim Countries," *Duke Law Journal* 52 *Thirty-Second Annual Administrative Law Issue—Politics and Policy: Executive Privilege and the Bush Administration* (2002): 423. More recently, the U.S. Commission on International Religious Freedom has been accused by some of its past members (commissioners and staff) of having an anti-Muslim bias—a charge that its Chairman vigorously denies. Michelle Boorstein, "Agency That Monitors Religious Freedom Abroad Accused of Bias," *The Washington Post*, February 17, 2010.

83. Fore, "Shall Weigh Your God and You," 434.

84. Ibid., 436–38.

85. Indeed, some of America's most influential champions of religious liberty have expressed a corresponding concern: namely, by linking religious freedom with the strict separation of religion from public life, the U.S. foreign policy establishment has

B. The European Court of Human Rights

Established in 1959, the European Court of Human Rights (ECHR) is the most developed multinational judicial body presently protecting religious freedoms.[86] It was created to interpret and apply the 1953 European Convention for the Protection of Human Rights and Fundamental Freedoms (Convention), which was "designed to give binding effect to some of the rights and freedoms set out in the United Nations' Universal Declaration of Human Rights."[87] Under Article 9 of the Convention, religious freedom is afforded much the same protection as under Article 18 of the UDHR, with the exception—at times significant—that freedom to manifest one's religion or beliefs is subject to certain limitations (e.g., public safety, public order, protection of the rights and freedoms of others).[88]

Other Convention provisions for religious freedom include Article 14, which prohibits discrimination on the basis of religion (among other classifications) with regard to ECHR-acknowledged rights, and Article 2 of the first Protocol, giving parents the right to regulate their children's

---

undermined its ability to influence countries hostile to such separation. For a related discussion, see Zachary R. Calo, "The Internationalization of Church-State Issues," in *Church and State Issues in America Today*, ed. Ann W. Duncan, and Steven L. Jones (Westport, CT: Praeger, 2008), 135–66.

86. Smith, "The Perplexities of Promoting Religious Freedom through International Law," 752. For a discussion of the ECHR in the context of European history, see Malcolm D. Evans, *Religious Liberty and International Law in Europe* (Cambridge: Cambridge University Press, 1997). For a comprehensive treatment of the ECHR and religious liberty laws in Europe, a subject beyond the scope of this book, see Carolyn Evans, *Freedom of Religion under the European Convention on Human Rights* (New York: Oxford University Press, 2001). On current tensions within the ECHR framework, see Malcolm D. Evans, "Freedom of Religion and the European Convention on Human Rights: Approaches, Trends and Tensions," in *Law and Religion in Theoretical and Historical Context*, ed. Peter Cane, Carolyn Evans and Zoe Robinson (Cambridge: Cambridge University Press, 2008), 291–315.

87. Willi Fuhrmann, "Perspectives on Religious Freedom from the Vantage Point of the European Court of Human Rights," *Brigham Young University Law Review* 2000 (2000): 829. On the application of the Convention in individual European states, as well as the jurisprudential relationship between states and the ECHR, see Achilles Emilianides, ed., *Religious Freedom in the European Union: The Application of the European Convention on Human Rights in the European Union* (Leuven, Belgium: Peeters, 2011).

88. Jónatas E. M. Machado, "Freedom of Religion: A View from Europe," *Roger Williams Symposium* (2005): 472–73. It is arguably possible, given these Article 9(2) limitations, for "almost any specific purpose pursued by national authorities [to be] justified according to the wide and ambiguous meaning attributed to limitation-concepts by the ECHR." Javier Martinez-Torron, "Limitations on Religious Freedom in the Case Law of the European Court of Human Rights," *Emory International Law Review* 19 (2005): 634.

religious education.[89] Moreover, in addition to the Convention, the European Union's progressive integration of national, regional, and international law in support of religious freedom led to the 1998 Oslo Declaration on the Freedom of Religion and Belief—a binding document for EU states, and one held (because of its detailed and specific account of freedom of religion and conscience) to be the most advanced legal document on religious freedom to date.[90]

As a general matter, the ECHR's religious liberty jurisprudence has "established that freedom of thought, conscience and religion are fundamental to the Convention."[91] However, this has been done with a view to "securing pluralism and tolerance as the hallmarks of democratic society,"[92] and thus the Court has in some cases "protected the rights of minority religious groups when confronted with a dominant religion," while in others recognized "the responsibility of states to protect the religious sensibilities of the majority."[93] The resulting tension is magnified by two additional factors: the secularization of Europe and its growing Muslim minority population.[94]

As Europe becomes increasingly secular, there are indications that religious expression is correspondingly devalued. This shift is furthered by church-state models that do not always conduce to religious liberty, especially in the cases of "religious dissidents, conscientious objectors to military service, and persons who seek exemptions from legal restraints

89. Carloyn Evans and Christopher A. Thomas, "Church-State Relations in the European Court of Human Rights," *Brigham Young University Law Review* 2006 (2006): 703–05. On the issue of religious instruction in schools as adjudicated by the ECHR, see Eugenia Relano, "Educational Pluralism and Freedom of Religion: Recent Decisions of the European Court of Human Rights," *British Journal of Religious Education* 32, no. 1 (2010): 19–29.

90. Daniel Wehrenfennig, "The Human Right of Religious Freedom in International Law," *Peace Review: A Journal of Social Justice* 18, no. 3 (July–September 2006): 404.

91. Fuhrmann, "Perspectives on Religious Freedom from the Vantage Point of the European Court of Human Rights," 838.

92. Ibid. This logic is consistent with the Court's opinion in *Kokkinakis v. Greece*, App. No. 14307/88, 260 Eur. Ct. H.R., 31 (1993), for example, which identified religious freedom as "a tool for protecting and advancing the goods of democratic pluralism." Zachary R. Calo, "Pluralism, Secularism and the European Court of Human Rights," *Journal of Law and Religion* 26 (2010–11): 102.

93. Fuhrmann, "Perspectives on Religious Freedom from the Vantage Point of the European Court of Human Rights," 838.

94. For example, see Malcolm D. Evans, "From Cartoons to Crucifixes: Current Controversies Concerning the Freedom of Religion and the Freedom of Expression before the European Court of Human Rights," *Journal of Law and Religion* 26 (2010–11): 345–70. A full analysis of these dynamics is beyond the scope of this book. Instead, they will occupy center-stage in the work that is to follow.

they deem to be contrary to their consciences."[95] For example, France's commitment to *laïcité* has resulted in many restrictions on religious liberty.[96] Germany, which has an established church, has also been criticized for restricting religious freedom, notably with regard to its ban on proselytism.[97] A 1997 law passed in Austria created a second class of religions that are not entitled to the full benefits and protections afforded traditional religions,[98] while a 2004 ECHR decision (*Leyla Şahin v. Turkey*, upholding a Turkish ban on wearing headscarves in universities and other educational and state institutions) evidenced the difficulty in balancing religious human rights protection with the demands of political context.[99]

Indeed, one ECHR judge, writing explicitly in his personal rather than professional capacity, observed that the Court's "main limitations to the right of religious freedom . . . are motivated by the need to protect democratic societies from the danger of Islam and sects." He then notes the language of the ECHR in *Refah Partisi v. Turkey*, which stated: "sharia, which faithfully reflects the dogmas and divine rules laid down by religion, is stable and invariable," and thus incompatible with "[p]rinciples such as pluralism in the political sphere or the constant evolution of public freedoms."[100] This is complicated by the fact that while Muslim minorities

95. Robert F. Drinan, *Can God and Caesar Coexist? Balancing Religious Freedom and International Law* (New Haven, CT: Yale University Press, 2004), 86.

96. See Elizabeth F. Defeis, "Religious Liberty and Protections in Europe," *Journal of Catholic Legal Studies* 45 (2006): 113; Christina A. Baker, "French Headscarves and the U.S. Constitution: Parents, Children, and Free Exercise of Religion," *Cardozo Journal of Law and Gender* 13 (2007); Jean Bauberot, "Secularism and French Religious Liberty: A Sociological and Historical View," *Brigham Young University Law Review* 2003 (2003).

97. *See* Defeis, "Religious Liberty and Protections in Europe," 113; Gerhard Robbers, "The Permissible Scope of Legal Limitations on the Freedom of Religion or Belief in Germany," *Emory International Law Review* 19 (2005).

98. Christopher J. Miner, "Losing My Religion: Austria's New Religion Law in Light of International and European Standards of Religious Freedom," *Brigham Young University Law Review* 1998 (1998).

99. *Şahin v. Turkey*, App. No. 44774/98, 44 Eur. H.R. Rep. 5 (2005); Christopher D. Belelieu, "The Headscarf as a Symbolic Enemy of the European Court of Human Rights' Democratic Jurisprudence," *Columbia Journal of European Law* 12 (2006). See also Jilan Kamal, "Justified Interference with Religious Freedom: The European Court of Human Rights and the Need for Mediating Doctrine under Article 9(2)," *Columbia Journal of Transnational Law* 46 (2008); Isabelle Rorive, "Religious Symbols in the Public Space: Religious Symbols in the Public Space: In Search of a European Answer," *Cardozo Law Review* 30 *Symposium: Constitutionalism and Secularism in an Age of Religious Revival: The Challenge of Global and Local Fundamentalism* (2009) [hereinafter *Cardozo Symposium* (2009)]: 2680–85.

100. Françoise Tulkens, "The European Convention on Human Rights and Church-State Relations: Pluralism vs. Pluralism," *Cardozo Symposium* (2009): 2587–88. Judge Tulkens situates these remarks in a discussion of *Refah Partisi v. Turkey*, 37 Eur. H.R.

in Western European states have experienced difficulty in suing their governments, the Court has found in favor of the rights of Muslim communities in European states such as Greece and Bulgaria.[101] Hence, while the ECHR "gives every person of faith and every faith-based body the right to go to an all-European tribunal to get relief," at least some of its precedents appear to reflect "the view of a continent that has been Christian for centuries," a posture that seems "unlikely to encourage Muslims and other non-Christians—an ever-growing portion of Europe's population—to hope for rulings supporting a new pluralism based on a more expansive right to the free exercise of religion."[102]

Nevertheless, the ECHR remains deeply committed to international human rights law and, in some though possibly not all respects,[103] to religious freedom. Because of its inherently diverse body politic, it serves as a crucial, dynamic experiment in confronting the challenges and complexities of religious liberty under conditions of increasing pluralism. It also provides a necessary forum for ongoing debates *within* the Western world as to the foundations and ultimate scope of religious freedom and human rights.

III. *DIGNITATIS HUMANAE*: THE CATHOLIC CHURCH AND THE MORAL CASE FOR RELIGIOUS FREEDOM

Recalling Maritain's observation that members of the 1946 UNESCO Committee on the Theoretical Bases of Human Rights could agree on

Rep. 1, 44 (2003) (a case discussed in Chapter 5 of this book). After this, he cites Karen Meerschaut and Serge Gutwirth's observation that "the Refah judgment implies a radical denial of any legal pluralism that pursues the accommodation of Islamic law and human rights: it leaves no place [or] space for 'compatibilisation' of different legal traditions." Karen Meerschaut and Serge Gutwirth, "Legal Pluralism and Islam in the Scales of the European Court of Human Rights: The Limits of Categrorical Balancing," in *Conflicts between Fundamental Rights*, ed. Eva Brems (Antwerp, Belgium: Intersentia, 2008): 439. Similar concerns appear to be animating national laws regarding Islamic practice, e.g., the Swiss ban on constructing minarets and the French ban on wearing the burqa in public.

101. Haldun Gülalp, "Secularism and the European Court of Human Rights," *European Public Law* 16, no. 3 (2010): 458, 471. Gülalp suggests that this difference in treatment may reflect unspoken assumptions by the Court about its willingness to defer to the Latin Christian states of the West, while insisting upon higher levels of "European supervision" of Orthodox Christian states in the East.

102. Drinan, *Can God and Caesar Coexist?*, 93–94.

103. See Carolyn Evans, "Individual and Group Religious Freedom in the European Court of Human Rights: Cracks in the Intellectual Architecture," *Journal of Law and Religion* 26 (2010–11): 321–44.

certain rights provided they were not asked why,[104] one of the great difficulties plaguing modern international human rights law is the problem of foundation. A strictly positivist approach to human rights law limits obligations to those that have been voluntarily assumed.[105] Consent is thus an essential element of jurisprudence based on individual and political will. But does a state's refusal to sign and ratify a human rights treaty allow its leaders to engage in the persecution of religious minorities, for example, without legal consequence?

The answer to that hypothetical depends on one's choice of jurisprudence and its corresponding moral and political philosophy. Yet one observation seems to follow from both logic and historical experience: the greater the dependence of jurisprudence upon political will and the greater the diversity of its subjects, the less likely the law will be obeyed or enforced absent the strong arm of a coercive state. That is one reason why tradition (or custom) and shared norms have played such vital roles in the evolution and efficacy of international law.

Applying this reasoning to a discussion of religious liberty, and further, to one of all human rights, the absence of agreement about the meaning of the UDHR created a significant problem. As Pope John Paul II explained in a 1989 address to the Vatican Diplomatic Corps, "the 1948 Declaration does not contain the anthropological and moral bases for the human rights that it proclaims."[106] Thus, apart from reliance upon military power or political maneuvering, it was difficult to understand how one would resolve entrenched rights-based conflict. Conceptualized differently, states and societies would have to depend more on power and political will (prone as they are to volatility) and less on reason (a generally stabilizing force). The international community was offered a means of escaping that burden, however, by the appearance nearly two decades later of another human rights treatise—one that offered an explicit argument for the relationship between human rights, human dignity, and human conscience.[107]

With the publication of *Dignitatis Humanae*, the Second Vatican Council (1962–1965) boldly proclaimed the dignity of the human person, "known

104. Kevin J. Hasson, "Religious Liberty and Human Dignity: A Tale of Two Declarations," *Harvard Journal of Law and Public Policy* 27 (2003): 81, quoting Jacques Maritain, *Man and the State* (Chicago: University of Chicago Press, 1956), 77.

105. K. Lee Boyd, "Are Human Rights Political Questions?," *Rutgers Law Review* 53 (2001): 312.

106. Mary Ann Glendon, "Foundations of Human Rights: The Unfinished Business," *The American Journal of Jurisprudence* 44 (1999): 12.

107. Hasson, "Religious Liberty and Human Dignity," 84–85.

through the revealed word of God and by reason itself."[108] Religious free-dom is an essential element of this dignity: an individual "should not be coerced to act against his own conscience nor be impeded to act according to [it]," while religious communities "have the right not to be hindered from publicly teaching and testifying to their faith both by the written and the spoken word."[109] Though Sir Thomas More had centuries earlier devel-oped a limited theory of religious freedom based upon rational principles in *Utopia*,[110] the theology of Vatican II fused natural law teaching with a strong Christological focus.[111] A series of sweeping new doctrinal state-ments and initiatives followed, transforming the Church's theological atti-tude toward and social actions respecting human rights and democracy.[112]

This remarkable transformation resulted in part from the influence of American Jesuit priest and theologian John Courtney Murray, who was initially barred by the Vatican from writing on church-state relations (particularly on efforts to reconcile Catholicism with American-style

108. Vatican Ecumenical Council II, *Dignitatis Humanae*; Johan D. van der Vyver, "Morality, Human Rights, and Foundations of the Law," *Emory Law Journal* 54 (2005): 194. See also Drinan, *Can God and Caesar Coexist?*, 96–112; Herminio Rico, *John Paul II and the Legacy of Dignitatis Humanae* (Washington, DC: Georgetown University Press, 2002).

109. Wood, "The Relationship of Religious Liberty to Civil Liberty and a Democratic State," 495. See also George Weigel, "Comment by George Weigel," in *The Influence of Faith: Religious Groups and U.S. Foreign Policy*, ed. Elliott Abrams (Lanham, MD: Rowman & Littlefield Publishers, Inc. & The Ethics and Public Policy Center, 2001).

110. Thomas More, *Utopia*, ed. George M. Logan and Robert M. Adams (Cambridge: Cambridge University Press, 2009); Sanford Kessler, "Religious Freedom in Thomas More's Utopia," *The Review of Politics* 64, no. 2 (Spring 2002): 207–29.

111. Charles Villa-Vicencio, "Christianity and Human Rights," *Journal of Law and Religion* 14 (1999–2000): 592. See also M. John Farrelly, "Religious Culture and Historical Change: Vatican II on Religious Freedom," *The Heythrop Journal* (2008): 731–41. More recently, Pope Benedict XVI has reasserted that natural law is the foun-dation of human rights. Keith Fournier, "Pope Calls for Universal Recognition of the Natural Law as the Basis of Human Rights," *Catholic Online* (May 7, 2009). Natural law emphasizes the accessibility of truth to reason—a point of great importance, as will be elaborated in Chapter 6 and the Conclusion.

112. John Witte, Jr., "A Dickensian Era of Religious Rights: An Update on Religious Human Rights in Global Perspective," *William and Mary Law Review* 42 (2001): 729–31. See also Louis-Leon Christians, "Religious Law and Secular Law in Democracy: The Evolutions of the Roman Catholic Doctrine after the Second Vatican Council," *Brigham Young University Law Review* 2006 (2006); Russell Hittinger, "Theology, Law, and the Self-Governance of Religious Communities: Dignitatis Humanae, Religious Liberty, and Ecclesiastical Self-Government," *The George Washington Law Review* 68 (2000); Robert J. O'Donnell, "The Church Learning and the Church Teaching: Vatican II and the Liberal Tradition of Religious Freedom," *Journal of Ecumenical Studies* 29, no. 3–4 (Summer-Fall 1992): 399–417.

separation).[113] Murray, resisting the privatization of religion and religious indifference that flowed from Enlightenment notions of toleration, sought to change the terms of the debate from "religious toleration" to "religious liberty"—ideas that significantly impacted Catholic thinking.[114] To support his position, Murray relied upon theological and philosophical argument, but also and especially upon the favorable experience of the Catholic Church in the United States, which showed that "the Church could flourish without enjoying a position of legal privilege, in the context of a political order guaranteeing wide-ranging religious freedom and in a social environment characterized by far-reaching pluralism."[115]

Religious freedom thus joined human dignity, democracy, and human rights as a cornerstone of *Dignitatis Humanae*. These principles were to become the life's work and legacy of John Paul II,[116] as he transferred the document's complete renunciation of the use of coercion in the defense of truth into the political center of his pontificate.[117] Guided by a deep commitment to advancing "the great cause of justice and peace,"[118] he repeatedly spoke on the importance of religious liberty as a condition of peace.[119]

113. Agostino Bono, "Religious Freedom: Vatican II Modernizes Church-State Ties," *Catholic News Service* (October 12, 2005). Murray was eventually invited to join the Vatican's Secretariat for Promoting Christian Unity (the Vatican agency that had drafted *Dignitatis Humanae*).

114. Claire Wolfteich, "The American Experiment: Religious Liberty, Roman Catholics, and the Vision of John Courtney Murray," *Journal of Human Rights* 2, no. 1 (March 2003): 31–47. See also Kenneth L. Grasso, "John Courtney Murray, 'the Juridical State,' and the Catholic Theory of Religious Freedom," *The Political Science Reviewer* 33 (2004): 1–61.

115. Kenneth L. Grasso, "An Unfinished Argument: John Courtney Murray, *Dignitatis Humanae*, and the Catholic Theory of the State," in *Catholicism and Religious Freedom: Contemporary Reflections on Vatican II's Declaration on Religious Liberty*, ed. Kenneth L. Grasso and Robert P. Hunt (Lantham, MD: Rowman and Littlefield Publishers, Inc., 2006), 161–88. See also John T. McGreevy, *Catholicism and American Freedom: A History* (New York: W.W. Norton, 2003).

116. Renato Raffaele Martino, "John Paul II and the International Order: Human Rights and the Nature of the Human Person," *Notre Dame Journal of Law, Ethics and Public Policy* 21 (2007). See also John J. Coughlin, "Law and Human Dignity: The Twenty-Second Annual Student Federalist Society Symposium on Law and Public Policy–2003: Pope John Paul II and the Dignity of the Human Being," *Harvard Journal of Law and Public Policy* 27 (2003); Avery Dulles, "Religious Freedom: Innovation and Development," *First Things* (December 2001).

117. James Carroll, "The Pope's True Revolution," *Time*, April 11, 2005. See also Gerald J. Beyer, "Freedom, Truth, and Law in the Mind and Homeland of John Paul II," *Notre Dame Journal of Law, Ethics & Public Policy* 21 (2007).

118. John Paul II, "On the Value and Content of Freedom of Conscience and of Religion" (November 14, 1980). See also Randy Lee, "Coming to Grips with What Law Means in the Hands of God," *Journal of Catholic Legal Studies* 25 (2006).

119. John Paul II, "To Serve Peace, Respect Freedom" (January 1, 1981).

Religious freedom is an essential requirement of human dignity, he taught, and just as the freedom of individuals and communities to profess and practice religion is necessary for peaceful coexistence, so, too, the violation of religious freedom (like the violation of other fundamental human rights) damages the cause of peace.[120]

This was the message John Paul II carried everywhere, as he steadfastly but nonviolently opposed Soviet communism, supported the Polish resistance movement, and sought to reverse Christianity's denigration of Judaism.[121] Indeed, through his quest for reconciliation with the Temple of Israel, the Pope affirmed a new Catholic commitment to pluralism—one that extends beyond Jews to Protestants, Muslims, and many others. George Weigel summarizes the teaching of the Second Vatican Council and John Paul II on religious freedom thus:

> The human person has an inalienable right to seek the truth without coercion, and a fundamental moral duty to act upon the truth when it is found. The right and the duty are part of the same package. The truth is not taken to be *my* truth, nor am I taken to be the norm of truth. The truth cannot be truly apprehended unless it is apprehended freely. Any appeal to religious freedom as a means of coercing others is a false appeal.[122]

Subsequently and repeatedly, these principles have been supported and elaborated by representatives of the Holy See at international fora including the Third Committee (Social, Humanitarian and Cultural) of the U.N. General Assembly,[123] the International Consultative Conference on School Education in Relation to Freedom of Religion or Belief, Tolerance and Non-Discrimination,[124] a conference organized by the Embassy of the United

120. John Paul II, "Religious Freedom: Condition for Peace" (January 1, 1988). See also Gerard Bradley, "Pope John Paul II and Religious Liberty," *Ave Maria Law Review* 6 (2007).

121. Carroll, "The Pope's True Revolution."

122. Weigel, "Comment by George Weigel," 67.

123. Celestino Migliore. United Nations Commission on Human Rights, *Statement* (October 26, 2004); Renato Raffaele Martino, The Third Committee (Social, Humanitarian and Cultural) of the 57th Session of the United Nations General Assembly, *Statement on Religious Freedom* (November 8, 2002); Renato Raffaele Martino, Statement at the Third Committee (Social, Humanitarian and Cultural) of the 52nd Session of the United Nations General Assembly, *Human Rights Questions: Freedom of Religion* (November 15, 1997).

124. Holy See Delegation, "Intervention of the Holy See Delegation at the International Consultative Conference on 'School Education in Relation to Freedom of Religion or Belief, Tolerance and Non-Discrimination'" (November 24, 2001).

States to the Holy See at Gregorian University,[125] and the Commission of the United Nations on Human Rights on the Elimination of All Forms of Religious Intolerance.[126] Hence, while the early echoes of religious liberty sounded in the upheaval accompanying the Protestant Reformation, and while they resonated through the American Founding and the birth of modern international human rights law, they came at last to ring in the nonviolent revolution of this Successor of Peter and the Catholic Church. The question now is whether they can be heard outside of the Western world, and, as will be discussed in the Conclusion, whether even in the West they have begun to fall on increasingly deaf ears.

125. See Giovanni Lajalo, "Holy See: Modern Challenges to Religious Freedom" (December 3, 2004). This address took place at the conference on "Religious Freedom, Cornerstone of Human Dignity."

126. Silvano Maria Tomasi, United Nations Commission on Human Rights, "Statement on the Elimination of All Forms of Religious Intolerance" (April 2, 2005).

CHAPTER 4
Religious Liberty and *Shari'a*

Islam has two sharply contrasting aspects within itself: an aspect of respecting the liberty of choosing one's faith, and an aspect of discrimination and punishment of the apostate that includes the death penalty . . . the aspect of *the freedom to choose one's faith* and the aspect of *oppression* with regard to faith . . . These two aspects are so diametrically opposed that I can hardly reconcile them in a single living tradition, Islam.
—*Masao Abe*[1]

Christendom and Islam are in many ways sister civilizations, both drawing on the shared heritage of Jewish revelation and prophecy and Greek philosophy and science, and both nourished by the immemorial traditions of Middle Eastern antiquity . . . But as well as resemblances, there are profound disparities between the two . . . Nowhere are these differences more profound—and more obvious—than in the attitudes of these two religions, and of their authorized exponents, to the relations between government, religion, and society . . . In the universal Islamic polity as conceived by Muslims, there is no Caesar but only God, who is the sole sovereign and the sole source of law . . . The Ayatollah Khomeini once remarked that "Islam is politics or it is nothing." Not all Muslims would go that far, but most would agree that God is concerned with politics, and this belief is confirmed and sustained by the shari'a, the Holy Law, which deals extensively . . . with what we in the West would call constitutional law and political philosophy.
—*Bernard Lewis*[2]

In 1981, Iran's representative to the U.N. General Assembly declared that the Universal Declaration of Human Rights represented a secular interpretation of Judeo-Christian tradition that could not be implemented

---

1. Masao Abe, "A Buddhist Response to Mohamed Talbi," in *Religious Liberty and Human Rights in Nations and in Religions*, ed. Leonard Swidler (Philadelphia: Ecumenical Press & Hippocrene Books, 1986), 189.
2. Bernard Lewis, *The Crisis of Islam: Holy War and Unholy Terror* (New York: The Modern Library, 2003), 5, 7–8.

by Muslim states.[3] At UNESCO in September of that same year, the Arab League proclaimed the Universal Islamic Declaration of Human Rights—a document based on the Qur'an and the *Sunnah*, and compiled by Muslim scholars, jurists, and representatives of Islamic movements and schools of thought.[4] This was followed in August 1990 by the Cairo Declaration on Human Rights in Islam, proposed by member states of the Organization of the Islamic Conference.

These and other formulations of Islamic human rights law diverge notably from accepted international legal standards of religious liberty, thereby challenging the characterization of human rights as universal or, alternatively, as neutral with respect to the religious beliefs of those to whom they are (intended to be) applied. In other words, recalling the discussion in the Introduction, they appear to pose "the dilemma of religious freedom"—a seemingly intractable trade-off between universal religious human rights, on the one hand, and recognition of and respect for religious and cultural differences regarding the scope and content of religious liberty, on the other.

Properly assessing the extent and gravity of this dilemma necessitates careful analysis of the relationship between Islam, Muslim states, and religious freedom. This chapter—the first of three dedicated to exploring that relationship—traces the evolution of Islamic law and thought as it relates to religious liberty. It opens with a discussion of basic principles of Islamic law. This is followed by specific analysis of freedom of religion in Islam, with special emphasis on two contentious issues: the rights of religious minorities and apostasy. Chapter 4 concludes by looking at the ideas of Muslim intellectuals who are working to transform the tradition, whose writings are perceived as containing the groundwork for a so-called "Islamic Reformation."

Just as the Protestant Reformation and the American constitutional experiment provided the backdrop against which modern religious human rights law emerged, so, too, the development of Islamic law and thought from the classical through the modern periods constitutes the religious-intellectual history within which the relevant legal-political institutions of

3. David G. Littman, "Human Rights and Human Wrongs," *National Review Online* (January 19, 2003); U.N. GAOR, 36th Sess., 3d Committee, paras. 10–19, U.N. Doc. A/C.3/36/SR.29 (Nov. 4, 1981); U.N. GAOR, 39th Sess., 3d Committee, paras. 91–95, U.N. Doc. A/C.3/39/SR.65 (Dec. 17, 1984). See also remarks by another Iranian representative, Mr. Zarif, regarding the relationship of the Islamic Revolution in Iran to human rights. U.N. GAOR, 37th Sess., 3d Committee, paras. 50–55, U.N. Doc. A/C.3/37/SR.56 (Dec. 2, 1982).

4. Ibid.

Muslim states (Chapter 5) and corresponding formulations of Islamic international law (Chapter 6) emerged. Hence, understanding the law and politics of religious freedom in the Muslim world first requires knowledge of the teachings and traditions of Islam, as well as their significance for Muslim followers.

I. PRINCIPLES OF ISLAMIC LAW—A BRIEF OVERVIEW

In the Middle East especially, but in other parts of the Muslim world as well, "national identification is still largely a function of religious affiliation."[5] Similarly, and in keeping with other non-Western faiths, the Islamic tradition can neither conceive of nor accept a system of rights that excludes religion.[6] Unlike Christianity, a religion of orthodoxy that emphasizes correct belief,[7] Islam is a religion of orthopraxy emphasizing correct action. This distinction is in part responsible for the tremendous importance Muslims accord religious law.[8] Thus, while Christians "despair when they see Muslim minorities in the West exploiting the freedom Christians themselves do not enjoy under Islam . . . when they see Muslims overtly and covertly extending elements of Shari'a law wherever they are," they need also to recognize that *Shari'a* is constitutive of Islam in a way that Western law is not (with respect to Christianity or even some forms of Judaism).[9]

Within Islam, "law" is usually expressed by one of three words: *fiqh* (i.e., jurisprudence)[10]; *qanun* (law as statutes or positive legal provisions in actual

5. Barry Rubin, "Religion and International Affairs," in *Religion, the Missing Dimension of Statecraft*, ed. Douglas Johnston and Cynthia Sampson (New York: Oxford University Press, 1994), 22. Religion governs private and public spheres, but the state is explicitly prohibited from intruding on the private sphere. Imad-ad-Dean Ahmad, "American and Muslim Perspectives on Freedom of Religion," *University of Pennsylvania Journal of Constitutional Law* 8 (2006): 361.
6. John Witte, Jr., "Law, Religion and Human Rights," *Columbia Human Rights Law Review* 28 (1996): 12.
7. Although this traditional distinction holds at a general level, it should be noted that Christianity certainly has orthopraxic elements (e.g., the canon law of Roman Catholicism).
8. Islam teaches that the world was made perfect with laws intact. In his most recent work, Noah Feldman controversially argues that the call for *Shari'a* should be understood as a call—particularly in the face of widespread political corruption—for rule of law. See Noah Feldman, *The Fall and Rise of the Islamic State* (Princeton, NJ: Princeton University Press, 2008).
9. Peter Stuart, "A Christian Perspective on Religious Freedom in a Pluralist World," *Stimulus* 15, no. 2 (May 2007): 35–42.
10. One legal scholar asserts that while *fiqh* (jurisprudential interpretation or "discussion of Islamic issues") can be "regarded as a methodology of revealing more detailed regulatory aspects of legal postulates," it "can in no way be treated as a source of

operation in contemporary Middle Eastern societies and states); and the more familiar *Shari'a* (a general term for Islamic law).[11] *Shari'a* appears in a variety of manifestations, including: *fiqh* compendia, judgments, manuals for *qadis* (judges) and *muftis* (Islamic scholars who interpret and expound religious law),[12] *fatwas* (legal pronouncements from religious scholars on specific issues), contracts and formularies, and literary and historical texts.[13] While the content of Islamic law derives primarily from the Qur'an and *Hadith* or *Sunnah* (the Prophet's commandments to his companions),[14] it has also been sourced by consensus (among Caliphs and jurists),[15] analogy (e.g. the prohibition against wine transmuted into a prohibition against alcohol),[16] and, increasingly, by custom.[17]

Islamic law." Maimul Ahsan Khan, *Human Rights in the Muslim World: Fundamentalism, Constitutionalism, and International Politics* (Durham, NC: Carolina Academic Press, 2003), 145. Senior advocate and practicing Pakistani lawyer Abrar Hasan defines *fiqh* instead as "understanding," and writes that it "implies an understanding of Islam in a general way . . . what a prudent person is likely to conclude from obvious evidences." Abrar Hasan, *Principles of Modern Islamic Jurisprudence* (Karachi, Pakistan: Pakistan Academy of Jurists, 2004), 11.

    11. Chibli Mallat, "From Islamic to Middle Eastern Law: A Restatement of the Field (Part I)," *American Journal of Comparative Law* 51 (2003): 718.

    12. "The domain of legal procedure, including adversarial cases, rules of evidence, binding judgments, and state enforcement, belongs to the judge," while "the issuance of nonbinding advisory opinions (*fatwas*) to an individual questioner (*mustafti*), whether in connection with litigation or not, is the separate domain of the jurisconsult (*mufti*)." Muhammad Khalid Masud, Brinkley Messick, and David S. Powers, "Islamic Legal Interpretation: Muftis and Their Fatwas," in *Islamic Legal Interpretation: Muftis and Their Fatwas,* ed. Muhammad Khalid Masud, Brinkley Messick, and David S. Powers (Cambridge, MA: Harvard University Press, 1996), 3. See also Hasan, *Principles of Modern Islamic Jurisprudence.*

    13. Chibli Mallat, "From Islamic to Middle Eastern Law: A Restatement of the Field (Part II)," *American Journal of Comparative Law* 52 (2004): 262. On the connection between *fatwas* and their social background, as well as their selective incorporation into positive law, see Wael B. Hallaq, "From *Fatwas* to *Furu*: Growth and Change in Islamic Substantive Law," *Islamic Law and Society* 1, no. 3 (1994): 29–65.

    14. The *Sunnah* embodies the ideas and practices of the oldest Islamic community and hence functions as the most authoritative interpretation of the Qur'an. Ignaz Goldziher, *Introduction to Islamic Theology and Law,* trans. Andras and Ruth Hamori (Princeton, NJ: Princeton University Press, 1981), 38. But, on the incorporation by some early Muslim jurists of naturalistic reasoning and rules without foundation in the Qur'an or *Sunnah,* see Anver M. Emon, "*Huquq Allah* and *Huquq Al-'Ibad*: A Legal Heuristic for a Natural Rights Regime," *Islamic Law and Society* 13, no. 3 (2006): 321–95.

    15. Majid Khadduri, *Islamic Jurisprudence: Shafi'i's Risala* (Baltimore, MD: The Johns Hopkins Press, 1961), 285–87.

    16. Mohammad Hashim Kamali, *Principles of Islamic Jurisprudence* (Cambridge, UK: Islamic Texts Society, 1991), 197–228. For a critical view of Kamali's theory of Muslim law, see Wael B. Hallaq, review of "Principles of Islamic Jurisprudence, Revised Edition," by Mohammad Hashim Kamali, *Islamic Law and Society* 2, no. 2 (1995): 209–10.

    17. Feisal Abdul Rauf, "What Is Islamic Law?," *Mercer Law Review* 57 (2006): 603–04.

Shari'a, grounded by principles of spiritual benefit and social welfare,[18] is divided into two broad categories of commandments: first, *'ibadat*, which covers both proper belief and liturgical acts of worship (i.e., Love of God); and second, *mu'amalat*, consisting of laws that deal with worldly affairs ranging from the treatment of human beings to the treatment of animals— the relational component of which includes everything from personal status, contract, and criminal law to governance and international law (i.e., Love of Neighbor).[19] Of the two, *'ibadat* is more familiar to most non-Muslims, as it incorporates not only acknowledgment of belief in God, angels, Scripture, and prophets, but also the highly visible practices of five-times daily prayers (*salah*), fasting during the month of Ramadan, and the pilgrimage to Mecca (*hajj*). These basic obligations form the "Pillars of Islam."[20] As Imam Rauf, leader of a large mosque in New York explains, the Prophet Muhammad taught that there is no action more pleasing to God than adhering to the prescriptive commandments of *Shari'a*, that God's love is in fact acquired by increasing the frequency of such performance.[21]

Importantly, non-Islamic law and normative practices are evaluated in terms of their degree of *Shari'a* compliance, which effectively means that Islamic law is both primary and determinate within its sphere of influence.[22] This is particularly relevant for questions at the intersection of international and religious law. While *Shari'a* treatment of religious freedom is examined in greater detail below, a few preliminary observations about its legal-historical cousin—separation of church (or mosque) and state—help frame the debate as it is popularly understood. Specifically, separation is a legal principle interpreted by many in the Muslim world as "the West's atheistic repudiation of religion and removal of religion and religious symbolism from all aspects of life," and one that, when attempted in Islamic communities, has produced "mixed and often bad results."[23] This response derives in part from traditions rooted in early Islamic jurisprudence.[24]

18. Akbar Ali Malik, *A Theoretical & Practical Approach to Islamic Law* (London: Unique Books, 2001), 55.
19. Rauf, "What Is Islamic Law?," 600–01.
20. Albert Hourani, *A History of the Arab Peoples* (New York: Warner Books, 1991), 65–66.
21. Rauf, "What Is Islamic Law?," 601.
22. Ibid., 604–05.
23. Ibid., 611–12.
24. But, for the argument that modern Islamic rules reflect competing influences in Muslim society rather than a "resurrection of classical rules" (a central inquiry of Chapter 5), see Haider Ala Hamoudi, "The Muezzin's Call and the Dow Jones Bell: On

In his careful and illuminating analysis of the doctrine of separation of church and state in classical Islamic legal thought, Babak Rod Khadem makes three primary arguments.[25] First, classical Islam's conception of religion failed to separate mosque and state, holding instead that the legitimacy of the state derived from its compliance with the dictates of religious law. Second, the role of the state was fundamentally executive in nature, and its function was ultimately "to execute the legislative and judicial models that had been determined a priori through revelation."[26] Third, this hierarchy, which privileged religious canonical teachings above government, generated a distinctively Islamic understanding of separation—one in which the state (and not the mosque) was to be separate from (indeed, subservient to) the Islamic judiciary (*futya*).[27] Khadem acknowledges that religious jurists and government judges frequently overlapped in practice; nevertheless, at least in theory, the Islamic judiciary "enjoyed inherent structural independence from the executive power and was responsible for the development and even the application of the substantive law. These features enabled it . . . to effectively safeguard the sacred law from what was understood to be the corrupting hands of the ruling authorities."[28]

These lines of inquiry bear centrally on the themes of this book. For example, in arguing that political legitimacy derived from religious compliance, Khadem traces the chronology of Islam and illustrates how Qur'anic prescriptions (e.g., Allah's sovereignty extends to the realm of governance) guided the early community in Medina under the leadership of Muhammad

the Necessity of Realism in the Study of Islamic Law," *American Journal of Comparative Law* 56 (2008).

25. Babak Rod Khadem, "The Doctrine of Separation in Classical Islamic Jurisprudence," *UCLA Journal of Islamic and Near Eastern Law* 4 (2004–05): 96.

26. Ibid. See also Noel J. Coulson, *A History of Islamic Law* (New York: Columbia University Press, 1995).

27. Khadem, "The Doctrine of Separation in Classical Islamic Jurisprudence," 96–97.

28. Ibid. For the analysis that the historical scope of *Shari'a* was in fact narrow, but that the gap between the sacred and secular spheres was "filled almost universally (within Sunni Islam) by the tyrannical despotism of caliphs who saw themselves as vice-regents of the will of Allah," see John Milbank, "Shari'a and the True Basis of Group Rights: Islam, the West, and Liberalism," in *Shari'a in the West*, ed. Rex Ahdar and Nicholas Aroney (New York: Oxford University Press, 2010), 150. Milbank draws on the following sources: Sayyed Mohammed Khatami, *La Religion et la Pensée Prises au Piège de L'Autocracie* (Louvain-Paris: Peeters, 2005); Aziz al-Azmeh, *Muslim Kingship: Power and the Sacred in Muslim, Christian and Pagan Polities* (London: IB Tauris, 2001); Bernard Lewis, *The Political Language of Islam* (Chicago: University of Chicago Press, 1991).

through the political challenges and hostilities it faced.[29] Over the ten years of the Prophet's Islamic government, the polity grew "to encompass virtually the whole of Arabia up to the borders of Byzantium."[30] Religious law and politics were thus linked from the outset of the tradition with historically remarkable results. This holds similarly true for Khadem's second argument, in which he notes that classical Islam's most legitimate government (however utopian) would be one in which the state executed the *Shari'a* faithfully with respect to both itself and society as a whole.[31]

Particularly against the backdrop of modernity, the foregoing raises key questions with regard to this project's primary concern—freedom of religion.[32] On the relationship between religious liberty and church-state separation, Imam Rauf asserts that "[f]rom the Islamic point of view, separation of church and state is neither a coherent nor [an] effective legal vehicle to guarantee the fundamental right of religious freedom."[33]

At the policy level, it is crucial here to distinguish between the religious freedom of groups and that of individuals. For example, constitutional provisions in many countries where Islam is the declared state religion are unclear, such that while groups are afforded general protections, individuals are not necessarily guaranteed the right to dissent from established religious doctrine (i.e., to profess a different faith or no faith at all, to enjoy freedom of conscience).[34] This issue arose in the context of the new Iraqi

---

29. Khadem, "The Doctrine of Separation in Classical Islamic Jurisprudence," 96–97. See also Seyyed Hossein Nasr, *Islamic Life and Thought* (Albany, NY: SUNY Press, 1981), 19–25; Wael B. Hallaq, *The Origins and Evolution of Islamic Law* (New York: Cambridge University Press, 2005), 20–25.

30. Khadem, "The Doctrine of Separation in Classical Islamic Jurisprudence," 109. See also W. Montgomery Watt, *Islamic Political Thought* (Edinburgh, UK: Edinburgh University Press, 1968), 4.

31. Khadem, "The Doctrine of Separation in Classical Islamic Jurisprudence," 113. In contrast, Islamic law scholars Haider Ala Hamoudi and Lama Abu-Odeh strongly caution against the view that "the Muslim world must somehow be understood *solely* through the lens of *shari'a* and that legitimacy in law cannot be achieved without it." Haider Ala Hamoudi, "The Death of Islamic Law," *Georgia Journal of International and Comparative Law* 38 (2010): 337 (italics in original). Hamoudi adapts this notion from Lama Abu-Odeh, "The Politics of (Mis)Recognition: Islamic Law Pedagogy in American Academia," *American Journal of Comparative Law* 52 (2004). See also Haider Ala Hamoudi, "Dream Palaces of Law: Western Constructions of the Muslim Legal World," *Hastings International and Comparative Law Review* 32 (2009).

32. Michael J. Perry, "A Right to Religious Freedom? The Universality of Human Rights, the Relativity of Culture," *Roger Williams University Law Review* 10 *Symposium: Religious Liberty in America and Beyond: Celebrating the Legacy of Roger Williams on the 400th Anniversary of His Birth* (2005): 385.

33. Rauf, "What Is Islamic Law?," 613.

34. Tad Stahnke and Robert C. Blitt, "The Religion-State Relationship and the Right to Freedom of Religion or Belief: A Comparative Textual Analysis of the Constitutions

constitution. Noah Feldman and Roman Martinez capture the complex debates there especially well:

> All Iraqis engaged in the constitutional negotiations believed in the importance of protecting group rights to religious freedom . . . [A]ll agreed that the constitution should prevent future governments from interfering with any group's right to affirmatively practice its particular religious tradition . . . The individual right to religious freedom, by contrast, was much more controversial. Such an individual right implies the right not to be religious at all—or, even more problematic from an Islamic perspective, the right to convert from Islam to other faiths.[35]

By implication, even if free exercise is part of Islamic law, there remain real and significant differences of interpretation as to its limits.[36]

Thus, in order to appreciate fully the policy dimensions of this debate, consideration must be given to the scope and content of religious liberty rights in the teachings and traditions of Islam. Indeed, because *Shari'a* recognizes no clear division between legal and religious norms, and because the creed of Islam underpins most doctrines and institutions of *Shari'a*, "the freedom of whether or not to embrace and practise Islam is the most sensitive and controversial area of all individual liberties."[37]

of Predominantly Muslim Countries," *Georgetown Journal of International Law* 36 (2005): 965.

35. Noah Feldman and Roman Martinez, "Constitutional Politics and Text in the New Iraq: An Experiment in Islamic Democracy," *Fordham Law Review* 75 (2006): 907. See also Forrest Hansen, "The Iraqi Constitution: Upholding Principles of Democracy While Struggling to Curtail the Dangers of an Islamic Theocracy," *Roger Williams University Law Review* 12 (2006); Joseph Khawam, "A World of Lessons: The Iraqi Constitutional Experiment in Comparative Perspective," *Columbia Human Rights Law Review* 37 (2006).

36. Ahmad, "American and Muslim Perspectives on Freedom of Religion," 361–62.

37. Mohammad Hashim Kamali, *Freedom of Expression in Islam* (Cambridge, UK: Islamic Texts Society, 1997), 47. Such controversy has attracted global attention in recent times. For example, Sudanese protestors called for the death penalty in the case of 54-year old British teacher Gillian Gibbons, who was charged with blasphemy for allowing schoolchildren to name the class teddy bear Muhammad. See Ayaan Hirsi Ali, "Islam's Silent Moderates," *The New York Times*, December 7, 2007; Andrew Heavens, "Sudanese Protesters Demand Death for Teddy Teacher," *The Washington Post*, November 30, 2007. Also, in Denmark, two Tunisians and a Dane were arrested to prevent a "terror-related assassination" of one of the twelve cartoonists responsible for caricatures of the Prophet Muhammad that sparked furious protests across the Muslim world when they were published in 2005. See Dan Bilefsky, "3 Arrested in Plot to Kill Cartoonist," *The New York Times*, February 13, 2008; "Q&A: The Muhammad Cartoons Row," *BBC News* (February 7, 2006).

II. FREEDOM OF RELIGION IN ISLAMIC LAW

To the extent that Islam granted Muslims religious liberty in the seventh century, it was a new idea[38]—one grounded in the divinely ordered nature of humanity and the unique capabilities and obligations of human beings.[39] The Qur'anic verse "Let there be no compulsion in religion" (2:256) implies, first, that no one is compelled to adopt Islam as his or her religion and, second, that upon embracing Islam, a person should not be forced to follow what others believe.[40] Faith is to be a free and voluntary act. Additionally, the Qur'an establishes guidelines for preaching: "invite all to the way of God with wisdom and beautiful preaching; and argue with them in ways that are best and most gracious" (16:125).[41] It teaches that when the Prophet Muhammad could not persuade delegates from non-Muslim tribes to embrace Islam, God commanded him to tell them that they and he could go their separate ways: this is the origin, for example, of Article 25 of the historic Constitution of Medina ("To the Jews their religion (*din*) and to the Muslims their religion").[42]

Yet as the constitutional and political history of religious liberty in Islamic countries evinces, Muslim scholars and policymakers do not agree upon the proper interpretation of these general precepts, nor is there consensus regarding such matters as conversion, blasphemy, tolerance, or the relative position of non-Muslims. Many of these issues are related. Thus, for purposes of analytical clarity, two broad groupings—religious minorities and apostasy—are treated in turn, followed by contrasting perspectives from Muslim reformers.

38. M. Cherif Bassiouni, "Evolving Approaches to Jihad: From Self-Defense to Revolutionary and Regime-Change Political Violence," *Chicago Journal of International Law* 8 (2007): 133.

39. Mohamed Talbi, "Religious Liberty: A Muslim Perspective," in *Religious Liberty and Human Rights in Nations and in Religions*, ed. Leonard Swidler (Philadelphia: Ecumenical Press & Hippocrene Books, 1986), 177.

40. Niaz A. Shah, "Freedom of Religion: Koranic and Human Rights Perspectives," *Asia-Pacific Journal on Human Rights and the Law* 1 & 2 (2005): 71. Shah cites the following translation of the Qur'an: A. Yousaf Ali, *The Meaning of the Holy Qur'an* (Maryland: Amana Corporation, 1991).

41. Shah, "Freedom of Religion: Koranic and Human Rights Perspectives," 71. Unlike Christianity, Islam has neither an institutional church nor a concept of redemption; consequently, there is no special set of individuals charged with dispensing salvation, and in that sense, all Muslims are laypersons. Josef van Ess, *The Flowering of Muslim Theology*, trans. Jane Marie Todd (Cambridge, MA: Harvard University Press, 2006), 13.

42. Shah, "Freedom of Religion: Koranic and Human Rights Perspectives," 71–72.

A. The Rights of Religious Minorities

Unlike jurisprudence under the First Amendment of the U.S. Constitution, which instructs the government to respect the religious identities of all citizens (including religious minorities and non-believers),[43] Islamic law differentiates between Muslims and non-Muslims, as well as between different types of non-Muslims. For example, classical Islam extended tolerance of a limited sort to "People of the Book"—members of the revealed religions specifically mentioned in the Qur'an (Jews and Christians).[44] During periods when Muslim power was ascendant, members of these groups (and sometimes Zoroastrians) occupied positions of trust and influence; they also performed many useful functions (e.g., lending money and charging interest, which was forbidden to Muslims).[45] Often, however, the state treated Jews and Christians as inferior members of the Islamic body politic, and though nineteenth century reforms in the Ottoman Empire granted them formal political equality, those who actually insisted on their legal rights were bitterly opposed.[46] Moreover, Muslim groups other than the majority Sunnis (e.g., the Shi'as, Ismailis, 'Alawis, and Druzes) faced even stronger opposition, since they were seen as unorthodox and therefore a greater threat to the unity of the *umma* (or Islamic community).[47]

In general, *Shari'a* during the period of Islamic conquest bestowed full citizenship only upon Muslim males.[48] Jews, Christians, and Zoroastrians qualified for limited citizenship rights, but they were compelled to submit to Muslim sovereignty under the compact of *dhimmh* (a charter of rights

43. Daniel O. Conkle, "The Establishment Clause and Religious Expression in Governmental Settings: Four Variables in Search of a Standard," *West Virginia Law Review* 110 (2007): 319.

44. Firuz Kazemzadeh, "The State of Religious Freedom: Remarks by Firuz Kazemzadeh," *World Affairs* 147, no. 4 (1985): 243.

45. Ibid., 244.

46. Paul Weller, "'Human Rights,' 'Religion,' and the 'Secular': Variant Configurations of Religions, States and Societies," *Religion and Human Rights* 1 (2006): 37–38. Despite their officially inferior status, certain groups, including the Balkan Christians in the seventeenth century, frequently opted to pursue their claims before Islamic judges rather than in church courts, largely because the former were (in those instances) able to provide more favorable dispute resolutions. Rossitsa Gradeva, "Orthodox Christians in the Kadi Courts: The Practice of the Sofia Sheriat Court, Seventeenth Century," *Islamic Law and Society* 4, no. 1 (1997): 37–69.

47. Kazemzadeh, "The State of Religious Freedom," 38. Note that while the origin of the Druze religion is related to the Ismaili sect of Islam, it also incorporates Gnostic and neo-Platonic elements and is thus held by some Islamic scholars to be a non-Muslim religion.

48. Ved P. Nanda, "Islam and International Human Rights Law: Selected Aspects," *American Society of International Law Proceedings* 87 (1993): 328.

and obligations with the Muslim state).[49] *Dhimmis* were required to pay a *jizya* (a poll tax or tribute demonstrating their submission to Islamic authority), comply with all Islamic holiday observances, refrain from proselytizing or publicly preaching their faith, and hold no positions of authority over Muslims (e.g., public office).[50]

Moreover, even this restricted status was denied to nonbelievers, who, according to the Qur'an, could be killed on sight unless they were granted *aman* (safe conduct) by Muslims in an Islamic state.[51] In cases where *Shari'a* conflicted with non-Muslim law, Islamic law controlled.[52] For these reasons, though *dhimmi* means "protected people" (and has been cited as evidence of *Shari'a* tolerance), *dhimmitude* is more commonly understood (at least in the West) as "the institutionalized subjugation of non-Muslim minorities,"[53]—its two-tier citizenship model a clear violation of religious freedom.[54] As Middle Eastern scholar Habib C. Malik writes, "[t]he best thing that can be said in its favor is that it entails violence 'with a human face.' The gradual dehumanization of non-Muslim minority communities— which is what the *dhimmi* system achieves—represents a form of cumulative abuse . . . .. Over time, [it] has functioned as a means not of tolerance but of liquidation."[55] In place from the seventh century until modern times, the legacy of the *dhimmi* system persists today for religious minorities

49. Ibid., 328–29.

50. Ibid., 329. For a contrasting perspective, see Ahmad Yousif, "Islam, Minorities and Religious Freedom: A Challenge to Modern Theory of Pluralism," *Journal of Muslim Minority Affairs* 20, no. 1 (2000): 36–37. Ahmad Yousif maintains that non-Muslims are permitted the following religious freedoms: full freedom of conscience and belief, the right to worship and practice in safety, freedom to celebrate religious festivals and ceremonies, permission to build and maintain places of worship, freedom to conduct missionary activities and propagate their faith, freedom to raise their children according to the tenets of their own faith, and the right to judicial autonomy. This presentation of the rights of non-Muslims follows Yousif's extensive criticism of Western religious freedom, which includes repeated mention of the granting of special privileges to Christians and Jews.

51. Nanda, "Islam and International Human Rights Law: Selected Aspects," 329.

52. Melanie D. Reed, "Western Democracy and Islamic Tradition: The Application of Sharia in a Modern World," *American University International Law Review* 19 (2004): 508.

53. Robert Spencer, *Onward Muslim Soldiers: How Jihad Still Threatens America and the West* (Washington, DC: Regnery Publishing, Inc., 2003), 174.

54. George Weigel, "Comment by George Weigel," in *The Influence of Faith: Religious Groups and U.S. Foreign Policy*, ed. Elliott Abrams (Lanham, MD: Rowman & Littlefield Publishers, Inc. & The Ethics and Public Policy Center, 2001): 67.

55. Habib C. Malik, "Political Islam and the Roots of Violence," in *The Influence of Faith: Religious Groups and U.S. Foreign Policy*, ed. Elliott Abrams (Lanham, MD: Rowman & Littlefield Publishers, Inc. & The Ethics and Public Policy Center, 2001), 117.

in countries like Saudi Arabia, Iran, Sudan, Egypt, Nigeria, and even Turkey.[56]

B. Apostasy and Islam

While free speech is an essential corollary of the Western concept of the autonomous individual, "the socially situated self of Islamic society necessarily rejects free speech in favor of prohibitions against insult and defamation."[57] According to orthodox Muslim scholars, Islamic law constitutes "an eternal, correct and immutable truth"; therefore, "any allegation that Islam is less than ideal would inevitably be perceived as a disloyal act of treason against Allah and the values of the believing community."[58] Under classical *Shari'a*, Muslims who renounced their belief in Islam (as well as some who refused to judge or be judged by Islamic law) were guilty of apostasy[59]—one of the seven *hudud* offenses against God necessitating punishment involving physical pain or death.[60] While no passage in the Qur'an actually specifies any temporal penalty per se for apostasy (instead condemning the guilty to eternal damnation),[61] converts to other religions

56. John L. Allen, Jr., "No Retreat from 'Reciprocity' Challenge," *National Catholic Reporter*, October 13, 2006. For a discussion of Egyptian intellectuals who, in the 1980s and 1990s, challenged traditional Islamic views on relations between Muslims and non-Muslims, see Jorgen S. Nielsen, "Contemporary Discussions on Religious Minorities in Islam," *Brigham Young University Law Review* 2002 (2002): 362–66.

57. M. M. Slaughter, "The Salman Rushdie Affair: Apostasy, Honor, and Freedom of Speech," *Virginia Law Review* 79 (1993): 155. See also Thomas M. Franck, "Is Personal Freedom a Western Value?," *American Journal of International Law* 91 (1997).

58. Donna E. Arzt, "Heroes or Heretics: Religious Dissidents under Islamic Law," *Wisconsin International Law Journal* 14 (1996): 373. Patrick Sookhdeo, director of the International Institute for the Study of Islam and Christianity in Great Britain, states, "It is intrinsic within the very nature of Islam in its classical formulation that a Muslim may not choose to embrace another faith." "Does Islam Have Room for Religious Liberty?," *Christianity Today* (August 19, 1991), 51. Alternatively, Sayyid Mohammad Syeed of the International Institute of Islamic Thought near Washington, DC asserts that conversion should be allowed under classical understandings of the Qur'an, but he acknowledges that there are different views within Islam on this issue. Ibid., 52.

59. In contrast to apostasy, heresy emphasizes the content of belief: "Just as criticism or rejection of religion could be labeled as apostasy, attempts to reform or revise it could be considered heresy." Arzt, "Heroes or Heretics," 376–77. The concept of heresy originated in the conflict between Sunnis, Shi'as, and Kharijites over the legitimate successor to Muhammad.

60. Ibid., 373–74.

61. But see Ibn Warraq, "A General Overview of Apostasy," in *The Myth of Islamic Tolerance: How Islamic Law Treats Non-Muslims*, ed. Robert Spencer (Amherst, NY: Prometheus Books, 2005), 429. Warraq cites the venerated Islamic authority al-Shaf'i (the founder of one of the four doctrinal schools of Islam), who interpreted the

were considered apostates and subject in practice to execution (a worldly punishment provided for in the *Sunnah*).[62]

To be precise, Islamic law distinguishes between two kinds of infidelity, "original" (*kufr asli*) and "new" (*kufr tari*): "new infidelity" is the realm of apostasy, and it is legally worse than its "original" counterpart (the realm of non-Muslims).[63] The Arabic term for apostasy is *riddah* or *irtidad* and derives from the verb *radda* (to return from something and come back).[64] *Riddah* literally means to revert or turn away; hence, apostasy in *Shari'a* is the return of a person from the religion of Allah (*Din Allah*) to the religion of disbelief (*kufr*).[65] *Riddah* is described by various Islamic scholars as: "a disbelief or rejection of belief of a Muslim with explicit statement or a word that he inflicts on himself or an action which holds him responsible" (*Mawsu'ah al Islamiah*); "to cut off relationship with Islam by statement or action of a person by denying or rejecting the obligatory articles of belief and pillars of Islamic religion" (Al 'Ajuz); or simply "cut off from Islam (*qat'u*

following Qur'anic verse (Sura 2:217) as prescribing the death penalty for apostates: "But whoever of you recants and dies an unbeliever, his works shall come to nothing in this world and the next, and they are the companions of the fire for ever." Warraq also notes that Al-Thalabi, al-Khazan, and al-Razi concur in this interpretation. For an instructive overview of the doctrinal schools of Islamic law, including their distinguishing characteristics and geographic distribution, see H. Patrick Glenn, *Legal Traditions of the World*, 4th ed. (New York: Oxford University Press, 2010): 207–11. As Glenn notes, the schools differ in terms of substantive content and with regard to the sources of law.

62. Arzt, "Heroes or Heretics," 375–76. See also Abm. Mahbubul Islam, *Freedom of Religion in Shari'ah: A Comparative Analysis* (Kuala Lumpur: A.S. Noordeen, 2002), 181. Despite the Qur'anic principle of equal responsibility for men and women, all schools of *Shari'a* agree that a woman apostate should not be stoned to death. They differ only on how long women should be held in prison until they recant, whether they can be beaten there, etc. Shah, "Freedom of Religion: Koranic and Human Rights Perspectives," 79. Mohammad Omar Farooq argues that the traditional position of Muslim jurists on this issue confused apostasy as "an issue of pure freedom of faith and conscience" from apostasy as "treason against the community or the state"—only the latter of which should have been punishable by death. He characterizes this "misunderstanding" as "excusable" on the part of classical scholars (a contestable claim in the view of this book), but nevertheless is unforgiving of contemporary scholars who make the same mistake. Thus, he has compiled an interesting list of Muslim scholars (past and present) who similarly agree that only apostasy as treason warrants capital punishment or who reject death as a penalty for apostasy altogether. The list includes excerpts of and citations to these scholars' works and public comments on the subject. Mohammad Omar Farooq, "On Apostasy and Islam: 100 + Notable Islamic Voices Affirming the Freedom of Faith" (Apr. 2, 2007). http://apostasyandislam.blogspot.com.

63. Yohanan Friedmann, *Tolerance and Coercion in Islam: Interfaith Relations in the Muslim Tradition* (New York: Cambridge University Press, 2003), 123.

64. Islam, *Freedom of Religion in Shari'ah*, 179.

65. Ibid., 179–80.

al Islam) or turning back from Islam (*ruju' 'an al Islam*)" (Abdul Qadir).[66] A *murtadd* (apostate) is one who commits *riddah*.

Shari'a teachings on apostasy are at the center of many contemporary debates about the international law of religious freedom. Commenting on Article 18 of the UDHR, Sultanhussein Tabandeh of Iran writes that while its provisions are largely acceptable,[67] important difficulties remain.[68] First, under an Islamic state, followers of religions contrary to Islam (i.e., all religions except for Judaism, Christianity, and Zoroastrianism) have no official right to freedom of religion; and second, both Sunnis and Shi'as object to the right to change one's religion, arguing for the superiority of Islam, the absence of a right to apostasy in the Qur'an, and the need to keep people within the fold of Islam (since, as the true and final religion, it offers the only path to salvation).[69] These objections are not esoteric.[70]

In 1989, Ayatolllah Khomeini broadcast a *fatwa* on Tehran radio sentencing Salman Rushdie to death for apostasy and declaring that anyone who carried out the sentence would be "a martyr and go directly to heaven."[71] In Egypt, Muslim intellectuals accused of apostasy include Farag Fuda (murdered in 1992), Nagib Mahfouz (stabbed in the neck in 1994), Nasr Hamid Abu Zaid (ordered to divorce his wife in 1995), the feminist leader Nawal al-Saadawy (who has received death threats), and Ahmed Subhy Mansour (fired from his position at Al-Azhar University in 1987 and briefly jailed).[72] A Malaysian woman who converted to Christianity, Lina Joy, fought for seven years to legalize the change and is now in danger of being jailed for apostasy after Malaysia's highest court ruled that she does not have a constitutional right to convert from Islam.[73] And in Afghanistan,

66. Ibid., 180–81.

67. Sultanhussein Tabandeh, *A Muslim Commentary on the Universal Declaration of Human Rights*, trans. Francis John Goulding (London: F. J. Goulding & Company, 1970), 1, 9, 85.

68. Ibid., 70, 72.

69. Abdullah Saeed and Hassan Saeed, *Freedom of Religion, Apostasy and Islam* (Burlington, VT: Ashgate, 2004), 15–16.

70. For a powerful collection of testimonies written by Muslim apostates from around the world, see Ibn Warraq, ed., *Leaving Islam: Apostates Speak Out* (Amherst, MA: Prometheus Books, 2003).

71. Said Amir Arjomand, "Religious Human Rights and the Principle of Legal Pluralism in the Middle East," in *Religious Human Rights in Global Perspective: Legal Perspectives*, ed. Johan D. van der Vyver and John Witte, Jr. (Boston: Martinus Nijhoff Publishers, 1996), 342–43.

72. Ahmed Subhy Mansour, review of "Freedom of Religion, Apostasy and Islam," by Abdullah Saeed and Hassan Saeed, *Middle East Quarterly* (Fall 2005): 86.

73. "Malaysian Court Tells Convert She Must Stay Muslim," *Christian Century* (June 26, 2007).

where the constitution simultaneously recognizes the Hanafi school of Islamic jurisprudence and at least some degree of religious liberty, Christian convert Abdul Rahman was arrested in 2006 on charges of apostasy—spared from Afghani jihadists' demands for his trial and death by the sanctuary of asylum in Italy.[74]

III. RELIGIOUS LIBERTY AND ISLAMIC REFORMATION

As the situation of religious minorities and apostates under Islamic law makes clear, at least historically, *Shari'a* has proven inconsistent with accepted international standards of religious freedom. When considered alongside the legal and political background to be sketched in Chapters 5 and 6, it is thus fair to conclude that law, religion, and politics have tended to combine in the Muslim world in ways that are detrimental to religious human rights (for Muslims and non-Muslims alike). However, it is true as well that the Qur'an provides for religious liberty, even if its scope and content is subject to debate. Moreover, Islam is not just a religion of rules, but also (at least for some) one of interpretation[75]—a tradition in which study and discussion are valued, in which the evolution of ideas and practices is possible.[76]

74. Robert Spencer, "Demanding Death for Apostasy," *Human Events* 62, no. 37 (October 30, 2006): 12.

75. H. Patrick Glenn provides a helpful overview of the role of interpretation in Islamic law. In the century following the Prophet, intellectual effort or endeavor (*ijtihad*) prevailed, alongside the use of individual reason (*ra'y*). Together, in the two subsequent centuries, these practices contributed to the development by the schools of major doctrinal statements of law. However, once these great works were completed, and once the *Hadith* had been compiled, "further human invention appeared incompatible with the divine nature of law and the implementation which had already occurred." Glenn, *Legal Traditions of the World*, 202–05. Thus, the "gate" or "door of endeavor" was closed, thereby eliminating interpretation and affirmative forms of rationality in the ongoing development of *Shari'a*. This did not hold true for the Shi'a, however, for whom the practice of *ijtihad* is obligatory (albeit limited to erudite and capable scholars). Ibid., 210–11. This subject has generated a tremendous amount of controversy within Islamic legal thought over the last century, with scholars arguing, to paraphrase Glenn, that the door should be re-opened, that it is already open, or that it was never actually closed. Ibid., 215. Islamic reformation depends, in part, on the recovery/embrace of *ijtihad* and rationality.

76. Donna E. Arzt, "Religious Human Rights in Muslim States of the Middle East and North Africa," *Emory International Law Review* 10 (1996): 160. For an interesting and provocative selection of essays exhibiting such interpretive evolution, see Kari Vogt, Lena Larsen, and Christian Moe, *New Directions in Islamic Thought: Exploring Reform and Muslim Tradition* (London: I.B. Tauris, 2008). See also Tariq Ramadan, *Radical Reform: Islamic Ethics and Liberation* (New York: Oxford University Press, 2008).

Muslim scholars working within these interpretive spaces are frequently referred to as moderates or reformers. Because there are relevant differences between these individuals and the arguments they make, any single designation is problematic. What is arguably the greatest public controversy surrounds Tariq Ramadan—one of Europe's most influential Muslim intellectuals who is variously hailed as a brilliant bridge builder and interreligious diplomat extraordinaire, but also decried as a misogynistic anti-Semite intent on waging covert jihad against the secular, hypercapitalist West.[77] These controversies are related to others about whether or not Islam can even be reformed, and, if so, to what degree.[78] Except where these debates directly touch on the subject matter here, they are outside the scope of this book. Thus, to be clear, these chapters present the views of reformers as they define them, not challenging their sincerity, but also recognizing that it remains to be seen whether their ideas will acquire traction capable of achieving and sustaining legal and cultural transformation.

That said, Muslim reformers are central to strategies of change and accommodation, including those aimed at reconciling Western and Islamic notions of freedom, democratic institutions, and human rights laws.[79]

One scholar, Liaquat Ali Khan, argues for what he terms the "jurodynamics of Islamic law"—a spatiotemporal approach to divine texts that recognizes the Qur'an as primary and thus not subject to abrogation (the invalidation of prior rules found to be incompatible with subsequent rules), but allows that classical *fiqh* opinions may indeed be abrogated so long as the resulting *qanun* is consistent with the Basic Code (the Qur'an and the *Sunnah*). Liaquat Ali Khan, "Jurodynamics of Islamic Law," *Rutgers Law Review* 61 (2009). Note that this does not necessarily resolve the problem of conflicting interpretations of the Basic Code itself, particularly when some interpretations are consistent with international legal standards of religious liberty and others are not.

77. See Paul Berman, *The Flight of the Intellectuals* (Brooklyn, NY: Melville House, 2010); Andrew March, "Who's Afraid of Tariq Ramadan?," *The American Prospect* (May 19, 2010); Paul Berman, "Who's Afraid of Tariq Ramadan?," *New Republic*, June 4, 2007; Ian Buruma, "Tariq Ramadan Has an Identity Issue," *The New York Times*, February 4, 2007.

78. See, for example, Bassam Tibi, *Islam's Predicament with Modernity* (New York: Routledge, 2009); Ayaan Hirsi Ali, *Infidel* (New York: Free Press, 2008); Bassam Tibi, *Political Islam, World Politics and Europe* (New York: Routledge, 2008); Ibn Warraq, *Why I Am Not a Muslim* (Amherst, MA: Prometheus Books, 2003); Bassam Tibi, *Islam between Culture and Politics* (New York: Palgrave, 2001); Ibn Warraq, "Yes! Islam Can Be Reformed: But It Will Also Be Transformed," *Free Inquiry* 24, no. 3 (Apr./May 2004).

79. Alternative formulations of democracy, rights, and pluralism are the subject of a nascent but growing literature on Qur'anic political thought. See Noah Feldman, *After Jihad: America and the Struggle for Islamic Democracy* (New York: Farrar, Straus and Giroux, 2003); Khaled Abou El Fadl, "Islam and the Challenge of Democratic Commitment," *Fordham International Law Journal* 27 (2003). Scholars observe that democratic principles such as popular elections, electoral process, multiplicity of political parties, and the authority of popularly-elected parliaments have been accepted as religiously legitimate by Islamist parties in countries such as Jordan, Egypt, and

There are many possibilities for how such conversations could take place. Before proceeding to a specific discussion about religious rights, some general observations from leading Islamic reformers are illuminating. For example, Abdullahi A. An-Na'im suggests that "'what must be done is to clarify and specify the relationship between Islam and political authority on the basis of an Islamic approach to secularism .... From this perspective, the protection of human rights, especially freedom of belief, expression, and association, is an Islamic imperative—and not merely a requirement of international treaties—because these rights are prerequisites for the necessary discourse."[80]

Turkey. Charles McDaniel, "Islam and the Global Society," *Brigham Young University Law Review* 2003 (2003): 525–26. In contradistinction to Western democratic systems, Islamic democracy is based not on popular sovereignty, but on the sovereignty of Allah and the duty of the people to follow and obey religious law. Ibid., 524–25. This law, *Shari'a*, emphasizes the duties of members toward society over and above individual rights derived from society; rights thus adhere primarily in the group, rather than the person. See Reed, 'Western Democracy and Islamic Tradition;' Jason Morgan-Foster, 'Third Generation Rights: What Islamic Law Can Teach the International Human Rights Movement,' *Yale Human Rights and Development Law Journal* 8 (2005); Ali Iyad Yakub, 'The Islamic Roots of Democracy,' *University of Miami International and Comparative Law Review* 12 (2004). Muslim scholars also note that in the Islamic tradition, pluralism within human societies is well recognized and that, in the Qur'an itself, there are principles of tolerance and respect for difference. Ali S. Asani, 'So That You May Know One Another: A Muslim American Reflection on Pluralism and Islam,' *Annals of the American Academy of Political and Social Science* 588 (July 2003): 42. See also Tassaduq Hussain Jillani, 'Democracy and Islam: An Odyssey in Braving the Twenty-First Century,' *Brigham Young University Law Review* 2006 (2006): 739–49.

80. Abdullahi A. An-Na'im, "Political Islam in National Politics and International Relations," in *The Desecularization of the World: Resurgent Religion and World Politics*, ed. Peter L. Berger (Grand Rapids, MI: Ethics and Public Policy Center & Wm. B. Eerdmans Publishing Co., 1999), 120. An-Na'im has recently elaborated upon his vision of secularism, making the following general arguments: Muslims need the opportunity to comply with Shari'a voluntarily, and thus the state should be secular; a secular state must preclude an institutional link between Islam and state institutions, but may allow faith to play a role in society; an Islamic state (a "postcolonial innovation") is actually a logical impossibility, as state actions are secular, politically motivated and backed by violence, whereas compliance with Shari'a cannot be coerced; there is a need for civic reason so that Muslims who openly agree or disagree with a policy proposal do not risk having their piety impugned; Shari'a is a changing product of human consensus, and because human judgment is fallible, there is always the potential for a new consensus to emerge; and, finally, Muslims should act upon their right to engage in consensus-building around a transformative reinterpretation of Shari'a that incorporates constitutionalism, human rights, and citizenship. Abdullahi A. An-Na'im, *Islam and the Secular State: Negotiating the Future of Shari'a* (Cambridge, MA: Harvard University Press, 2008). For the argument that Islam does not conflict with secularism because of its internal commitment to pluralism, freedom of conscience, and human rights, see Nehaluddin Ahmad, "The Modern Concept of Secularism and Islamic Jurisprudence: A Comparative Analysis," *Golden Gate University School of Law Annual Survey of International & Comparative Law* 15 (2009).

Likewise, to build a case for tolerance in Islam, Khaled Abou El Fadl maintains that Qur'anic verses should be read not in isolation, but rather in light of the moral imperatives of the text, including mercy, justice, kindness, and goodness.[81] Critics of Abou El Fadl argue that Islamic "intolerance" is the principled resistance of Muslims standing up for justice, and that he concludes erroneously that "the state has co-opted the clergy . . . reduced the clergy's legitimacy, and produced a profound vacuum in religious authority."[82] In response, Abou El Fadl writes that the former charge demonstrates a striking lack of concern for the suffering Muslims experience at the hands of extremists, while the latter is belied by groups like the Taliban, "who carry the banner of Islamic authenticity and legitimacy, [but] are far more anti-Western than they are pro-Islamic."[83] He then poignantly articulates the challenge to Muslims reformers:

> As a Muslim intellectual, I have no moral choice but to confront the following question: Do the bin Ladens of the Muslim world actually find justification for the ugliness that they perpetrate in any interpretive tradition in Islam? Does this level of intolerance and criminality find support, regardless of how flimsy or absurd, in some of the traditional interpretations? I think that, unfortunately, the answer must be yes — it would be dishonest to say otherwise. But fortunately, Muslims have the power to deconstruct and reject those interpretations.[84]

One renowned Muslim scholar who has been engaged in just such acts of deconstruction and interpretation, while also crafting new visions of Islamic freedom and democracy, is Abdolkarim Soroush. Soroush has been called "the Luther of Islam," and like Martin Luther, Soroush was an early supporter of the institutions he now critiques. In an article on Islamic reformation, foreign policy analyst Robin Wright describes the political

81. Khaled Abou El Fadl, "The Place of Tolerance in Islam," in *The Place of Tolerance in Islam*, ed. Joshua Cohen and Ian Lague (Boston: Beacon Press, 2002), 13–14. On the nexus of kindness and justice in Islam, see Muhammad Fathi Al-Dirini, "Justice in the Islamic Shari'a," in *Justice and Human Rights in Islamic Law*, ed. Gerald E. Lampe (Washington, DC: International Law Institute, 1997), 49–50.
82. Abid Ullah Jan, "The Limits of Tolerance," in *The Place of Tolerance in Islam*, ed. Joshua Cohen and Ian Lague (Boston: Beacon Press, 2002), 45. See also Qamar-ul Huda, "Plural Traditions," in *The Place of Tolerance in Islam*, ed. Joshua Cohen and Ian Lague (Boston: Beacon Press, 2002), 82.
83. Khaled Abou El Fadl, "Reply," in *The Place of Tolerance in Islam*, ed. Joshua Cohen and Ian Lague (Boston: Beacon Press, 2002), 97–104.
84. Ibid., 111. See also Khaled Abou El Fadl, "Islam and the Challenge of Democracy," in *Islam and the Challenge of Democracy*, ed. Joshua Cohen and Deborah Chasman (Princeton, NJ: Princeton University Press, 2004), 3–48.

context of Soroush's transformation, which I paraphrase here:[85] After initially supporting Iran's revolution in 1979 (e.g., revising university curricula), Soroush began increasingly to articulate ideas that the regime considered highly controversial. Leaders, including Ayatollah Khamenei, implicitly but unmistakably framed public remarks in response to Soroush's articles and speeches, including ideas of his that were viewed as heretical (e.g., a 1995 address by Khamenei commemorating the 1979 takeover of the U.S. Embassy devoted more time to condemning Soroush's teachings than it did to attacking either the United States or Israel). Indeed, "[a] new law imposing severe penalties on anyone associating with critics and enemies of the Islamic Republic [of Iran] was widely thought to be aimed at undermining Soroush's growing support."[86]

Several of Soroush's ideas are relevant to the relationship between Islam and religious freedom. For example, he asserts that those who criticize Islamic democracy make three "dark and dangerous" errors: they equate democracy with extreme liberalism; they sever *Shari'a* from its foundations; and they equate religious democratic government with religious jurisprudential (*fiqhi*) government.[87] Instead, Soroush advocates democracy for the Muslim world based on two related principles. First, true belief requires freedom (including freedom to leave a chosen faith), and this freedom is the basis for democracy.[88] Second, religious understanding does and must continue to evolve, for while sacred texts do not change, their interpretation is subject to the influence of the age and the conditions in which believers live; correspondingly, everyone is entitled to his or her own understanding, and no interpretation is automatically more authoritative than others.[89]

Furthermore, "given his belief in the unity of truth," Soroush asserts "the necessity of religious toleration in societies claiming to uphold human

85. Robin Wright, "Islam and Democracy: Two Visions of Reformation," *Journal of Democracy* 7, no. 2 (1996): 64–75.

86. Ibid., 66.

87. Abdolkarim Soroush, *Reason, Freedom and Democracy in Islam: Essential Writings of Abdolkarim Soroush*, ed. and trans. Mahmoud Sadri and Ahmad Sadri (New York: Oxford University Press, 2000), 134.

88. Wright, "Islam and Democracy," 67. See also Soroush, *Reason, Freedom and Democracy in Islam*, 21–22, 35, 129.

89. Wright, "Islam and Democracy," 68. See also Soroush, *Reason, Freedom and Democracy in Islam*, 22, 30, 69, 100; Abdolkarim Soroush, "The Changeable and the Unchangeable," in *New Directions in Islamic Thought: Exploring Reform and Muslim Tradition*, ed. Kari Vogt, Lena Larsen, and Christian Moe (London: I.B. Tauris, 2008), 14–15.

rights" and the requirement of a plurality of voices if justice is to prevail.[90] Practically, Soroush calls for the end of financial support for religious leaders from the state (in most Sunni countries) and from the people (in Shi'ite communities), so that they will no longer be compelled to propagate official or popular interpretations of Islamic law.[91] In support of these positions, Soroush cites the Qur'an and the Prophet Muhammad, but also Jalal al-Din Rumi, Muhammad Iqbal, Jurgen Habermas, and Alexis de Tocqueville.[92] And though he is criticized for not taking into account such factors as the form of the state, the existence of civil institutions, the presence of a tolerant political culture, the nature of the economic system, or discrepancies in the socioeconomic and political status of various groups, Soroush succeeds in demonstrating how innovative interpretations of Islamic teachings and traditions might engender meaningful compatibility of Islam with freedom, democracy, and human rights.[93]

As in the West, where Christian theology and revolutionary constitutional politics contributed both form and substance to modern religious human rights law, the legal and political landscape of the Muslim world is similarly animated by Islam. Its teachings and traditions constitute the religious-intellectual history within which the pertinent legal-political institutions of Muslim states and corresponding formulations of Islamic international law have emerged and evolved. These domestic and global institutional developments (the subjects of Chapters 5 and 6, respectively) provide essential empirical content for determining whether different religious and political trajectories are indeed contributing to a world legal tradition, or whether they could.

90. Irene Oh, *The Rights of God: Islam, Human Rights, and Comparative Ethics* (Washington, DC: Georgetown University Press, 2007), 103.

91. Wright, "Islam and Democracy," 70. See also John von Heyking, "Mysticism in Contemporary Islamic Political Thought: Orhan Pamuk and Abdolkarim Soroush," *Humanitas* XIX, nos. 1 & 2 (2006): 71–96.

92. Soroush, *Reason, Freedom and Democracy in Islam*, 140–142; L. Carl Brown, review of *Reason, Freedom, and Democracy in Islam: Essential Writings of Abdolkarim Soroush*, by Abdolkarim Soroush, ed. and trans. Mahmoud Sadri and Ahmad Sadri, *Foreign Affairs* 79, no. 5 (September/October 2000): 148.

93. Mehrzad Boroujerdi, review of *Reason, Freedom, and Democracy in Islam: Essential Writings of Abdolkarim Soroush*, by Abdolkarim Soroush, ed. and trans. Mahmoud Sadri and Ahmad Sadri, *Middle East Institute* (Summer 2001). Bassam Tibi, while accepting the possibility of new interpretations of rights based on Islamic scripture and jurisprudence, cautions that "the mere existence of norms means nothing unless there are institutions to enforce them." Bassam Tibi, "The European Tradition of Human Rights and the Culture of Islam," in *Human Rights in Africa: Cross-Cultural Perspectives*, ed. Abdullahi A. An-Na'im and Francis M. Deng (Washington, DC: The Brookings Institution, 1990), 131.

CHAPTER 5

Between Religion and Law

Politics as an Intervening Variable

Although a disturbing record of assaults on the principle of religious freedom has been
accumulated by countries like Egypt, Iran, Pakistan, Saudi Arabia, and the Sudan, it would
be simplistic to blame Islam per se for these outcomes. After all, these countries' policies
are so inimical to religious freedom that professing Muslims may be prosecuted as heretics or blasphemers for what is actually political or theological dissent or may be arbi-
trarily declared apostates and executed. These outcomes have little to do with mandates
of Islamic law. It seems fairer to assess the violations . . . as a symptom of a pervasive lack
of respect for civil and political rights... . The real conflicts over religious freedom are
therefore not so much conflicts between Islamic law and international law as conflicts
waged between competing factions within Muslim societies.
                                   —Ann Elizabeth Mayer[1]

The first part of this book introduced the religious and philosophical
genesis of religious liberty in the West, followed by its institutionalization in the American constitution and in modern human rights law. The
second part opened with the contours of Islamic law as it pertains to freedom of religion. Thus, it might be expected that discussions of Muslim
state constitutions and international legal formulations would follow, and
they will. However, there is a crucial historical divergence that bears directly
on the central questions of this project.

The nation-states of the West developed as separate legal and political bodies
centuries before international religious human rights law was established.

---

1. Ann Elizabeth Mayer, *Islam and Human Rights: Tradition and Politics* (Boulder, CO:
Westview Press, 1999), 174.

As Chapters 2 and 3 illustrated, this makes it possible to tell a relatively clean story about that law's theological precursors, as well as to distinguish between the religious and political concerns motivating the scope and content of religious liberty. By contrast, the domestic constitutions of many states in the Muslim world evolved contemporaneously with declarations of Islamic international law. Individually and collectively, they were often drafted in response to the legacies of colonialism. In this compressed historical space, domestic and international political considerations are not easily distinguishable. Moreover, unlike their Western counterparts,[2] Muslims states have proven far less likely to separate mosque and state, which means that religious arguments are far more commonplace in legal and political discourse and exert independent influence (though whether they are piously and/or strategically motivated remains a matter of intense scholarly debate).

These differences are of the utmost importance for interpreting the "dilemma of religious freedom." In the West, particularly after the Second Vatican Council, Christian teachings and traditions regarding religious liberty largely and positively align with state constitutions (especially the American one) and with international legal standards.[3] Conversely, in the Muslim world, Islamic teachings and traditions as expressed in most state constitutions and Islamic international human rights declarations do not. If those legal texts accurately render Islamic principles, and if Islam itself is not subject to change, then the dilemma of religious freedom stands: there is an intractable conflict between Western and Islamic international law.

Therefore, it seems that there are two entry points for challenging the dilemma. The first, which was introduced in Chapter 4 and will be taken up again in subsequent sections, is directed toward alternative interpretations of Islam and religious reform. The second, which motivates Chapters 5 and 6, is to pry open the relationship between Islamic law and the constitutional texts of modern Muslim states thereby to uncover intervening political variables. Explanations that ignore politics risk conflating religious teachings and traditions with the political agenda of country elites. Similarly, explanations that discount the influence of Islam in favor of purely legal and political reforms underestimate the extent to which

2. The United States remains a special case, in that separation of church and state and the (partial) secularization of culture have not eliminated religious arguments from public discourse on law and politics.

3. Orthodox Christianity, insofar as it is aligned with ethnic and/or political groupings (e.g., Russian Orthodoxy), is a notable exception, but one whose intricacies are beyond the scope of this book.

religion conditions institutional possibilities. Thus, to anticipate, this book will argue that both entry points and their corresponding strategies are necessary to traversing the dilemma.

More immediately, by analyzing the political and cultural processes that drive the institutionalization of Muslim identity, this chapter and the next seek to demonstrate that Islamic law as it appears in these legal texts results from factors that are at least as much political as they are religious. In other words, they substantiate the possibility that the conflicts over religious freedom are ultimately between competing factions of Muslim society, including contesting schools of Islamic thought, and not between (all formulations of) Islamic and international law.

Recognizing that the construction and institutionalization of religious liberty rights is at once a political and a legal project, this chapter proceeds in two main sections. The first focuses on the political and socio-cultural processes in Muslim states that have interacted over time to institutionalize Islamic law and identity at national and transnational levels. This history is essential, not least because the modern constitutions of many relevant states were adopted during the 1970s and 1980s amidst struggles marked by Arab nationalism, Islamism, and Islamic identity formation. Hence, in the second section, the constitutional consequences of these historical-political processes are explored via specific examination of religious liberty in the laws and practices of four influential countries—Iran, Turkey, Egypt, and Pakistan. This, in turn, lays the groundwork for Chapter 6, which analyzes the development and implications of Islamic international law as an alternative/oppositional paradigm.

I. MIDDLE EAST MEETS WEST: POLITICAL CONTESTATION AND ISLAMIC IDENTITY[4]

More than one hundred fifty years passed between the first American settlement at Jamestown and adoption of the United States Constitution.

---

4. It should be noted at the outset that identifiers such as "Middle East" and "Arab" are somewhat amorphous. The Middle East generally refers to countries in southwest Asia and northern Africa, though precisely which states are included has shifted throughout history. There is no universally agreed upon definition at present. To give just three examples: 1) the 1957 Eisenhower Doctrine, which defined the Middle East as "the area lying between and including Libya on the west and Pakistan on the east and Turkey on the North and the Arabian peninsula to the south, plus the Sudan and Ethiopia." Roderic H. Davison, "Where Is the Middle East?," *Foreign Affairs* 38 (1960): 665–75; 2) the definition provided by the airline industry, maintained by the IATA

The political, economic, social, and religious struggles of the early Republic's history indelibly shaped the form and content of that founding document, including its First Amendment. The same is true for the constitutions of Muslim states in the Middle East and elsewhere. Although the time period is different, the resulting legal texts undoubtedly reflect the complex religious and political histories of their respective states. This is one reason why a discussion of politics precedes that of constitutional law in this chapter. Additionally, the political and socio-cultural processes presented below problematize the relationship between Islam and the laws of Muslim states by calling into question how accurately and exclusively the latter represent the former. In other words, by revealing religiously informed laws and social identities to be, in part, the products of political contestation, they illuminate the possibility of alternate social imaginaries and thus alternate institutional arrangements.

To that end, this section engages two interrelated lines of inquiry. The first is the historical development of Arab nationalism and Islamism, noting

standards organization, which includes Bahrain, Egypt, Iran, Iraq, Israel, Jordan, Kuwait, Lebanon, Occupied Palestinian Territory, Oman, Qatar, Saudi Arabia, Sudan, Syrian Arab Republic, United Arab Emirates, and Yemen; or 3) a geographic definition including Bahrain, Egypt, Iran, Iraq, Israel, Jordan, Kuwait, Lebanon, Oman, Palestine, Qatar, Saudi Arabia, Sudan, Somalia, Syria, Turkey, the United Arab Emirates and Yemen.

The incorporation of Iran, Pakistan, or Turkey into any of these definitions can be problematic, as these countries are not traditionally regarded as Arab states (e.g., Iran is Persian). This raises the question of how to define an Arab state. The United Nations Development Programme defines Arab States as including the following: Algeria, Bahrain, Djibouti, Egypt, Iraq, Jordan, Kuwait, Lebanon, Libya, Morocco, Palestinian Programme, Saudi Arabia, Somalia, Sudan, Syria, Tunisia, United Arab Emirates and Yemen. Members of the Arab League include all of the UNDP countries, plus Comoros, Mauritania, Oman, and Qatar. As this Chapter discusses, modern nationalist movements identified Arab peoples based on three features: 1) membership in an Arab state or a state with historic ties to Arabia; 2) command of the Arabic language; and 3) fundamental knowledge of Arabian traditions. Of course, these conceptual categories are not exhaustive.

The complex and contested nature of these definitions should be acknowledged, but cannot be altogether avoided. Throughout these chapters, a few guiding principles have been employed. First, when referencing the work of other scholars, this book has deferred to their terminology (i.e., their use of Arab or Middle East). Second, literature from and consultation with experts in the field whose own work at times focuses on Turkey or Iran, for example, has been sought—not because these are Middle Eastern or Arab states per se, but because their political and legal histories bear importantly on such phenomena as Arab nationalism or the rise of Islamism. Thus, the examples provided are intended first and foremost to illustrate the dynamics under consideration. Identity construction is itself a legal, religious, cultural, and political project. The intention here is to illustrate, not to define; the act of definition is left to others more appropriate to the task.

particularly the resurgence of Islamic law and politics in reaction to the secularism of Western imperial power. This is important because it raises questions about whether and to what degree Islamic states and their constitutions represent authentic religious law versus political strategy, and also whether they may more appropriately be understood as anti-Western (rather than pro-Islam). The second line of inquiry is the contemporary development among Muslim communities of movements tied to Islam and Islamic identity, including their various instantiations at global, state, and local levels. This simultaneously provides evidence of transnational Muslim identity (which might be expected to strengthen Islamic international law) and of Muslim particularism (which challenges the notion of "Muslim" or "Islamic" as homogenous categories).

Although they do not specifically address religious freedom, these two queries are inextricably related to it. In fact, they fundamentally inform the subsequent analysis of legal texts at both state and international levels. That is because academic and policy conversations about religious liberty rights in and across Muslim states almost invariably raise some version of the following questions: Do these laws accurately represent Islam and, by extension, Muslim society? How have their form and content been influenced by non-religious factors (i.e., how have domestic political struggles, international relations, and social movements impacted the institutionalization and practice of religious norms)? And, in terms of strategic recommendations, how can the West most productively engage Islamic states and communities on the issue of religious freedom? These questions, which will occupy the remainder of this book, cannot be properly answered without first attending to the history presented here.

A. Arab Nationalism and Islamism

Any serious study of legal and political life in the Middle East must take account of both Arab nationalism and Islamism.[5] The two socio-political

5. Various scholars of nationalism differently identify its origins. Thus, Elie Kedourie points to the rise of consensual politics and the national idea, Ernest Gellner to industrialization, Benedict Andersen to print capitalism, and Michael Mann to the consequences of Great Power war. Yet in the Middle East—a region that saw in the past century an articulated national idea, economic industrialization, the introduction of mass media, and several major wars—nationalism (along with the development of nation-states) and religion (particularly religious law) have been linked in a manner markedly different from the experience of the West. The general contours of this relationship were suggested by Charles Kupchan in his address on Nationalism at

forces strike an uneasy balance, and while their histories overlap with varying degrees of significance depending upon the time period in question,
they rest upon competitive ontologies. Political scientist Adeed Dawisha,
analyzing this dynamic as it unfolded in the twentieth century, notes that
the essence of the tension is not one of correctness, but of primacy.[6]

On the one hand, Arab nationalism has been in most cases an avowedly
secular movement; still, it necessarily recognizes the particular role of
Islam in the Arab world (e.g., the majority Arabs are Muslims, and the most
dominant periods of Arab influence were tied to medieval Islamic empires).
On the other hand, Islamism champions religious law as the foundation of
all forms of organization, including those political; nevertheless, it is tied
historically to the Arabian Peninsula and linguistically to Arabic.[7] The question is thus not whether one doctrine or the other offers a complete identity, but rather which lays claim to greater authenticity and import in the
hearts and minds of Arab peoples.

However one answers this question, it definitively marks legal and political development in the Arab world in ways that are different from other
regions. While the rise of the modern state system in the West depended
on a certain disestablishment of legal, religious, and political identities, the
same has not been true in the Middle East.[8] Bernard Lewis, writing about
the overlapping identities of Middle Eastern peoples, defines a nation as
"a group of people held together by a common language, belief in a common
descent and in a shared history and destiny. They usually but not necessarily inhabit a contiguous territory; they often enjoy, and if they do not enjoy
they commonly seek, sovereign independence in their own name."[9] Nationalism, by extension, is the ideological force utilized in the movement from

Georgetown University (Washington, DC, September 15, 2003). See also Ernest
Gellner, *Nations and Nationalism* (Ithaca, NY: Cornell University Press, 1983), 82;
Elie Kedourie, *Nationalism* (Cambridge, MA: Blackwell, 1993); Benedict Anderson,
Imagined Communities: Reflections on the Spread of Nationalism (New York: Verso, 1990);
Michael Mann, *The Sources of Social Power: Volume 2, The Rise of Classes and Nation-States*
(New York: Cambridge University Press, 1993).

6. Adeed Dawisha, "Arab Nationalism and Islamism: Competitive Past, Uncertain
Future," *International Studies Review* 2 (Fall 2000): 79.

7. Bassam Tibi notes that given Islamism's diversity and fragmentation, it is empiri-
cally more accurate to speak of it in the plural as Islamic fundamentalisms. Bassam
Tibi, "The Fundamentalist Challenge to the Secular Order in the Middle East," *The
Fletcher Forum of World Affairs* 23, no. 1 (1999): 194.

8. For an interesting discussion of this difference, see Daniel Philpott, "The Challenge
of September 11 to Secularism in International Relations," *World Politics* 55 (October
2002): 66–95.

9. Bernard Lewis, *The Multiple Identities of the Middle East* (New York: Schocken
Books, 1999), 81.

a nation to a sovereign, independent nation-state (as well as in the reconceptualization of an existing nation-state).

The significance of this for the Arab Middle East, a region where "the
nation" is inextricably bound up with religion—via language, descent from
the Prophet Muhammad, the historical spread of Islamic empire, etc.—lies
in competing loyalty claims.[10] The nation-state as such is undermined in
several ways, both from below (agrarian states, familial orientation, tribal
bonds) and above (Islamic culture and law). This is especially true because
the constitution of "Arab" identity, which has undergone considerable geographic shifts over time, came in the middle of the twentieth century to be
understood as comprising the following: the historical bonds under early
Islamic rule; the proximity of their manners and traditions; and their ability to claim Arabic as their mother tongue (a language whose diffusion and
evolution was greatly facilitated by Islam).[11] Identity thus conceived is primarily legal-cultural and only secondarily political.

However, even this is too simplistic, for various components of the complex identities engaged here have shifted historically, such that the mid-
twentieth century saw primacy given to secular Arab nationalism (with
religious identity being marginalized), while more recent decades have seen
a resurgence of Islamic identity alongside state or regional ones.[12] This
leads some scholars to ask why inhabitants of the Arab world have "*imagined* themselves to constitute a *deep, horizontal* solidarity."[13] Answering this
question requires elaboration of both the early origins of Arab nationalism
and its subsequent encounters with Islamism.

Arab nationalism first emerged as a coherent ideology in the 1920s
under the leadership of Sati' al-Husri, a Syrian who was at that time in
charge of educational policies for the newly independent kingdom of Iraq.[14]
Upon surveying the intellectual traditions of European thought, he came
to favor German nationalist writings from the Romantic era over their

10. On the relationship between religion and nationalism, see Anthony D. Smith,
"The 'Sacred' Dimension of Nationalism," *Millennium: Journal of International Studies*
29, no. 3 (2000): 791–814.
11. Dawisha, "Arab Nationalism and Islamism," 81.
12. Ibid., 82. See also Rashid Halidi, *Palestinian Identity: The Construction of Modern
National Consciousness* (New York: Columbia University Press, 1997).
13. Dawisha, "Arab Nationalism and Islamism," 82. See also Ernest Renan, "What
Is a Nation?," in *Nation and Narration*, ed. Homi Bhabha (New York: Routledge, 1990),
8–22.
14. Dawisha, "Arab Nationalism and Islamism," 82. See also William Cleaveland,
*The Making of an Arab Nationalist: Ottomanism and Arabism in the Life and Thought of
Sati' Al-Husri* (Princeton, NJ: Princeton University Press, 1971); Bassam Tibi, *Arab
Nationalism: A Critical Inquiry* (New York: St. Martin's Press, 1990).

Anglo-French counterparts, thus privileging the former's emphasis on cultural and linguistic identity over the latter's focus on political institutions. Within the context of the Arab world, this preference may have emerged organically, for, as Elie Kedourie observes, German Romanticism resolved the tension between individuals and society in communal terms—a feature of Arab law and culture(s) that pre-dates Arab nationalism by several centuries.[15] According to al-Husri, the Arab peoples represented one nation that had been torn apart by the imperialism of Western European powers (especially the British and the French).[16]

This idea gained currency throughout the first half of the twentieth century, culminating with the leadership of Egyptian President Gamal Abdel Nasser.[17] Egypt's nationalization of the Suez Canal Company in 1956 and demonstrations across the Middle East against subsequent military hostilities by the British, French, and Israelis led many Arabs to believe that their nationalism would be triumphant against the forces of Western imperialism.[18] Ironically, this challenge to European political power occurred alongside those directed at traditional values and customs; nevertheless, while competing political ideologies such as liberalism and Marxism fell by the wayside, Islam and Islamic law remained a submerged, but still crucial, component of Arab identity.[19] Thus, when secular Arab nationalism began to waver in the late 1960s, political Islam was ready in the wings.

After Syria, Egypt, and Jordan were defeated by Israel in the Six-Day War, Islam reemerged as a (perhaps *the*) defining feature of Arab national identity.[20] Arab nationalism reconsidered within this religious light led to pan-Arab nationalism, and secularism gave way to Islamic-centeredness. In historical terms, this shift occurred rapidly, thereby marking the 1967 War as a critical juncture; indeed, by the time of the Yom Kippur War (called the Ramadan War by Arabs) just six years later, Islam served as the central

15. Elie Kedourie, *Nationalism* (Cambridge, MA: Blackwell, 1993), 30–32.
16. Stephen R. Humphreys, *Between Memory and Desire: The Middle East in a Troubled Age* (Los Angeles: University of California Press, 1999), 67–68. See also Bernard Lewis, "What Went Wrong?," *The Atlantic Monthly*, January 2002.
17. Youssef M. Choueiri, "The Middle East: Colonialism, Islam and the Nation-State," *Journal of Contemporary History* 37 (2002): 660.
18. Dawisha, "Arab Nationalism and Islamism," 86. See also Michael N. Barnett, *Dialogues in Arab Politics: Negotiations in Regional Order* (New York: Columbia University Press, 1998); Adeed Dawisha, *Egypt in the Arab World: The Elements of Foreign Policy* (New York: Macmillan Press, 1967).
19. Dawisha, "Arab Nationalism and Islamism," 87.
20. Kristel Halter, "Robin Wright's Perspective on Religious Extremism," *Washington Report on Middle East Affairs* 21 (April 2002): 91.

source of Arab identity—legally, politically, and militarily.[21] From that point through the present, Islam has continued to function as a crucial element of Arab identity and Middle Eastern law and politics; as with early Arab nationalists, pan-Arab nationalists of the 1980s invoked Islam and Islamic law as political tools for combating the influence and perceived oppression of the West.[22]

This political history is important because it raises questions about whether and to what degree Islamic states and their constitutions represent authentic religious law versus political strategy, and also whether they may more appropriately be understood as anti-Western (rather than pro-Islam). One important debate in the field of Middle East studies is thus focused on the character of political Islam. John Esposito and John Voll represent those who argue that Islam is centered by certain concepts and images, which in turn provide the foundation for a particular Islamic perception of democracy.[23] Further, they suggest that these core concepts are central to the legal and political positioning of nearly all Muslims, and that a culturally authentic Islamic democracy has as its core a consensual, rather than a win-or-lose majoritarian, political architecture.[24] Their analysis is guided, at times more explicitly than others, by a claim about Muslim identity—that it is inherent to the faith, common across regions and sects, and that it can find political expression in one particular regime type.

These tenets are strongly contested by another school of thought exemplified by the writings of Daniel Brumberg. He challenges this univocal view of Muslim identity, arguing that it necessarily yields neither a political trump card nor a preference for religiously based politics. Instead, Brumberg observes that political identity in the Middle East is shaped by a myriad of factors (of which religion is but one), and that the Islamist invocation of "authenticity" points in fact to a politically constructed Islam that borrows from both Western and Islamic political thought.[25] Under such a reading,

21. Ibid., 92.
22. Ibid., 92. For an insightful analysis of Islamic fundamentalism, as well as the argument that Sayyid Qutb's political thought was a critique of modernity (one shared by many Western thinkers) and not just a response to Western oppression and corrupt Middle Eastern governments, see Roxanne L. Euben, *Enemy in the Mirror* (Princeton, NJ: Princeton University Press, 1999).
23. John L. Esposito and John O. Voll, *Islam and Democracy* (New York: Oxford University Press, 1996), 23.
24. Ibid., 18–19.
25. Daniel Brumberg, "Islamists and the Politics of Consensus," *Journal of Democracy* 13 (2002): 109.

the construction of domestic and international Islamic law is first and foremost a political, rather than a religious, project.

B. (Re)Constructing Middle Eastern Identity in Response to the West

Parallel to these political developments, Muslim communities have witnessed the growth and flourishing of a vast number of movements tied to Islam and Islamic identity. According to historian Ira M. Lapidus, some of these are revivals of past movements, while others are new and highly creative in their methodology, organization, and objectives.[26] As with the tension between Arab nationalism and Islamism, Muslim identity movements are oriented by two divergent strains. The first, more universalistic in character, is based on the devotional components of Islam, as well as common beliefs, rituals, and social practices.[27] This includes ritual commandments (such as the *hajj*, or pilgrimage), but also the Islamist call for a return to *Shari'a*. Geopolitics also contribute greatly, if unintentionally, to this growing support for a universal Islamic identity. The situation of Muslim minorities in non-Muslim states, as well as conflicts in areas like Afghanistan, Palestine, Bosnia, Chechnya, and Iraq, help generate transnational Muslim identification.[28]

Such identification is supported by the rapid diffusion of mass communications and media technology, decreasing transportation costs, and widespread migratory patterns, but also through an enormous global network of Islamic organizations.[29] Examples include those that specialize in publication and propaganda (e.g., the Muslim World League and the Islamic Call Society), proselytism (e.g., missionary societies like *Tablighi Islam*), finance (e.g., Muslim banks), the needs of emigrant communities, and Sufi brotherhoods.[30] Additionally, there are explicitly political groups, such as

26. Ira M. Lapidus, "Between Universalism and Particularisms: The Historical Bases of Muslim Communal, National, and Global Identities," *Global Networks* 1 (2001): 37.

27. Ibid., 37. But see Olivier Roy, *The Failure of Political Islam*, trans. Carol Volk (Cambridge, MA: Harvard University Press, 1998).

28. Lapidus, "Between Universalism and Particularisms," 38. See also Dale F. Eichelman and James Piscatori, *Muslim Politics* (Princeton, NJ: Princeton University Press, 1996).

29. These factors have been particularly successful at consolidating the support of younger generations, who increasingly adopt a more conservative Islam than that of their parents. Michael Slackman, "Jordanian Students Rebel, Embracing Conservative Islam." *The New York Times*, December 24, 2008.

30. Lapidus, "Between Universalism and Particularisms," 38. See also John L. Esposito, *The Islamic Threat: Myth or Reality?* (New York: Oxford University Press, 1992).

the Institute for Muslim Minority Affairs, the Society of Muslim Brothers (the Muslim Brotherhood), and the Islamic Liberation Party (which, among other things, calls for the unity of Muslims in all countries against secular and imperial power). Of course, there are also militant and terrorist groups, many of whose members are recruited from among the large Arab population of rural poor, in addition to veterans of Islamic wars.[31]

Despite this proliferation of transnational activity, however, a deeper analysis reveals that many Islamic organizations are tied to the power, money, and influence of particular nation-states. One political economic example of this type of operation is the Organization of the Islamic Conference. This vast association sponsors a wide range of activities, including relief efforts, political interventions, and the Islamic Development Bank (which draws its guidelines from both secular and religious models); ultimately, though, the OIC derives its authority from the national governments that sponsor it.[32] Many other organizations are state-sponsored, including some of those listed above (e.g., the Muslim World League by Saudi Arabia and the Islamic Call Society by Libya). Also, several international movements share broad mandates, financial architecture, and intellectual capital, while nevertheless operating within the existing legal and socio-political frameworks of particular states. In this way, universal religious orientation and national political bodies are integrated in mutually supporting relationships.

Stepping back from this organizational focus, the tension between Islamic universalism (emphasizing the community of Muslims worldwide) and particularism (emphasizing local communities of Muslims with shared legal, political, and cultural histories) manifests itself in other ways, as well. Modern history has pulled Islam in competing directions—between global integration and nation-state consolidation—that are mediated by cultural identity and legal-political institutions.[33] Education plays a powerful

---

31. However, it is important to note that many of the bombers and strategists alike are university-educated professionals and other members of the intelligentsia, as observed by religious historian Scott Appleby in some of his recent research. Scott Appleby, "Rethinking Fundamentalism in a Secular Age" (paper presented at the Working Group on Religion and Politics, Yale University, New Haven, CT, 2008). See also Charles W. Collier, "Terrorism as an Intellectual Problem," *Buffalo Law Review* 55 (2007).

32. Lapidus, "Between Universalism and Particularisms," 38. See also Saad S. Khan, *Reasserting International Islam: A Focus on the Organization of the Islamic Conference and Other Islamic Institutions* (New York: Oxford University Press, 2001).

33. This is true in the U.S. and Europe, too, where there is tension between the competing claims of national sovereignty and international law, as well as between individual human rights and group politico-religious traditions. On the former,

role here. In the West, the decoupling of religious and political identity corresponded with the splintering of religious authority (following the Reformation), the rise of industrial capitalism, and thus the need for universal public education (which is largely, and in some areas exclusively, secular).[34]

During roughly the same historical period, Muslims have experienced a re-consolidation of Islamic concepts, norms, and practices across geographical boundaries, including the call (originating in the eighteenth century) to conform to common texts of Islam—the Qur'an, selected *Hadith*, and the principles of *Shari'a*.[35] Moreover, public education *is* religious education in some states (e.g., Saudi Arabia and Pakistan), and religion strongly influences the educational system in others, even where it is not formally linked. Islamic universalism is additionally facilitated by the globalizing economy, supported by systems of transport, communications, and technology.[36] These material factors facilitate cohesive Muslim identity in ways unthinkable a century ago.

However, it would be incorrect to draw from this any sense that religious and political particularism (i.e., localism) does not thrive in the Arab world. Indeed, the case is quite the opposite, owing in no small part to a long history of loyal adherence to families, tribes, ethnic groups and, more recently, to states.[37] Muslim identity provides the foundation for religious communities, but these communities exist in relation to legal and political institutions. That is, Islam provides the universal identity, while law and politics provide a particular or local identity. This is a reflection of the lack of centralization in Islam itself, and the resulting ambiguity among overlapping identities makes various institutional arrangements of law, religion, and politics tenable (thus challenging the notion of "Muslim" or "Islamic"

see Paul W. Kahn, "Speaking Law to Power: Popular Sovereignty, Human Rights, and the New International Order," *Chicago Journal of International Law* 1 (2000). On the latter, see Adamantia Pollis, "Eastern Orthodoxy and Human Rights," *Human Rights Quarterly* 15, no. 2 (1993): 339–56.

34. Ernest Gellner, *Nations and Nationalism* (Ithaca, NY: Cornell University Press, 1983), 24–38.

35. Lapidus, "Between Universalism and Particularisms," 49. See also James Piscatori, *Islam in a World of Nation-States* (New York: Cambridge University Press, 1993); Olivier Carre, *Islam and the State in the World Today* (Columbia, MO: South Asia Books, 1987).

36. Lapidus, "Between Universalism and Particularisms," 49.

37. Ibid., 50. See also Montgomery W. Watt, *Muhammad at Medina* (New York: Clarendon Press, 1953); Eric R. Wolf, "The Social Organization of Mecca and the Origins of Islam," *Journal of Anthropology* 7 (1951): 329–56.

as homogenous categories).[38] Such institutional diversity is evident in the constitutions of Muslim states, although in practice it has often meant that international legal standards of religious liberty, far from being protected by creative legal-political arrangements, are instead undermined in an extraordinary variety of ways.

II. RELIGIOUS LIBERTY IN THE CONSTITUTIONS OF MUSLIM STATES

The rise of political Islam and the proliferation of movements connected to Muslim identity affected law and politics at multiple levels. Internationally, these forces inspired efforts to develop Islamic alternatives to Western international law, while domestically, Islamists sought to institutionalize their religious authority and political power in state constitutions, with profound legal and practical consequences for freedom of religion in those countries. The two levels are intimately related. As Ann Elizabeth Mayer explains, "[t]he treatment of human rights in constitutions is critical, because international human rights law relies for its implementation on national law and institutions. The international standards are meant to serve as models for the rights protected under the constitutions and other domestic laws in individual countries."[39]

Keeping this relationship in mind, the origin and evolution of Islamic international law as it pertains to human rights will be treated in Chapter 6. Throughout the remainder of this chapter, some of the state constitutions that contributed to and were informed by Islamic international declarations and their corresponding political movements are examined. Specific constitutional arrangements in Iran, Turkey, Egypt, and Pakistan are illustrative.[40] First, however, some general observations help approximate the global scale of the dilemma.

38. Lapidus, "Between Universalism and Particularisms," 50–51. See also Hasan Kayali, *Arabs and Young Turks* (Los Angeles: University of California Press, 1997); Michael Brett, ed., *Northern Africa, Islam and Modernization* (Portland, OR: International Scholarly Book Services, Inc., 1973).

39. Mayer, *Islam and Human Rights*, 19.

40. These and other examples presented throughout the paper are not intended as case studies. Case studies are intensive examinations that, while unable to constitute the basis for valid generalizations, form the foundation for further comparative research. They are a central component of the comparative method in political science, itself a method of discovering empirical relationships among variables (not a method of measurement or specialized technique). See Arend Lijphart, "Comparative Politics and the Comparative Method," *The American Political Science Review* 65 (September 1971): 682. The examples sketched here are illustrative: they offer windows through

A. Freedom of Religion in Muslim States—A Brief Overview

In 2005, the U.S. Commission on International Religious Freedom conducted an extensive comparative analysis of the relationship between religion and state and the right to freedom of religion or belief in forty-four predominantly Muslim countries. Generally, the Commission found that the constitutional arrangements in such countries vary considerably, ranging from Islamic republics in which Islam is the official state religion to secular states with strict separation of religion and state.[41] Additionally, the study found the following: 1) greater than half of the global Muslim population (est. 1.3 billion) lives in countries that are neither Islamic republics nor that have declared Islam to be the state religion; 2) countries in which Islam is the declared state religion may constitutionally guarantee the right to freedom of religion or belief and may also constitutionally protect related rights to freedom of expression, association, assembly, and equality or nondiscrimination with regard to religion and gender; and 3) several constitutions of predominantly Muslim countries reference or incorporate international human rights instruments.[42]

Of the forty-four countries studied, thirty-two of them (which claim 602.5 million—approximately fifty-eight percent—of the Muslims living in predominantly Muslim countries) are either declared Islamic states or states in which Islam is the declared state religion.[43] For example, declared Islamic states include Afghanistan, Iran, Pakistan, and Saudi Arabia, while states in which Islam is the declared state religion include Egypt and Iraq (TAL—transitional administrative law). Noteworthy outliers include Turkey, a declared secular state, and Indonesia, which has no constitutional declaration regarding religion.

which to view institutions and processes that are particularly relevant to the research question. However, they are necessarily limited by their lack of depth and scope. This book suggests that they reveal critical variables requiring further detailed examination, but makes no claim of causal relationships or generalizability.

41. U.S. Commission on International Religious Freedom. 2005. *The Religion-State Relationship and the Right to Freedom of Religion or Belief: A Comparative Textual Analysis of the Constitutions of Predominantly Muslim Countries*. http://www.uscirf.gov/images/stories/pdf/Comparative_Constitutions/Study0305.pdf. See also Tad Stahnke and Robert C. Blitt, "The Religion-State Relationship and the Right to Freedom of Religion or Belief: A Comparative Textual Analysis of the Constitutions of Predominantly Muslim Countries," *Georgetown Journal of International Law* 36 (2005).

42. U.S. Commission on International Religious Freedom. 2005. *The Religion-State Relationship and the Right to Freedom of Religion or Belief*.

43. Ibid. For a complete listing and map of states categorized according to the constitutional role for religion, see page 7.

In analyzing the religious liberty provisions of various state constitutions, the Commission compared them to what it deemed to be the minimum international standards for constitutional provisions—Article 18 of the Universal Declaration of Human Rights and Article 18 of the International Covenant on Civil and Political Rights.[44] This resulted in five categories of constitutional provisions, which are consolidated here into three broader groups: 1) provisions that generally compare favorably, establishing specific safeguards against religious coercion; 2) the absence of provisions or provision only for the right to worship, and/or provisions that do not define rights on an individual basis or that limit rights to one or more enumerated groups; and 3) provisions that permit limitations not enumerated under international standards of religious freedom.[45] Group one includes the constitutions of Iraq (TAL), Pakistan, and Turkey. Group Two includes those of Egypt, Iran, Saudi Arabia, and Afghanistan. The third group (numbering fifteen states total) includes state constitutions from each of the first two groups, such as those of Turkey, Iran, and Afghanistan.

The study's findings are relevant to this book across several dimensions. Consider, for example, three states whose constitutions generally compare favorably with international religious liberty standards—Iraq (TAL), Pakistan, and Turkey. Under the transitional administrative law, Islam is the declared state religion in Iraq; in that way, it diverges not only from American constitutionalism, but also and more significantly from Western movements in favor of secularism and strict separation. Pakistan affords very little, if any, protection to religious minorities, and though Turkey is constitutionally secular, it too restricts religious freedoms—for majority *and* minority religious groups. Thus, even some of the Muslim-majority countries whose constitutions compare most favorably with international laws of religious freedom nevertheless deviate in significant ways from Western theory and practice. The reasons for, and implications of, this are more readily apparent when state constitutions are considered individually. Four such examinations follow, beginning with the Constitution of the Islamic Republic of Iran.

B. The Islamic Republic of Iran

When the Ayatollah Ruhollah Khomeini, following more than fourteen years in exile, led Iran's Islamic revolution to victory in 1979, he represented a

44. Ibid., 12–18.
45. Ibid., 15. A complete country listing, broken out by category, is available at page 15.

new form of nationalism—one that embraced religion and the brother-hood (or *umma*) of all Muslims. Khomeini was deeply committed to the nation of Iran, believing that it was appropriate "to love one's fatherland and its people and to protect its frontiers."[46] However, his devotion to Iran stemmed not from the secular Arab nationalism common to the region in previous decades, but from a militant anti-Americanism born in response to American and British relations with the Shah and the Iranian Parliament he would ultimately depose.

This denunciation extended beyond the context of Iran to include Western domination of the Islamic world, and in this sense, Khomeini's nationalism (at least initially) bridged legal, religious, and political identity.[47] In Islam, he found and articulated a new identity and dignity for Arab peoples with charisma that mobilized tremendous levels of support.[48] Of course, power politics played an important role, and clerics who had fought to separate religious institutions from political control in the 1920s allied with Khomeini when they realized that under his leadership, Islam would dominate, rather than be subject to, political mechanisms of authority.[49]

Yet regardless of its intentions and ultimate manifestation, the Ayatollah's message linked Islam with nationalist sentiment in resistance to foreign domination, thereby paving the way for a new pan-Arab nationalism. As historians Edmund Burke III and Ira M. Lapidus summarize, "[o]nly in the Iranian revolution did historical conditions allow an effective junction of Islamic symbols, leaders, and political action ... . In that moment, Islamic symbols could again express . . . the integration of cultural identity and world actuality."[50]

This quest for political and cultural integration through Islam found institutional expression in the Constitution of the Islamic Republic of Iran,[51] which was affirmed by 98.2 percent of eligible voters in a referendum

46. Ruh Allah Khomeini, *Islam and Revolution in the Middle East: Writings and Declarations of Imam Khomeini*, trans. Hamid Algar (Berkeley, CA: Mizan Press, 1981), 302.

47. Henry Munson, "Islam, Nationalism and Resentment of Foreign Domination," *Middle East Policy* 10 (Summer 2003): 43.

48. Bernard Lewis, *Islam and the West* (New York: Oxford University Press, 1993), 40.

49. Arang Keshavarzian, "Turban or Hat, Seminarian or Soldier: State Building and Clergy Building in Reza Shah's Iran," *Journal of Church and State* 45 (2003): 111.

50. Edmund Burke, III and Ira M. Lapidus, *Islam, Politics, and Social Movements* (Los Angeles: University of California Press, 1988), 16.

51. International Constitutional Law. Constitution of the Islamic Republic of Iran. http://www.servat.unibe.ch/icl/ir00000_.html.

held in March 1979 (after, as the text proclaims, "the victorious Islamic Revolution").[52] Article 1 establishes the form of government as that of an Islamic Republic, "endorsed by the people of Iran on the basis of their longstanding belief in the sovereignty of truth and Koranic justice."

Unlike the liberal democracies of the West, whose constitutions locate sovereignty in the people and legislative power in their elected representatives, the Iranian constitution is built upon a theological interpretation of government wherein the legal and political authority of (religious) truth is absolute. Hence, under Article 2, sovereignty and the right to legislate are the exclusive province of "the One God," while human freedom consists in the exercise of God-given rights in accordance with other constitutional and religious principles—foremost among which is the necessity of submitting to God's commands, which are known by divine revelation.[53] The purpose of the Constitution is thus, in part, to create the conditions necessary for the development of human beings in accordance with the principles of Islam.[54]

Because sovereignty is based on truth and truth is known by divine revelation, Article 4 stipulates the "Islamic Principle" that undergirds every legal and regulatory institution in Iran. Specifically, "[a]ll civil, penal, financial, economic, administrative, cultural, military, political, and other laws and regulations must be based on Islamic criteria." These criteria are rooted in the religious and legal edicts of the Qur'an, which, while historically progressive with regard to some rights and practices, has come with time to be interpreted more restrictively.[55] This is especially true in view of the Iranian

---

52. The creation of an explicitly Islamic constitution is also not surprising in view of Iran's earlier constitutional history, one in which Western influence persisted despite efforts to create an independent state. Consider, for example, the Iranian Constitution of 1906—part of the Persian Constitutional Revolution. In August 1906, Mozaffareddin Shah allowed a parliament to be established. The parliament met for the first time in October of that year, during which time the body transformed itself into a constitutional assembly intent on crafting an Iranian constitution. The aging Shah was in poor health, so time was of the essence. His subordinates, knowing of his desire to have a constitution, went to the British Embassy to borrow one. There, however, they were informed that the British did not have a written constitution, but hearing that the Belgians did, they literally went next door to borrow a copy from the Embassy of Belgium. This is why Iran's first constitution was based on the Belgian model. Special thanks to Joe Brand, attorney at Patton Boggs LLP and an international practitioner with decades of experience in the Middle East, for this anecdote.
53. S. I. Strong, "Law and Religion in Israel and Iran: How the Integration of Secular and Spiritual Laws Affects Human Rights and the Potential for Violence," *Michigan Journal of International Law* 19 (1997): 151.
54. Ibid., 152.
55. Ibid., 167.

emphasis on traditional, literal interpretations of religious law.[56] The "Islamic Principle" applies "absolutely and generally" to the entire content of the Constitution, and also to all other legal and regulatory rules and actions.[57] There is quite literally no legal space outside the primary authority of Islam.[58] Clearly, this bears importantly on the question of religious freedom in Iran, specifically, but it also elucidates the institutional and practical status of religious liberty in an Islamic republic more generally.[59]

For example, consider the situation of religious minorities. Although Article 12 declares Islam and the Twelver Ja'fari school (a Shi'a jurisprudence) to be the official and "eternally immutable" religion of Iran, it also maintains that other Islamic schools are to be respected, that their followers are "free to act in accordance with their own jurisprudence in performing their religious rights," and that they have official legal status in matters pertaining to religious education and affairs of personal status. Further, Article 23 provides for freedom of belief, insofar as it prohibits the investigation of individuals' beliefs and forbids individuals from being attacked based on their beliefs. On their own, these provisions might be perceived as a religiously sanctioned alternative vision of religious freedom, one limited but nevertheless at least somewhat accommodating.

However, when these two articles are read in tandem with Article 64 (which authorizes political representation for Zoroastrians, Jews, and certain Christian groups), the result is that religious minorities who are not explicitly protected are subject to persecution. Iran's most well-known such group, and its largest non-Muslim minority, is the Baha'i—a community considered to be apostate and thus not a true religion worthy of

56. Ibid.
57. Thus, under Article 170, the judiciary is "obliged to refrain" from executing any government statutes or regulations that conflict with the law or even the norms of Islam.
58. Moreover, all aspects of the Constitution related to the Islamic character of the political system and criteria for law formation are unalterable. As Article 177(5) declares: The contents of the articles of the Constitution related to the Islamic character of the political system; the basis of all the rules and regulations according to Islamic criteria; the religious footing; the objectives of the Islamic Republic of Iran; the democratic character of the government; the holy principle; the Imamate of Ummah; and the administration of the affairs of the country based on national referenda, official religion of Iran and the religious school are unalterable.
59. For additional discussion of the incongruence between Iranian and Western law as it pertains to religious liberty, see Jennifer F. Cohen, "Development: Islamic Law in Iran: Can It Protect the International Legal Right of Freedom of Religion and Belief?," *Chicago Journal of International Law* 9 (2008).

state protection.[60] In addition to the Baha'i, Iran also targets Sufi Muslims and Evangelical Christians in "systematic, ongoing, and egregious violations of religious freedom, including prolonged detention, torture, and executions based primarily or entirely upon the religion of the accused."[61] As a result, significant numbers of religious minorities have fled the country in the years since the 1979 revolution—[62] a main point of contention for human rights observers, and the subject of a day-long series of meetings at the Vatican in January 1997 between Iranian Minister of Foreign Affairs Ali Akbar Velayati and Cardinal Angelo Sodano and other church officials.[63] Then as now, the constitutional status of Islam (and especially the Shi'a doctrine of the Twelver Ja'fari school) has been used to permit and even legitimate widespread curtailment of religious freedom. This led the State Department in 1999 to designate Iran as a "country of particular concern."

Other abuses of religious liberty perpetrated by Iranian judicial and political officials are documented at some length by the U.S. Commission on International Religious Freedom in its Annual Reports.[64] They include, but are certainly not limited to, the following: the sentencing of hundreds of prominent Muslim activists and dissidents from the Shi'a majority advocating political reform to lengthy prison terms by the Revolutionary Court on charges of blasphemy or seeking to overthrow Iran's Islamic system; the targeting of Shi'a religious leaders who oppose religious tenet and practices of the Iranian government for house arrest, detention without charge, trial without due process, and torture; the repression of Sunni minorities (including bans, despite Article 12, on Sunni teachings in public schools and Sunni religious literature even in predominantly Sunni areas);

60. Jose Casanova, "Civil Society and Religion: Retrospective Reflections on Catholicism and Prospective Reflections on Islam," *Social Research* 68, no. 4 (Winter 2001): 29.

61. U.S. Commission on Religious Freedom. 2007. *Annual Report*. http://www.uscirf. gov/images/AR_2007/annualreport2007.pdf, 212.

62. Ibid.

63. "Vatican and Iran Discuss Religious Liberty," *Church & State* 50, no. 3 (March 1997).

64. U.S. Commission on Religious Freedom. 2007. *Annual Report*, 211–17; 2008. *Annual Report*.

http://www.uscirf.gov/images/annual%20report%202008-final%20edition.pdf, 138–45; 2009. *Annual Report*.

http://www.uscirf.gov/images/final%20ar2009%20with%20cover.pdf, 32–38; 2010. *Annual Report*.

http://www.uscirf.gov/images/annual%20report%202010.pdf, 54–66; 2011. *Annual Report*.

http://www.uscirf.gov/images/book%20with%20cover%20for%20web.pdf, 74–87.

discrimination against non-Muslims in education, government jobs and services, and the armed services; prohibition of public religious expression and persuasion by non-Muslims among Muslims; virulent harassment and imprisonment of, and physical attacks upon, non-Muslim religious minorities, including the constitutionally protected Jews, Christians, and Zoroastrians; prolonged detention, torture, and executions based primarily or entirely upon the religion of the accused; and a striking rise in anti-Semitism.[65]

Because Iran remains the only Muslim-majority country "to have undergone the political metamorphosis from an Islamic revolution to the establishment of an Islamic Republic and, finally, the emergence of a post-revolutionary society," one crucial question raised by these violations of religious human rights is to what extent actions taken in the name of this or any other Islamic republic are attributable to Islam itself, rather than to (corruptions of) the political process.[66] There is little agreement regarding the answer.

Thus, some scholars and practitioners highlight the singularity of the Iranian Revolution and the "uniquely Iranian leadership, the independent and well respected *ulama* [clerics] who 'had always acted as the spokes[men] of the collective consciousness.'"[67] Others contend that Khomeinism in the domestic politics of Iran:

> reveals the disparity between traditional principles of Shari'a and the principles
> recently implemented in response to the necessities of governance and under
> the guise of divinity. A claim to divinity is thus understood as an attempt by
> the governing and authoritarian elites to respond to the economic, social and

65. U.S. Commission on Religious Freedom. 2007. *Annual Report*. On the question of religious liberty and the relation between Jews and Muslims in Israel, see Natan Lerner, "Religious Liberty in the State of Israel," *Emory International Law Review* 21 (2007). There are occasional exceptions to these patterns of persecution. For example, the Revolutionary Tribunal in Bandar-Anzali recently acquitted eleven Church of Iran members charged with "action against the order of the country" and drinking alcohol, after it was determined that their house church meeting and taking of communion wine fell within their rights under Article 13 of the Constitution. Meanwhile, six other members of the Church of Iran in Shiraz are awaiting word on whether their blasphemy charges are legally valid. "Iranian Court Acquits 11 Christians," *Christianity Today* (May 20, 2011).

66. Robert W. Hefner, ed. *Remaking Muslim Politics: Pluralism, Contestation, Democratization* (Princeton, NJ: Princeton University Press, 2005).

67. Carolyn Cox Cohan, "International Mavericks: A Comparative Analysis of Selected Human Rights and Foreign Policy Issues in Iran and the United States," *George Washington International Law Review* 33 (2001). See also Albert Hourani, *A History of the Arab Peoples* (New York: Warner Books, 1992), 457–58.

political realities of the twentieth century while remaining within the ostensibly legitimate confines of Islam.[68]

Indeed, upon Khomeini's death in July 1989, a great struggle over the legitimate locus of authority ensued. His institutionalization of conflicting legal, religious, and political symbols left unclear how legal and political relationships in Iran should be constructed between Islamist and non-Islamist groups, but also among competing Islamist visions on the right and the left.[69]

Importantly, this absence of agreement cautions scholars and policymakers to consider the authorizing voices behind international Islamic human rights pronouncements. As will be seen in Chapter 6, Iran has played a leading role in the development of Islamic international law. To the extent that its constitutional jurisprudence and religious liberty practices are colored by political contestation, there are grounds to doubt both the necessity of its interpretation of Islam and the extent to which it represents the views of Muslim communities. Put differently, Iran is essential to any explanation of religious liberty provisions in Islamic human rights instruments, but its official interpretations and applications of *Shari'a* are neither determinate nor uncontested (even among its own population).[70]

---

68. Sarvenaz Bahar, "Khomeinism, the Islamic Republic of Iran, and International Law: The Relevance of Islamic Political Theology," *Harvard International Law Journal* 33 (1992): 179.

69. Daniel Brumberg, "Dissonant Politics in Iran and Indonesia," *Political Science Quarterly* 116 (Fall 2001): 388–89. To give one example of the institutionalized conflict, Islamic socialists were pivotal in both the Revolution and its subsequent ruling institutions, such that secular intellectuals drawing on the writings of Marx and Sartre arguably had as much to do with the working out of Khomeini's Islamic revolutionary vision as did religious scholars. Though many of them were ultimately discarded by Khomeini and his political supporters, the concepts they introduced were appropriated for strategic ideological and socio-political purposes. Yet those secular concepts clash, sometimes violently, with Islamist visions of social and political order. See Daniel Brumberg, "Is Iran Democratizing? A Comparativist's Perspective," *Journal of Democracy* 11 (2000).

70. For an impassioned plea for Muslim democracy and universal human rights from a former commander of the Islamic Revolutionary Guards Corps and "Iran's most famous dissident," see Akbar Ganji, *The Road to Democracy in Iran* (Cambridge, MS: MIT Press, 2008). Also, for a discussion of the evolution of human rights in Iran since the time of the Revolution, see Barb Rieffer-Flanagan, "The Janus Nature of Human Rights in Iran: Understanding Progress and Setbacks on Human Rights Protections since the Revolution," in *APSA Annual Meeting* (Toronto, September 3–6, 2009).

C. The Republic of Turkey

The historical evolution of the relationship between mosque and state in Turkey is arguably the most complicated and unique among Middle Eastern states.[71] The Turkish case is especially important because it seems to challenge the role of religion and religious law in the development of national identity and civil-political rights. When Atatürk first crafted the Republic, he resolutely intended to transform it into a secular society.[72] Consequently, Turkish elites refused to incorporate any facet of Islam into the state constitution. However, as in the case of secular Arab nationalism, where Islam remained a submerged but nevertheless key component of the population's identity, there was a divergence between elite and popular opinion: "(w)hile the Young Turk elites succeeded in creating an ethnically-defined national state, the Turkish people continued to identify with Islam."[73] In practice, most Turks maintained a dual identity in which nationality was an expression of Muslim identification.[74] Before discussing the resulting controversies, however, it is important to understand the interplay of secularism and religious freedom in the Constitution.

71. For an excellent summary of this history, see Susanna Dokupil, "The Separation of Mosque and State: Islam and Democracy in Modern Turkey," *West Virginia Law Review* 105 (2002).

72. Lapidus, "Between Universalism and Particularisms," 47. See also Niyazi Berkes, *The Development of Secularism in Turkey* (Toronto: McGill University Press, 1964). On a related note, early attempts at secularizing Turkey included strong ethnic assimilation efforts, thus sparking the tension between "Turks" and the Kurdish population. See Mustafa Saatci, "Nation-States and Ethnic Boundaries: Modern Turkish Identity and Turkish-Kurdish Conflict," *Nations and Nationalism* 8 (2002): 549–64. Peoples who had previously perceived themselves primarily as Muslim were introduced to new forms of ethnic consciousness. Here, attempts to separate legal, religious, and political spheres contributed to the types of conflict usually associated with attempts to unite them.

73. Lapidus, "Between Universalism and Particularisms," 47. See also Serif Mardin, "Religion and Politics in Modern Turkey," in *Islam in the Political Process*, ed. James Piscatori (New York: Cambridge University Press, 1983), 138–59. In this predominantly Muslim country, Turkish scholar Nurham Sural argues that it is this bifurcation between bureaucratic elites and the masses (not religious pluralism) that fuels conflicts like the headscarf debate. See Nurhan Sural, "Country Studies: Turkey: Islamic Outfits in the Workplace in Turkey, a Major Muslim Country," *Comparative Labor Law and Policy Journal* 30 (2009).

74. Regarding the ways in which Islamic identity is conferred upon Turkish people by the "secular" state, thereby complicating the meaning and practice of secularization, see Huldun Gulalp, "Whatever Happened to Secularization?: The Multiple Islams in Turkey," *South Atlantic Quarterly* 102, no. 2/3 (2003): 381–95.

Turkey's present Constitution,[75] ratified in 1982, strives to preserve Atatürk's founding vision of a secular state (*laik*)—one that was itself modeled on the French system of *laïcité*.[76] Its Preamble describes the Constitution as embodying the principle of secularism, which requires that there be "no interference whatsoever by sacred religious feelings in state affairs and politics." This version of church-state separation is extreme when compared not only to Muslim state constitutions, but also to most Western ones.[77] It is affirmed in Article 2, where the Republic of Turkey is characterized as "a democratic, secular and social state governed by the rule of law." Loyalty to the nationalism of Atatürk is also explicitly mentioned.

Such strict secularism is problematic when evaluated according to international legal standards of religious liberty—an assessment that is warranted by the constitutional text itself. Specifically, Article 14 prohibits the abuse of fundamental rights and freedoms, and 14(1) holds in pertinent part: "none of the rights and freedoms embodied in the constitution shall be exercised with the aim of . . . endangering the existence of *the democratic and secular order of the Turkish Republic based upon human rights*" (emphasis mine). The difficult ambiguity of this provision emerges more clearly when it is read alongside Article 24, which grants everyone the right to freedom of conscience, religious belief, and conviction (24(1)), but permits acts of worship, religious services, and ceremonies only insofar as they do not violate Article 14 (24(2)). Article 24(5) additionally forbids anyone from exploiting or abusing religion or religious feelings, or things held sacred by religion, "for the purpose of personal or political influence, or for even partially basing the fundamental, social, economic, political and legal order of the state on religious tenets."

75. Constitution of the Republic of Turkey, http://www.anayasa.gov.tr/images/loaded/pdf_dosyalari/THE_CONSTITUTION_OF_THE_REPUBLIC_OF_TURKEY.pdf.

76. Peter L. Berger, "Secularization Falsified," *First Things* (February 2008): 25. Interestingly, Atatürk's secularism in turn influenced the Pahlavi regime that preceded the Iranian revolution of 1979, where it proved unable legally, culturally, and politically to prevent the rise of political Islam. Ibid., 26. For a systematic comparison of the French and Turkish approaches to secularism, see Ahmet T. Kuru, *Secularism and State Policies toward Religion: The United States, France, and Turkey* (Cambridge: Cambridge University Press, 2009).

77. Political scientist M. Hakan Yavuz characterizes secularism in Turkey as a "conscious political ideology," rather than the outworking of transformative technological, economic, and social forces, as it was elsewhere. He also identifies the tension between secularism and Islamism as the "fundamental framework of Turkish politics." See M. Hakan Yavuz, *Secularism and Muslim Democracy in Turkey* (New York: Cambridge University Press, 2009).

The trouble originates with Article 14's grounding of the secular state in human rights. This alone creates a potentially serious institutional tension between the claims of secularism and the claims of religious human rights law—a tension that, depending on how it is read, could effectively render the provision unintelligible. Moreover, Article 24 invokes Article 14 to demarcate permissible religious practice, which makes little sense jurisprudentially given that Article 14 offers what might loosely be understood as two opposing legal tests. Ultimately, then, whether or not the Turkish Constitution accords with international legal standards of religious freedom depends a great deal on how Article 14 is interpreted and enforced (i.e., when in conflict, whether the demands of secularism or human rights are given priority).

These difficulties are constitutive of the broader challenge posed by Turkish secularism to religious liberty. While Western-style secularism generally allows neither the state nor religion to intrude upon the sphere of the other, Turkey's system of *laik* allows the state to access and regulate religion, whereas religion does not have a reciprocal authority to do so.[78] This is an ambitious form of secularism, not least because ninety-nine percent of the population is Muslim.[79] The other one percent is governed by a highly complex legal framework such that different regulations apply to different non-Muslim religious communities. In that sense, not all religious rights are universally held.

Fortunately, under the current government led by the Justice and Development Party, and in response to European Union membership requirements,[80] many laws granting new rights to religious minorities have been proposed.[81] Also, in positive contrast with Iran, there are few reported problems in Turkey regarding freedom to gather and worship, religious literature, or the rights to assemble and express belief, and there are no religious prisoners.[82] At the same time, majority and minority religions encounter real and serious limitations on their religious liberty,[83]

78. Adrien Katherine Wing and Ozan O. Varol, "Is Secularism Possible in a Majority-Muslim Country? The Turkish Example," *Texas International Law Journal* 42 (2006): 6.

79. Ergun Ozsunay, "The Permissible Scope of Legal Limitations on the Freedom of Religion or Belief in Turkey," *Emory International Law Review* 19 (2005).

80. See James C. Harrington, *Wrestling with Free Speech, Religious Freedom, and Democracy in Turkey* (Lanham, MD: University Press of America, 2011).

81. Ilhan Yildiz, "Minority Rights in Turkey," *Brigham Young University Law Review* 2007 (2007): 807–10.

82. U.S. Commission on Religious Freedom. 2007. *Annual Report,* 14–15.

83. A factor that led the U.S. Commission on International Religious Freedom to place Turkey on its Watch List beginning in 2009.

including: the prohibition against wearing certain kinds of Muslim religious garb in state institutions (which until very recently included public and private universities[84]); the lack of legal recognition of religious minorities, which creates difficulties for them involving property rights and the selection and training of clerical leaders; problems opening, maintaining, and operating houses of worship; state expropriation of religious properties without compensation; and public, sometimes violent anti-Semitism.[85]

Another area of serious legal contention involves the intersection of religious identity and the political process. Republican Turkey has been defined by the dual (and at times competing) legacies of Atatürk's secularism and Ottoman Islam: the struggle of the former to limit and contain the latter is reflected, for example, in the Constitution's prohibition against religious political parties (Article 68).[86] However, the re-emergence of Islamist movements marks the persistence of Islam as a foundational component of Turkish identity. One example of particular importance is the rise and subsequent dissolution of the Islamist Refah Partisi (Welfare or Prosperity Party).

Established in 1983, Refah Partisi was led by Necmettin Erbakan (who would become Turkey's first Islamist Prime Minister in 1996) and derived its support from a broader spectrum of society than just the traditional base of lower-income groups and religious conservatives.[87] Over time, Erbakan's popularity grew, owing to a combination of factors including national party divisions, a general resurgence of Islamic fundamentalism, and anti-Western sentiment.[88] Refah Partisi consistently improved its results at the polls, owing its political successes to three primary factors: 1) mounting public dissatisfaction with pro-secular parties; 2) efficient

84. Sabrina Tavernise, "In Turkey, a Step to Allow Head Scarves," *The New York Times*, January 29, 2008. Tavernise reports that Turkey's governing political party, led by Prime Minister Recep Tayyip Erdogan, reached an agreement to lift a ban on the wearing of headscarves by women attending universities in place since a court ruling in the late 1990s.

85. U.S. Commission on Religious Freedom. 2007. *Annual Report*, 14–26; 2008. *Annual Report*, 277–81; 2009. *Annual Report*, 202–12; 2010. *Annual Report*, 303–17; 2011. *Annual Report*, 317–38. See also Talip Kucukcan, "State, Islam, and Religious Liberty in Modern Turkey: Reconfiguration of Religion in the Public Sphere," *Brigham Young University Law Review* 2003 (2003).

86. Mustafa Akyol, "Render Unto Ataturk," *First Things* (March 2007): 16.

87. Dokupil, "The Separation of Mosque and State," 105. See also Sencer Ayata, "Patronage, Party and State: Politicization of Islam in Turkey," *Middle East Journal* 50 (1996): 40–56.

88. Dokupil, "The Separation of Mosque and State," 106. See also Sabri Sayari, "Turkey's Islamist Challenge," *Middle East Quarterly* 3 (1996): 35–43; Fred Coleman, "Will Turkey Be the Next Iran?," *U.S. News & World Report*, June 6, 1994.

party organization built atop strong grassroots membership; and 3) an increased role for and visibility of religion in the country.[89] This surge culminated in the Islamists' 1995 electoral victory, which, while short-lived, was fueled by plans both to change the constitutional and legal rules pertaining to regulation of religion and to expand the role of Islamic institutions, organizations, and education in Turkish society.[90] But such was not to be.

In 1998, the Turkish Constitutional Court (TCC) held that Refah Partisi should be dissolved.[91] After 15 years of existence, Refah held the most seats in the Turkish Parliament and was part of a national coalition government, while Erbakan was Prime Minister; however, the TCC held that "Refah was inconsistent with Turkey's constitutional commitment to secularism, which, in Turkish constitutional tradition, calls for a radical separation between church and state."[92] On appeal in 2001, a chamber of the European Court of Human Rights (ECHR) affirmed the dissolution, finding that "the prohibition had been prescribed by law, in support of a legitimate aim, and 'necessary in a democratic society.'"[93] Further, in 2003, a grand chamber of the ECHR unanimously upheld the initial chamber's ruling.[94]

This series of decisions has been characterized as the authorization of "militant democracy" in support of legal pluralism.[95] It raises profound questions about the locus of self-determination, the disjuncture between elite and popular opinion regarding religion and state, and the very possibility of "Islamic democracy"—issues that continue to provoke violence in Turkey. For example, in May 2006, Alparslan Arslan (himself a lawyer) shot and killed prominent Turkish Council of State Judge Mustafa Yucel Ozbilgin, also wounding five of Ozbilgin's colleagues in Turkey's highest administrative court.[96] Arslan was allegedly responding to the Court's

89. Dokupil, "The Separation of Mosque and State," 107.

90. Ibid., 109, 15.

91. Patrick Macklem, "Militant Democracy, Legal Pluralism, and the Paradox of Self-Determination," *International Journal of Constitutional Law* 4 (July 2006): 490; Case of Refah Partisi (The Welfare Party) and Others v. Turkey, App. Nos. 41340/98, 41342/98, 41343/98, 41344/98, 35 Eur. H.R. Rep. 3 (2001) (including a joint dissenting opinion by Judges Fuhrmann, Loucaides, and Sir Nicolas Bratza).

92. Macklem, "Militant Democracy," 507. See also Dicle Kogacioglu, "Progress, Unity and Democracy: Dissolving Political Parties in Turkey," *Law and Society Review* 38 (2004): 433–61.

93. Macklem, "Militant Democracy," 508.

94. Ibid.

95. On the nature of militant democracy and legal pluralism, Ibid., 510–14. See also Kevin Boyle, "Human Rights, Religion and Democracy: The Refah Party Case," *Essex Human Rights Law Review* 1 (2004).

96. "Judge Dies in Turkey Court Attack," *BBC News* (May 17, 2006).

recent decisions confirming Turkey's ban on the *hijab* in public institutions such as government buildings and universities.[97]

Thus, even in this Middle Eastern state that has moved most closely and consistently toward secularism, Islam remains an immediate and powerful force animating legal, social, and political action, and especially debates about the scope and content of religious freedom.[98] These debates are responsible, in part, for propelling the popularity of religious candidates for political office.[99] For example, President Abdullah Gül, a Muslim whose wife is the first to wear the *hijab*, won election despite repeated threats from the secular military establishment.[100] While from the perspective of *laik*, this rise of Muslim political influence and the softening of strict secularism appears as a form of "backsliding," contemporary religious politics may represent a middle ground between secular democracy and Islamic theocracy—one that, however troubling to the EU, the ECHR, and Turkey's secular elite,[101] could evolve into a new form of Islamic democratic politics.[102] Therefore, Turkish religious rights are best understood as being in a state of flux, and Turkey—simultaneously an applicant for EU membership and a member of the Organization of the Islamic Conference—as the site of a live experiment at the intersection of international and Islamic human rights law.

D. The Arab Republic of Egypt

As mentioned in the first section of this chapter, early twentieth-century Islamist organizations, including the Muslim Brotherhood, were defined in part by their desire for a return to Islamic law. However, rather than

---

97. "Court Backs Turkish Headscarf Ban," *BBC News* (November 10, 2005).

98. For an interesting discussion of recent Turkish protests in favor of secularism, see Claire Berlinski, "In Turkey, a Looming Battle over Islam," *The Washington Post*, May 6, 2007, B1. Berlinski cautions that Western observers "tempted to sigh with approval, imagining this as an outpouring of sympathy with liberal Enlightenment values" would be mistaken, noting the various successes of the religiously-affiliated party in power (the AKP) and warning that Turkish secularism is decidedly *not* "liberal, democratic and friendly to the West" (emphasis added).

99. Sabrina Tavernise and Sebnem Arsu, "A Religious Candidate Is Ascendant in Turkey," *The New York Times*, August 28, 2007.

100. Thomas Ryan, "A Shift to a More Democratic and More Muslim Turkey," *National Catholic Reporter*, August 17, 2007.

101. Government Policy Netherlands Scientific Council, "The European Union, Turkey and Islam" (Amsterdam: Amsterdam University Press, 2004).

102. Elizabeth Shakman Hurd, "Theorizing Religious Resurgence," *International Politics* 44 (2007): 647–65.

opposing the adoption of Western governmental structures (e.g., civil legal systems) by Arab states, Islamists in Egypt (and elsewhere) framed their organizational demands in constitutional terms.[103] By incorporating Islamic law into state constitutions, they aspired to institutionalize the link between religious law and political power. Legal scholars Nathan Brown and Clark Lombardi observe that this demand for the constitutionalization of Islamic law resonated especially in Egypt: the constitution disseminated originally in 1971 under the authority of Anwar Sadat was the first Egyptian constitution to mention Islamic law and to provide it with an explicit role.[104] At that time, Article 2 announced that Islamic *Shari'a* was henceforth "a" principal source of Egyptian legislation.[105]

Islamism gained in strength over the years that followed, so much so that the constitution was crucially amended in 1980, at which time Article 2 declared Islam as the religion of the state, Arabic as the official language, and the principles of Islamic *Shari'a* as "the" (no longer merely "a") principal source of legislation (a designation that the new Provisional Constitution of the Arab Republic of Egypt, adopted March 30, 2011, preserves in its own Article 2).[106] Not surprisingly, this third prong, "aimed at bringing all Egyptian laws [and Executive Authority decrees] in conformity with Islamic Shari'a," generated widespread debate and controversy.[107] For example, it was unclear exactly what was meant by "Islamic Jurisprudence"— whether it referred to a particular *fiqh* (schools of thought representing human knowledge or comprehension of the *Shari'a*, of which there are many), or whether it encompassed broad interpretation of the *Shari'a* by Egyptian religious authorities without reference to any particular *fiqh*.[108]

103. Clark B. Lombardi and Nathan J. Brown, "Do Constitutions Requiring Adherence to Shari'a Threaten Human Rights? How Egypt's Constitutional Court Reconciles Islamic Law with the Liberal Rule of Law," *American University International Law Review* 21 (2006): 389.

104. Ibid., 389–90. That constitution was in effect until the 2011 revolution.

105. Aly Mokhtar, "An Egyptian Judicial Perspective," *Denver University Law Review* 80 (2003): 778.

106. Provisional Constitution of the Arab Republic of Egypt, http://www.cabinet. gov.eg/AboutEgypt/ConstitutionalDeclaration_e.pdf. Kristen A. Stilt, "Islamic Law and the Making and Remaking of the Iraqi Legal System," *George Washington International Law Review* 36 (2004): 722–23. However, Yale professor of theology and history Lamin Sanneh suggests that this view would have been shocking to the original architects of *Shari'a* jurisprudence, who were independent scholars rather than clients of the state. Lamin Sanneh, 'Religion, Politics and the Islamic Tradition: A Comparative Intellectual Critique, with Special Reference to Nigeria' (paper presented at the Working Group on Religion and Politics, Yale University, New Haven, CT, September 20, 2007), 8.

107. Mokhtar, "An Egyptian Judicial Perspective," 778.

108. Stilt, "Islamic Law," 721–23. See also Joseph Schacht, *An Introduction to Islamic Law* (New York: Oxford University Press, 1983); Roy Parviz Mottahedeh,

This ambiguity was significant because it necessarily affected subsequent interpretation of case law.

A second example of the controversy involved the term "principal." As Islamic law scholar Kristen Stilt elaborates, the intentionally ambiguous phrase represented a compromise between groups who favored more or less reliance on the general principles versus the specific teachings of the *Shari'a* (with direct implications for substantive law and constitutional litigation).[109] In 1996, Egypt's Supreme Constitutional Court (SCC) articulated a test for constitutionality under Article 2.[110] In May of that year, a father brought a challenge against a Ministry of Education decree that prohibited girls (including his two daughters) from attending school while wearing a *niqab* (a face covering, as opposed to the permitted *hijab*, or hair covering). The father argued that he believed the *niqab* to be required by Islam, and thus the prohibition of it violated the principles of the *Shari'a*, as well as Article 2. In response, the SCC developed a two-part test for whether post-1980 legislation was constitutional.

The first part required that the authenticity of the referenced text be proven beyond doubt. Of course, the authenticity of the totality of the Qur'an was granted, so this prong only arose when the law derives from the *Hadith* or *Sunnah* (i.e., the Prophet's commandments to his companions).[111] The second part of the test required that there be one absolutely clear meaning of the text. When the revealed texts were uncertain in their meanings (thereby necessitating *ijtihad*, or interpretation), then no judge could reverse the decision of another (i.e., there is no *ijtihad* hierarchy).[112] However, when the revealed texts were unambiguous and authentic, there was by definition no room for *ijtihad*, and any judge could reverse a decision that contradicted what God has commanded.

Because few texts met the latter criteria, the SCC seldom invalidated legislation for contradicting Article 2. Nevertheless, the court often upheld

"Introduction," in *Lessons in Islamic Jurisprudence*, ed. Muhhamad Baqir As-Sadr (Oxford, UK: Oneworld Publications, 2003).

109. Stilt, "Islamic Law," 723–24.

110. Ibid., 725–27; Supreme Constitutional Court of Egypt, Case No. 8, Judicial Year 17 (May 18, 1996), al-Jarida al-Rasmiya [Official Gazette], No. May 21, 30, 1996, 1026, 1028. Stilt presents a detailed explanation of the case and its jurisprudential implications, which is summarized in these two paragraphs. All source material for these paragraphs is drawn from her article.

111. *Hadith* (narrations and approvals) and *Sunnah* (the way or deeds of Muhammad) are related but not always interchangeable. Use of these terms throughout the book reflects the particular sources engaged at any point.

112. As addressed in Chapter 4, it is to this notion that many turn when looking for the seeds of a so-called Islamic Reformation.

legislation against an Article 2 challenge, finding Qur'anic justification for propositions including the following: polygamy as the right of the husband; the requirement that women cover most of their bodies (perhaps everything but their face and hands); that the father alone has responsibility for the maintenance of minor children; and that women have no immunity from state interference in the matter of religious dress requirements.[113]

Part of what makes Egypt such an interesting example is the perception that, in its present form and unlike Iran or Saudi Arabia, it represents (or at least has the potential to represent) the legal institutionalization of moderate Islam—one crafted over decades through delicate compromise.[114] Moderate is of course a relative term here, as the preceding country comparisons indicate. Moreover, although the Egyptian judiciary remains largely independent from the state, the reliance of the SCC on subjective judgments means that if a faction (secularist or Islamist) took control of the judiciary, serious abuses of power could arise.[115] These concerns are heightened by continuous, widespread violations of religious freedom in Egypt—abuses that persist despite the fact that all Egyptian constitutions since 1923 have explicitly provided for religious liberty (presently in Article 11, which guarantees freedom of religious belief and practice).[116]

For example, in a recent Annual Report, the U.S. Commission on International Religious Freedom observed that while Egyptian officials have over the past few years adopted measures acknowledging religious pluralism and promoting interfaith activity, "the government has not taken sufficient steps to halt repression of and discrimination against religious believers, including the indigenous Coptic Orthodox Christians, or,

113. See also Frank E. Vogel, "Conformity with Islamic Shari'a and Constitutionality under Article 2: Some Issues of Theory, Practice, and Comparison,' in *Democracy, the Rule of Law and Islam*, ed. Eugene Cotran & Adel Omar Sherif (Cambridge, MA: Kluwer Law International, 1999), 525–44. These findings are consistent with the SCC's 1985 decision declaring President Sadat's 1979 decree-law (which, advocated by feminist groups, had improved the status of women and given them more rights in divorce and custody cases) to be unconstitutional and therefore void. Farhat J. Ziadeh, 'Book Review: Islam and Public Law,' *Islamic Law and Society* 2, no. 3 (1995): 348.

114. Lombardi and Brown, "Do Constitutions Requiring Adherence to Shari'a Threaten Human Rights?" Whether this will hold true in the wake of legal and political reforms following the 2011 revolution remains to be seen.

115. Clark Benner Lombardi, "Islamic Law as a Source of Constitutional Law in Egypt: The Constitutionalization of the Shari'a in a Modern Arab State," *Columbia Journal of Transnational Law* 37 (1998): 81–82.

116. Abdullahi A. An-Na'im, "Religious Freedom in Egypt: Under the Shadow of the Islamic *Dhimma* System," in *Religious Liberty and Human Rights in Nations and in Religions*, ed. Leonard Swidler (Philadelphia: Ecumenical Press & Hippocrene Books, 1986), 45–46.

in many cases, to punish those responsible for violence or other severe violations of religious freedom."[117] The Commission noted, for example, that a December 2006 ruling of the Supreme Administrative Court upheld Egypt's policy of prohibiting Egyptian Baha'is from obtaining a national identity card. Although the Constitution does not limit state protection to Islam, Christianity, and Judaism, government officials have interpreted the text in this way because these are the only religions recognized in Islam.[118]

Even still, vicious anti-Semitic material appears regularly in state-controlled and semi-official media, as well as in an education system increasingly under the influence of Islamic extremists.[119] Other violations of religious liberty rights include tight government control of all Muslim religious institutions (which are encouraged to promote an officially sanctioned interpretation of Islam), imprisonment and physical abuse of religious minorities, militant suppression of religious and political dissent, official discrimination against Christians, and use of the penal code to discourage proselytizing by non-Muslims.[120] Egypt therefore serves as a powerful reminder of the profound differences that can exist between constitutional protections for religious freedom and reality on the ground in countries where Islam is the declared state religion—not because of the official status of Islam per se, but instead because of the complex institutional relationships that propel Islamists to power and the interests that they represent.[121]

As this book goes to press, those relationships are under intense international scrutiny, owing to Egypt's prominent role in what is being termed the "Arab spring." Although the revolts initially appeared secular in character, there are increasing signs that Islam is a growing force—a fact that is making many within and outside of the region uneasy.[122] The Egyptian

117. U.S. Commission on Religious Freedom. 2007. *Annual Report*, 203. Coptic Egyptians, especially, have been the targets of brutal violence by Islamists. In the first four years of the 1990s alone, 1164 people were killed in Egypt for religious or political reasons, a significant portion of whom were Copts. See Scott Kent Brown, "The Coptic Church in Egypt: A Comment on Protecting Religious Minorities from Nonstate Discrimination," *Brigham Young University Law Review* 2000 (2000): 1069.

118. U.S. Commission on Religious Freedom. 2007. *Annual Report*, 206.

119. Ibid., 207.

120. Ibid., 201–10; 2008. *Annual Report*, 221–30; 2009. *Annual Report*, 161–68; 2010. *Annual Report*, 227–40; 2011. *Annual Report*, 49–66.

121. Recently, the rise of independent media has made it possible for more individuals inside Egypt to challenge conventional thinking on these and other questions. However, the majority community remains vocally conservative. See Michael Slackman, "Hints of Pluralism in Egyptian Religious Debates," *The New York Times*, August 31, 2009.

122. "Islam and the Arab Revolutions," *The Economist*, March 31, 2011.

government has continued to engage in and tolerate violations of religious freedom following President Hosni Mubarak's deposal in February 2011, including the use by military and security forces of excessive force and live ammunition targeting Christian places of worship and Christian demonstrators.[123] Religious clashes between Muslims and Coptic Christians have destroyed churches and left dozens dead, underscoring "the volatility and intensity of long-subdued rifts in Egyptian society that were unleashed by [the] uprising."[124]

The Muslim Brotherhood, an Islamist group once banned by the state, is acquiring new influence—institutional (possibly because of an early deal with the military, although open cooperation with the military has since ceased) and political (in part because of its well-regarded charitable works, but also due to its relatively sophisticated organizational capabilities).[125] The Brotherhood itself is internally divided between a conservative wing (including a Sheikh who recently called for the transformation of Egypt into an Islamic state governed by *Shari'a*) and a more moderate element that says it supports a civil state, rather than a religious one.[126] Many Egyptians, however, are less concerned about the Brotherhood and more troubled by the rise of Salafist groups, which believe in creating an Islamic state governed by *Shari'a* as it was practiced by the Prophet and his companions in the seventh century, and which are gaining in popularity among rural Egyptians (even as the groups shift from a religious focus to one that includes the call for political participation).[127]

Regardless of who ultimately ends up in power, the Christians in Egypt (as elsewhere in the Arab world) are "underrepresented and vulnerable"—as are Jews, non-dominant Muslim groups, and other

123. U.S. Commission on Religious Freedom. 2011. *Annual Report*, 49. These actions, in keeping with other violations, led the USCIRF in 2011 to designate Egypt for the first time as a "country of particular concern"—a status indicating systematic, ongoing, and egregious violations of religious freedom.

124. Ernesto Londono and Ingy Hassieb, "Scores Wounded in Latest Religious Clashes in Egypt," *The Washington Post*, May 15, 2011. See also David D. Kirkpatrick, "Clashes in Cairo Leave 12 Dead and 2 Churches in Flames," *The New York Times*, May 8, 2011; Liz Sly, "Reversals Challenge Hope of Arab Spring," *The Washington Post*, May 12, 2011; Anthony Shadid, and David D. Kirkpatrick, "Promise of Arab Uprisings Is Threatened by Divisions," *The New York Times*, May 21, 2011.

125. Michael Slackman, "Islamist Group Is Rising Force in a New Egypt," *The New York Times*, March 24, 2011; Fredrick Kunkle, "In Egypt, Muslim Brotherhood's Charitable Works May Drive Political Support," *The Washington Post*, April 12, 2011.

126. Michael Jansen, "Muslim Brotherhood Leader Talks of Applying Sharia Law," *The Irish Times*, April 19, 2011.

127. Owen Bennett Jones, "Salafist Groups Find Footing in Egypt after Revolution," *BBC News* (April 6, 2011).

religious minorities.[128] There are many reasons for this sectarian strife, including laws that treat Muslims differently from Christians and other non-Muslim minorities.[129] Indeed, in a multi-country survey undertaken by the Pew Research Center in March/April 2011, Muslims were asked whether they believed laws should be based strictly on the teachings of the Qur'an. A solid majority of Egyptians answered in the affirmative.[130] They were joined in this opinion by majorities in Jordan and Pakistan.

E. The Islamic Republic of Pakistan

When it was originally established in 1947, Pakistan was a Muslim-majority state, but not an explicitly Islamic one. Though it emerged partly out of the Hindu-Muslim divide in the 1940s, Pakistan also represented the positive idea—articulated by leading Indian Muslims of the time including Mohammad Ali Jinnah—of a sovereign and liberal Muslim state, "founded on consensual and pluralistic grounds, as a model of welfare, community, and popular sovereignty."[131] Jinnah explicitly challenged those who would become Pakistani Muslims to disregard religious differences in politics, which he blamed for being the greatest hindrance to the progress of India.[132] Indeed, the centrality of religious liberty to the struggle for an independent Pakistan inspired Muhammad Zafrullah Khan (Pakistan's first foreign minister, an Ahmadi, and the Pakistani representative to the U.N. General Assembly's drafting session for the UDHR) to support freedom of conscience and freedom to change one's religion against the vehement opposition of Saudi Arabia.[133]

Very little time passed, however, before Muslim fundamentalists in Pakistan sought to abridge the religious freedom of certain groups, beginning with the Ahmadis (whom they demanded be declared a non-Muslim minority and, eventually, wanted to have expelled from the country).

128. Gerald Butt, "Fears for the Middle East's Christians in the Wake of the Arab Spring," *The Guardian*, April 16, 2011.
129. David D. Kirkpatrick, "Egypt's Christians Fear Violence as Changes Embolden Islamists," *The New York Times*, May 30, 2011.
130. Pew Research Center, Global Attitudes Project. May 17, 2011. *Arab Spring Fails to Improve U.S. Image.* http://pewglobal.org/files/2011/07/Pew-Global-Attitudes-Arab-Spring-FINAL-May-17-2011.pdf.
131. Amjad Mahmood Khan, "Persecution of the Ahmadiyya Community in Pakistan: An Analysis under International Law and International Relations," *Harvard Human Rights Journal* 16 (2003): 220.
132. Ibid., 221.
133. Ibid., 221–22.

Throughout the 1950s and 1960s, the government clashed with Islamic revivalist movements, slowly but surely losing ground to those who envisioned a theocratic state.[134] In 1973, "[a]fter a bloody civil war and the separation of Bangladesh from Pakistan in 1971, the National Assembly approved a new constitution . . ., portions of which embodied the legal and political machinery of the *Shari'a* as espoused by the orthodox religious clergy."[135]

The 1973 constitution[136] formally announced the Islamic Republic of Pakistan, declaring Islam as the state religion (Article 2).[137] Then-Prime Minister Zulfiqar Ali Bhutto planned a full implementation of *Shari'a*, and while this was halted when Bhutto was overthrown by General Zia ul-Haq four years later, the General himself introduced ordinances and punishments based on Islamic criminal law (e.g., amputation, stoning), followed during his military rule in the 1980s by blasphemy laws subject to the death penalty.[138] These Penal Code provisions, propagated under martial law and by civilian government, were designed exclusively for the benefit of the Islamic faith and are still in place more than two decades later.[139] For example, Section 295C of the Code holds that "an offender may be punished with death or lifetime imprisonment if it is proved that he used derogatory language toward or regarding the Holy Prophet Muhammad.'"[140]

At a panel discussion titled "Apostasy, Human Rights, Religion, and Belief," convened in Geneva in April 2004 at the sixtieth session of the United Nations Committee on Human Rights, Muhammad Younus Shaikh presented the story of his own blasphemy trial.[141] A Pakistani citizen, doctor, and Muslim by birth, he observed that liberal and moderate Muslims are the first victims of Islamism, targeted for abuse by Islamic mullahs who

134. Ibid., 224–25.
135. Ibid., 225.
136. Constitution of the Islamic Republic of Pakistan,
http://www.mofa.gov.pk/Publications/constitution.pdf,
http://www.pakistani.org/pakistan/constitution/.
137. Paul Marshall, "The Islamists' Other Weapon," *Commentary* (April 2005), 62.
138. Ibid.
139. Farooq Hassan, "Religious Liberty in Pakistan: Law, Reality, and Perception (a Brief Synopsis)," *Brigham Young University Law Review* 2002 (2002): 292.
140. Ibid., 295–96.
141. As Pakistani scholar of law and policy Osama Siddique observes, the blasphemy laws were promulgated undemocratically, suffer from serious design and drafting issues, are problematically justified in the name of Islamic teachings, and have resulted in the persecution, confinement, exile, and even death of innocent people. See Osama Siddique and Zahra Hayat, "Unholy Speech and Holy Laws: Blasphemy Laws in Pakistan - Controversial Origins, Design Defects, and Free Speech Implications," *Minnesota Journal of International Law* 17 (2008).

capture the apparatus of the state and the civil law.[142] One consequence is that whereas the original law had been balanced and applied equally to all religions, the revised law provides for the death penalty only in cases of blasphemy against Islam.[143]

This legal disparity is consistent with Pakistan's larger nation-building project, which has relied heavily on "the Islamization of society and the enforcement of *Shari'a*. In effect, this has meant the politicisation of religion and forced assimilation of ethnic as well as religious minorities."[144] One religious minority group, the Ahmadis, has been subject to especially harsh and persistent persecution. The four million strong Ahmadi community, deemed by the Sunni Muslim majority to be heretical, has seen its mosques burned, its graves desecrated, and its existence criminalized.[145] Between 1999 and 2001 alone, at least two dozen adherents were charged with blasphemy for actions including wearing an Islamic slogan on a shirt, planning to build an Ahmadi mosque in Lahore, and distributing Ahmadi literature in a public square.[146]

Using Ahmadi-related jurisprudence, one legal scholar divides Pakistani protection of religious minorities into three periods (e.g., unequivocal protection from 1947–1972; deference to constitutional amendment and contraction of protection; and, most recently, complete judicial capitulation), arguing that the judicial branch in post-colonial settings like Pakistan is insufficiently insulated from political currents and contributes to the erosion of its own independence and legitimacy by capitulating to dominant political forces.[147] This is one reason why democratic reforms tied to the rule of law are particularly urgent, although events such as the assassination of Benazir Bhutto suggest that reform will not happen quickly or easily.[148]

---

142. Muhammad Younus Shaikh, "Pakistani Blasphemy Law," in *The Myth of Islamic Tolerance: How Islamic Law Treats Non-Muslims*, ed. Robert Spencer (Amherst, NY: Prometheus Books, 2005): 444–47.

143. Ibid., 446.

144. Javaid Rehman, "Nation-Building in an Islamic State: Minority Rights and Self-Determination in the Islamic Republic of Pakistan," in *Religion, Human Rights and International Law: A Critical Examination of Islamic State Practices*, ed. Javaid Rehman and Susan C. Breau (Boston: Martinus Nijhoff Publishers, 2007), 430.

145. Khan, "Persecution of the Ahmadiyya Community in Pakistan," 219.

146. Ibid.

147. Tayyab Mahmud, "Freedom of Religion & Religious Minorities in Pakistan: A Study of Judicial Practice," *Fordham International Law Journal* 19 (1995).

148. For example, see David Ignatius, "The Legacy of Benazir Bhutto," *The Washington Post*, December 28, 2007; Ahmed Rashid, "America's Bad Deal with Musharraf, Going Down in Flames," *The Washington Post*, June 17, 2007.

That said, Pakistan remains an interesting case because its Constitution combines the establishment of an Islamic state with comparatively robust legal provisions for religious liberty. Yet two features of Article 20 (which provides the right to profess, practice, and propagate one's religion) merit special attention: first, 20(a) makes the right available only to citizens of Pakistan; and second, religious liberty is construed as a constitutional right subject to law (i.e., sub-constitutional legislation may regulate the right for reasons of public morality or order, which the courts may, but are not required to, interpret in the light of Article 31's provisions for an "Islamic way of life").[149] The citizen clause raises questions about whether foreigners (and, by analogy, non-Muslims) are entitled to full religious rights. Moreover, the construction of religious liberty as a right subject to law could facilitate policies highly restrictive of non-state sanctioned religious practice. Violations of religious freedom by successive Pakistani government bear these concerns out.

For example, as the U.S. Commission on International Religious Freedom reports, "[d]iscriminatory legislation, promulgated in previous decades and persistently enforced, has fostered an atmosphere of religious intolerance and eroded the social and legal status of members of religious minorities, including Shi'as, Ahmadis, Hindus, and Christians. Government officials do not provide adequate protections from societal violence to members of these [groups], and, with some exceptions, perpetrators of attacks . . . are seldom brought to justice."[150] The Commission also notes that the government of Pakistan has in recent times directly encouraged religious intolerance.

Further findings include the following: substantial evidence exists that government officials have been complicit in sheltering Taliban members; present efforts to curb the content of the *madrassas'* extremist and violent curriculum are inadequate; religiously motivated violence remains a serious and chronic problem, despite some notable efforts of the government to condemn and prosecute perpetrators; blasphemy laws perpetuate lengthy detention of and violence against religious minorities, often without any meaningful due process in legal proceedings; and, geopolitically, Western efforts to fight the war on terrorism and promote democracy worldwide are seriously compromised by violations of religious freedom in Pakistan.[151] Also, in recent months, two high-profile members of the ruling

149. Hassan, "Religious Liberty in Pakistan," 288.
150. U.S. Commission on Religious Freedom. 2007. *Annual Report*, 246.
151. Ibid., 245–50; 2008. *Annual Report*, 146–53; 2009. *Annual Report*, 65–72; 2010. *Annual Report*, 91–102; 2011. *Annual Report*, 110–23. For a detailed analysis of the role

party (Shahbaz Bhatti, Pakistan's federal minorities minister and a Christian; and Salman Taseer, the Punjab province governor) were assassinated for advocating against the country's repressive blasphemy laws.[152] Thus, despite constitutional provisions that generally compare favorably with international standards of religious liberty, Pakistan remains dominated in consequential ways by radical Islamist parties (and culture) that have shown themselves hostile to human rights, pluralism, and religious freedom.[153]

In sum, the ascendency of Islamism and the development of transnational Muslim identity in the latter decades of the twentieth century enabled Islamists to seize political power and enshrine their authority in the domestic constitutions of Muslim states. The effects upon religious freedom, in law and/or in practice, have largely been dismal. This is especially relevant because, just as the U.S. Constitution contributed to Western human rights law, the political and constitutional experiences of Muslim-majority states such as Iran, Turkey, Egypt, and Pakistan have helped shape the discourse and instruments of Islamic human rights. However, a word of caution is here appropriate.

Considered on their own, the historical tides and country profiles sketched in this chapter would bode decidedly ill for the prospects of reconciling Islamic formulations of religious freedom with international legal standards. It is thus vital to recognize the existence of Islamic movements that are credibly seeking to develop alternative models of governance—in the Middle East, but also outside of it in countries like Indonesia.[154] Indonesia is the fourth most populous nation in the world and the largest Muslim-majority state; it also contains significant numbers of Hindus, Buddhists, and Christians (the other religions officially recognized and protected by the Indonesian government).[155]

and relative influence of these religious schools in Pakistan, see C. Christine Fair, *The Madrassah Challenge: Militancy and Religious Education in Pakistan* (Washington, DC: United States Institute of Peace Press, 2008).

152. Karin Brulliard, "Shahbaz Bhatti, Pakistan's Christian Minorities Minister, Is Assassinated in Islamabad," *The Washington Post*, March 2, 2011; Pamela Constable, "Pakistani Christian Official's Slaying Stirs Fear, Discord," *The Washington Post*, March 26, 2011.

153. To this day, Islamists in Pakistan are contending for authority to install *Shari'a* nationwide, including the abolition of all "un-Islamic laws and customs." See Pamela Constable, "Extremist Tide Rises in Pakistan," *The Washington Post*, April 20, 2009.

154. Peter L. Berger, "Religions and Globalisation," *European Judaism* 36, no. 1 (Spring 2003): 8.

155. Casanova, "Civil Society and Religion," 30–31.

In his scholarship on Indonesia, anthropologist Robert Hefner describes the movements there (e.g., Nudhat'ul-Ulama, with its millions of adherents) as part of "civil Islam"—a vision that unites Muslim belief, ritual, and morality with support for democracy, market economics, gender equality, separation of church and state, and religious freedom.[156] The resulting portrait of the "diversity of modern Muslim politics" reminds us that the many features traditionally associated with Muslim politics may "owe more to Middle Eastern circumstances than Muslim civilization as a whole."[157] Elsewhere, Hefner elaborates on the necessity for civil democratic politics not just of civil association, but also of "a broader pattern of political pluricentrism, in which no single social class or organization asserts monopoly control over the social, political, and moral resources of society."[158]

In some ways, however, this points back toward the original research question: do Islamic human rights instruments meaningfully provide for and protect the religious freedom and corresponding religious diversity that is understood (in the West) to be a fundamental condition of democratic pluralism? If not, could they? Answering these questions requires weaving together the religious teachings considered in Chapter 4 with the political and legal institutions considered in this chapter to analyze Islamic international law and its global implications. This is the task of Chapter 6.

156. Robert W. Hefner, *Civil Islam: Muslims and Democratization in Indonesia* (Princeton, NJ: Princeton University Press, 2000); Robert Hefner, "Human Rights and Democracy in Islam: The Indonesian Case in Global Perspective," in *Religion and the Global Politics of Human Rights*, ed. Thomas Banchoff and Robert Wuthnow (New York: Oxford University Press, 2011), 39–70. See also Azyumardi Azra and Wayne Hudson, eds., *Islam Beyond Conflict: Indonesian Islam and Western Political Theory* (Aldershot, UK: Ashgate, 2008). For an Islamist response, see Greg Fealy, "Indonesian Islamist Perspectives on Human Rights," in *Islam and Human Rights in Practice*, ed. Shahram Akbarzadeh, and Benjamin MacQueen (New York: Routledge, 2008), 142–53.

157. Robert W. Hefner, "Public Islam and the Problem of Democratization," *Sociology of Religion* 62, no. 4 (2001): 492. Even in Indonesia, however, the headscarf and other visible symbols of Islam are increasingly important elements of political discourse. See Norimitsu Onishi, "Head Scarf Emerges as Indonesia Political Symbol," *The New York Times*, July 3, 2009.

158. Robert W. Hefner, "On the History and Cross-Cultural Possibility of a Modern Ideal," in *Democratic Civility: The History and Cross-Cultural Possibility of a Modern Ideal*, ed. Robert W. Hefner (New Brunswick, NJ: Transaction Publishers, 1998), 39.

CHAPTER 6

Religious Liberty in Islamic International Law

Many regimes in the Muslim world today seek their legitimacy through portraying an adherence to Islamic law and traditions. Thus any attempt to enforce international or universal norms within Muslim societies in oblivion of established Islamic law and traditions creates tension and reactions against the secular nature of the international regime no matter how humane or lofty such international norms may be.

—*Mashood Baderin*[1]

More and more citizens in the Muslim world, or rather individuals aspiring to the status of modern citizenship, are engaged in a struggle for the separation of religion and politics, for the recognition of religious freedom and for the abolition of the *Sharia*.... This struggle should be viewed as part of the social, cultural and political evolution of societies which can no longer be described as one homogeneous, intangible "Muslim society."

—*Kai Hafez*[2]

The rise of political Islam in the 1970s and 1980s in reaction to secular Western imperial power had consequences at both the domestic and international levels. As illustrated in Chapter 5, Islamists sought to institutionalize their religious authority and political power in state constitutions, which in turn had tangible and often grave effects on the practical and legal status of religious freedom in those countries. Concurrently, the growing

1. Mashood A. Baderin, *International Human Rights and Islamic Law* (New York: Oxford University Press, 2003), 30.
2. Kai Hafez, ed. *The Islamic World and the West: An Introduction to Political Cultures and International Relations* (Leiden, The Netherlands: Brill, 2000), XII.

power of Islamism, coupled with the rise of national and transnational Islamic identity, inspired efforts to develop Islamic alternatives to Western international law. The resulting agreements—such as the Universal Islamic Declaration of Human Rights and the Cairo Declaration on Human Rights in Islam—have raised pressing questions about the compatibility of Islam and human rights, the status of women, non-Muslims and religious freedom in Islamic declarations, the nature of contemporary Islamic international law, and the implications of differences between Western and Islamic formulations for the universality of human rights. These questions are the subject of this chapter.[3]

I. ISLAM AND HUMAN RIGHTS—ORIGINS OF THE DEBATE

Because Islam as a system of belief separates religion neither from politics nor from law,[4] many Muslim states (as well as the scholars and movements advising them) have tended to formulate human rights in Islamic terms even after modernizing.[5] In so doing, they have drawn upon concepts, values, and principles that variously overlap with and diverge from those in Western civilization. For example, reflecting teachings and traditions dating from pre-modern times, Islamic thought is largely communitarian in emphasis.[6] Hence, in contrast with the modern West, where human rights have been shaped by the individualism of (Protestant) Christianity and liberal political thought, Islamic formulations of human rights are more frequently and explicitly accompanied by concerns for public

3. The status of women in Islam, though clearly related to debates about Islamic international law and human rights, is outside the scope of this book. For an excellent analysis of the keys issues and texts, see Ann Elizabeth Mayer, *Islam and Human Rights: Tradition and Politics* (Boulder, CO: Westview Press, 1999), 97–130. See also Leila Hilal, "The Cairo Declaration on Human Rights in Islam and International Women's Rights," *Buffalo Women's Journal of Law and Social Policy* 5 (1997).
4. But see Ali Abdul Raziq's 1925 work *Islam and the Foundation of Government* (*al-Islam wa naul al-hukum*), which Muslim modernists and realists build upon to argue for separating the institutions of religion and state. Peter A. Samuelson, "Pluralism Betrayed: The Battle between Secularism and Islam in Algeria's Quest for Democracy," *Yale Journal of International Law* 20 (1995): 337; Ali Abdul Raziq, *Islam and the Foundation of Government* (Cairo: Maktabat Misr, 1925).
5. Joelle Entelis, "International Human Rights: Islam's Friend or Foe?," *Fordham International Law Journal* 20 (1997): 1262.
6. Mayer, *Islam and Human Rights*, 43.

morality and order.[7] Such differences and their implications appear more clearly when their historical origins and evolution are considered.[8]

While international human rights law as such originated in the twentieth-century Western world, resonant theological and philosophical principles may be found in many pre-modern and non-Western civilizations, including that/those anchored by Islam. "The sources and methods of Islamic law contain common principles of good government and human welfare that validate modern international human rights ideals," Islamic law scholar Mashood Baderin explains. "Respect for justice, protection of human life and dignity are central principles inherent in the *Shari'ah* which no differences of opinion can exclude. They are the overall purpose of the *Shari'ah*, to which the Qur'an refers."[9] Nevertheless, even if public international law and Islamic law share what might be understood as a humanitarian orientation, "human rights as they are presently formulated in international law lack precise equivalents in the Islamic legal heritage."[10]

There are two especially relevant reasons for this. The first, as anthropologist Robert Hefner explains, is that *Shari'a* is underspecified regarding matters of governance.[11] Historically, *Shari'a* was developed during the end of the Umayyad dynasty (661–750 C.E.) and the beginning of its Abbasid successor (750–1258 C.E.). Unlike their predecessors, the Abbasids relied heavily on Persian political culture, with two consequences. One is that the

7. Although such provisions do exist in international human rights law as well (e.g., Article 18(3) of the ICCPR subjects freedom to manifest one's religion or belief "only to such limitations as are prescribed by law and are necessary to protect public safety, order, health, or morals or the fundamental rights and freedoms of others").

8. For example, Islam does not share the formal separation between church and state that exists in post-Reformation Christianity. Jan-Erik Lane and Hamadi Redissi, *Religion and Politics: Islam and Muslim Civilisation* (Burlington, VT: Ashgate, 2004).

9. Baderin, *International Human Rights and Islamic Law*, 13.

10. Ann Elizabeth Mayer, "Universal Versus Islamic Human Rights: A Clash of Cultures or a Clash with a Construct?," *Michigan Journal of International Law* 15 (1994): 321. Strong versions of this view are challenged by some Muslim scholars and practitioners. For example, Rajsoomer Lallah, a member of the Human Rights Committee of the Office of the U.N. High Commissioner for Human Rights, attempts to "explode the myth that human rights are a Western invention" by emphasizing that: 1) African and Middle Eastern societies historically employed standards of justice that were similar to those in modern human rights instruments; and 2) the UDHR and the ICCPR represent the contributions and aspirations of people from diverse cultural and religious traditions. A.Yasmine Rassam, "Islam and Justice: Debating the Future of Human Rights in the Middle East and North Africa. By Lawyer's Committee for Human Rights," *Pace International Law Review* 10 (1998): 192–93.

11. Robert Hefner, "Human Rights and Democracy in Islam: The Indonesian Case in Global Perspective," in *Religion and the Global Politics of Human Rights*, ed. Thomas Banchoff and Robert Wuthnow (New York: Oxford University Press, 2011), 43–44. All of the material in this paragraph is drawn from Hefner's chapter.

jurists limited their political pronouncements to well-established and uncontroversial matters, deferring to Abbasid leaders on most issues of governance; thus, the public law provisions of *Shari'a* are largely theoretical.[12] Another consequence is that the Abbasids themselves began to issue edicts covering areas of governance on which *Shari'a* was silent, which effectively bifurcated the law between religious jurisprudence and statutory legislation.[13] Yet, as Hefner clarifies, because *Shari'a* as a total system remained the ideal, jurists could neither draw upon nor give explicit normative sanction to this statutory legislation. The resulting underspecification of *Shari'a* helps explain why the Islamic legal heritage does not contain human rights formulations as such.

A second reason involves the historic subordination of Islam's rationalist thinkers to orthodox scholars who emphasized divine revelation. For example, as Ann Elizabeth Mayer documents, one of the most important rationalist currents in Islamic thought was associated with the Mu'tazila.[14] The Mu'tazilites "called for rational interpretation of the Islamic sources and demanded justice in both the political and social spheres. The community was to control the government, not blindly to defer to authority, and it was free to revolt against governments that denied fundamental liberties."[15] This group's influence peaked in the Sunni world in the ninth century, after which it was suppressed—sometimes brutally—by orthodox Sunnis (Ash'arites) who feared that emphasizing human reason would lead Muslims to stray from the truth of revelation.[16]

The orthodox position, also known as ethical voluntarism,[17] was asserted against Islamic philosophers (e.g., al-Farabi, d. 950, and Ibn Rushd "Averroës," d. 1190) and other rationalist thinkers, who were forced on the

---

12. In support of this analysis, Hefner also cites Sami Zubaida, *Law and Power in the Muslim World* (London: I.B. Tauris, 2003).

13. Ibid. Here, Hefner also draws upon Jonathan Berkey, *The Formation of Islam* (New York: Cambridge University Press, 2002).

14. Mayer, *Islam and Human Rights*, 43. On the discovery by Islam of Hellenic thought and the arguments for and from reason made by the Mu'tazilites, see Robert Reilly, *The Closing of the Muslim Mind* (Wilmington, DE: ISI Books, 2010), 11–39.

15. Mayer, *Islam and Human Rights*, 44.

16. Ibid., 43–44. For a detailed accounting of the overthrow of the Mu'tazilites, see Reilly, *The Closing of the Muslim Mind*: 41–58. But, for the important (counter)argument that it was not the case that all Ash'arites rejected legal interpretation and, moreover, that *ijtihad* is not the exclusive preserve of Islamic rationalists, see Wael B. Hallaq, "Was the Gate of Ijtihad Closed?" *International Journal for Middle East Studies* 16 (1984): 3–41.

17. It is also referred to by various scholars as voluntarism, nominalism, and theistic subjectivism, each of which has distinct theological and philosophical nuances.

defensive (where they have generally remained ever since).[18] Ethical voluntarism in turn generated an emphasis on the duties of obedience Muslims owe to God (*haqq Allah*) and to the community (*haqq al-nas*), rather than on what they are owed as human beings.[19] In other words, Islamic law has, throughout most of its history, been oriented by divine command—not by rationalism, natural law, or human rights.[20] The influence of the Mu'tazilites did survive (particularly in the Twelver Shi'a Islam of Iran), but those who argue too openly for the supremacy of reason over revelation or the precedence of justice (e.g., Abdolkarim Soroush) have always risked institutional persecution and physical violence.[21]

Separately and together, these two reasons for the absence of human rights in the Islamic legal heritage—the underspecificity of Islam and the divine command orientation of its ethical voluntarism—also suggest possible strategies for reconciling Western and Islamic international law. To anticipate, the underspecificity of Islam may point toward an interpretive space within which Islamic jurisprudence could be decoupled from its historical-political institutionalization and then used to inform a vision of human rights that is authentically Islamic, while also compatible with contemporary international legal standards. In order for this effort to succeed, Islamic jurisprudence would itself have to move beyond the strict ethical voluntarism of the orthodox scholars and embrace a role for reason, thereby opening a space for human freedom and hence rights alongside duties.

For the moment, however, it is enough to recognize that throughout most of its history, Islamic law did not recognize human rights. Indeed, the very concept of human rights (*huquq al-insan*) was not introduced into the Arabic language until the end of the nineteenth century, when Rifa'ah Rafi' al-Tahtawi included a European-inspired "Declaration of Human Rights" in his book *Takhlis al-Ibriz*.[22] As religious historian Yvonne Haddad notes, al-Tahtawi's ideas were subsequently adopted and developed by local

18. On what he characterizes as "Islam's rejection of philosophy," see Antony Black, *The West and Islam: Religion and Political Thought in World History* (New York: Oxford University Press, 2008).

19. Mayer, *Islam and Human Rights*, 45.

20. But, arguing against claims that Islam is a defining case of ethical voluntarism and that the prominent theory in Islamic ethical thought is Divine Command Theory, see Mariam al-Attar, *Islamic Ethics: Divine Command Theory in Arabo-Islamic Thought* (New York: Routledge, 2010).

21. Mayer, *Islam and Human Rights*, 44.

22. Yvonne Haddad, "Muslims and Human Rights," (Washington, DC: Georgetown University, 2008). See also `Abd al-Razzaq `Id, "Al-Nizam Al-Abawi Wa-`Alaqatuhu Bi-Huquq Al-Insan," in *Huquq Al-Insan Fi Al-Fikr Al-`Arabi: Dirasat Fi Al-Nusus,* ed. Salma al-Khadra' al-Jayyusi (Beirut: Markaz Dirasat al-Wahdah al-`Arabiyah, 2002).

secularist writers (both Christian and Muslim), particularly those who were educated in institutions run by missionaries or the colonial powers.[23] These ideas were consistent with European political thought, which may be one reason why Muslim countries appeared, for the most part, to accept the international consensus on human rights in the decades immediately following World War II.[24]

Even still, as discussed in Chapter 3, Muslim states did not hesitate to register specific objections to Western formulations of religious liberty rights. By the late 1960s and 1970s, as secular Arab nationalism increasingly gave way to political Islam, these preliminary objections developed into the much broader assertion that international human rights law was variously Judeo-Christian, Western, or secular, but in any case incompatible with Islam. This position was vigorously advocated by some Muslim states, most notably Iran after its 1979 Islamic Revolution.[25]

All of these factors—the growing salience of global human rights norms, Muslim concerns about the scope and content of religious freedom, the post-colonial reaction against the West, and the ascendency of Islamism—combined in the second half of the twentieth century to spark debate about the compatibility of Islam and human rights. This debate was fueled by publications from Islamic scholars.

For example, in *A Muslim Commentary on the Universal Declaration of Human Rights* (a pamphlet published originally in Persian in 1966, then in English translation four years later), Iranian religious leader Sultanhussein Tabandeh asserted not only that sacred Islamic theology and Shi'a beliefs were the authoritative sources of law, but also that, where discrepancies existed, the UDHR should be rewritten to conform to Islam.[26] Tabandeh presented his commentary to Muslim state representatives to the 1968 Tehran International Conference on Human Rights, in order to advise them of the positions they should adopt vis-à-vis various provisions of the UDHR according to the dictates of Islamic law.[27] Similarly, in the mid-1970s, Abu'l A'la Mawdudi (a prominent Sunni leader) published the pamphlet *Human Rights in Islam*, a document animated by his vociferous hostility to the West and his belief in the superiority of Islamic civilization.[28] Mawdudi also

23. Haddad, "Muslims and Human Rights."
24. Mayer, "Universal Versus Islamic Human Rights," 321.
25. Ibid., 322.
26. Mayer, *Islam and Human Rights*, 20, 102.
27. Ibid., 20.
28. Ibid., 20–21. See also Asma Afsaruddin, "Demarcating Fault-Lines within Islam: Muslim Modernists and Hardline Islamists Engage the Shari'a," in *Shari'a as*

founded the political group Jama'at-i-Islami, "whose members are committed to the reinstatement of Islamic law and the establishment of an Islamic state in Pakistan."[29]

Their arguments and others centered on the claim that international human rights are not in fact universal, but instead represent a political model that must be rejected by Muslim states. It is worth noting that the conflicts revolved around civil and political rights (including such issues as conversion, the right to unbelief, and the status of non-Muslims), whereas the compatibility of Islam with economic, social, and cultural rights was rarely raised.[30] This suggests, among other things, the centrality of religious freedom to conflicts between Western and Islamic international law.

In any event, as Islamists gained in influence, they used their political power to institutionalize alternate models of governance. This process was reflected at the domestic level by changes to state constitutions, which granted Islam official status and formulated rights with reference to Islamic law. Religious liberty rights in many Muslim states thus came to diverge from international legal standards either directly, as in the constitutions of Iran and Pakistan, or indirectly, as in the case of Egypt, where the constitutional privileging of Islamic jurisprudence has been interpreted to the practical detriment of religious freedom laws that are otherwise facially compatible with international norms.

These state-level processes simultaneously consolidated the national power of Islamist groups and facilitated their transnational cooperation, which they directed toward challenging the content of international human rights treaties and developing their own religiously based alternatives. Not surprisingly, religious liberty as it appears in Islamic human rights declarations embodies many of the same problems present in domestic constitutional counterparts.

Discourse: Legal Traditions and the Encounter with Europe, ed. Jorgen S. Nielsen and Lisbet Christoffersen (Burlington, VT: Ashgate, 2010), 30.

29. Mayer, *Islam and Human Rights*, 20. On Mawdudi's views in the context of Salafism, see Jorgen S. Nielsen, "Shari'a between Renewal and Tradition," in *Shari'a as Discourse: Legal Traditions and the Encounter with Europe*, ed. Jorgen S. Nielsen and Lisbet Christoffersen (Burlington, VT: Ashgate, 2010), 5.

30. Mayer, "Universal Versus Islamic Human Rights," 322. Some scholars and policymakers look to similarities between international law and Islamic declarations as regards the latter category of rights, and are then tempted to interpret disagreements on civil and political rights as matters that can be piecemeal negotiated. Such an approach misses the point. Insofar as Islamic law is posited as grounding an alternate paradigm of human rights, the legitimacy of each and all of those rights derives from Islam. What is at stake is the comprehensive foundation of law, not just its particular instantiations.

In 1981, after two decades of negotiation, the U.N. Declaration on the Elimination of All Forms of Intolerance and of Discrimination Based on Religion or Belief was adopted by the U.N. General Assembly without a vote. As discussed in Chapter 3, the language of the 1981 Declaration represented significant compromises by different groups of states, made necessary by ideological and religious conflict between Muslim countries, the Soviet Union, and the United States. The level of disagreement was sufficient to prevent the transformation of the 1981 Declaration into a legally binding instrument, although it has since acquired a certain degree of authority and influence.[31]

Of particular interest, the clause "this right includes the freedom to change his religion or belief" was left out of the 1981 Declaration (as was the compromise version of the clause in Article 18 of the ICCPR), in order to secure the support of Muslim countries, who were by this time gathered within the Organization of the Islamic Conference (OIC).[32] Speaking on behalf of the OIC after the 1981 Declaration was adopted, Iraqi representative Habib A. al-Qaysi expressed the organization's "reservations in connection with any provision or wording in the Declaration which might be contrary to Islamic Law (Shari'a) or to any legislation or act based on Islamic Law."[33]

While Muslim states had expressed their concerns about the scope and content of religious liberty in international treaty debates beginning with the UDHR, the year 1981 was an important turning point for several reasons. First, the OIC was able to wield its political power to change treaty language.[34] Second, as mentioned previously, the Iranian representative to the U.N. General Assembly characterized the UDHR as a secular interpretation of Judeo-Christian tradition that could not be implemented by Muslim states. And third, the Universal Islamic Declaration of Human Rights

31. Kevin Boyle, "Freedom of Religion in International Law," in *Religion, Human Rights and International Law: A Critical Examination of Islamic State Practices*, ed. Javaid Rehman and Susan C. Breau (Boston: Martinus Nijhoff, 2007), 45–46.

32. Ibid., 47.

33. Ibid., 48.

34. Founded in 1969 by Muslim heads of states and governments with the objective of "promoting Islamic solidarity among member states," the OIC currently has fifty-seven members. Its founding Charter entered into force on February 28, 1973. On February 1, 1974, the OIC Charter was registered as an international treaty with the U.N. in conformity with Article 102 of the U.N. Charter; it is thus evocable before the organs of the U.N. Baderin, *International Human Rights and Islamic Law*, 226.

(UIDHR) was proclaimed at the United Nations Educational, Scientific and Cultural Organization (UNESCO) in Paris. These three moments mark 1981 as a critical juncture in the development of an Islamic human rights paradigm, followed soon thereafter by the Cairo Declaration on Human Rights in Islam.

The UIDHR was prepared by representatives from Egypt, Pakistan, Saudi Arabia, and other countries in connection with the Islamic Council (a private, London-based organization affiliated with the Muslim World League, which is an international non-governmental organization headquartered in Saudi Arabia).[35] To the casual reader, it may appear comparable to the UDHR,[36] but many similarities turn out to be misleading, especially as the English version diverges from the Arabic original at key points.[37] Based on the Qur'an and the *Sunnah*, the UIDHR contains two provisions related to religious liberty. For example, under Article 12 (Right to Freedom of Belief, Thought and Speech), every person "has the right to express his thoughts and beliefs so long as he remains within the limits prescribed by the Law" (12.a); additionally, there "shall be no bar on the dissemination of information provided it does not endanger the security of the society or the state and is confined within the limits imposed by the Law" (12.c).

Whether one finds these English-version provisions in substantial conformity with international legal standards or not (they can arguably be construed either way[38]), their Arabic counterparts are strikingly different and reveal that Islamic criteria limit freedom of expression.[39] Translated, Article 12.a states: "Everyone may think, believe and express his ideas and beliefs without interference or opposition from anyone as long as he obeys the limits (*hudud*) set by the *Shari'a*. It is not permitted to spread falsehood

35. Douglas Hodgson, *Individual Duty within a Human Rights Discourse* (Burlington, VT: Ashgate, 2003), 51; David G. Littman, "Universal Human Rights and 'Human Rights in Islam,'" *Midstream Magazine* 2 (February/March 1999).

36. At least one scholar even goes so far as to argue that, despite the "noticeable presence of huge restrictions in these . . . texts," their "so-called incompatibility . . . with international [standards] is illusory." Baudouin Dupret, "Islam and Human Rights: Tradition and Politics. By Ann Elizabeth Mayer," *Journal of Law and Religion* 15 (2000–2001): 572. In light of all the evidence to the contrary, this view is difficult to comprehend.

37. Mayer, *Islam and Human Rights*, 21.

38. For an optimistic reading, see Susan C. Breau, "Human Rights and Cultural Relativism: The False Dichotomy," in *Religion, Human Rights and International Law: A Critical Examination of Islamic State Practices*, ed. Javaid Rehman and Susan C. Breau (Boston: Martinus Nijhoff Publishers, 2007), 160–61. Especially in view of the Arabic original text, this book is more skeptical.

39. Mayer, *Islam and Human Rights: Tradition and Politics*, 160.

(*al-batil*) or disseminate that which involves encouraging abomination (*al-fahisha*) or forsaking the Islamic community (*takhdhil li'l-umma*)."⁴⁰

As international law scholar Ann Elizabeth Mayer observes, at a minimum, proselytizing by non-Muslims and speaking disparagingly of the Prophet Muhammad would be forbidden, but because there are no established standards for how far the *Shari'a* limits may be extended, the provision is open-ended.⁴¹ Similarly, while the English version of Article 13 (Right to Freedom of Religion) holds that every person "has the right to freedom of conscience and worship in accordance with his religious beliefs," the Arabic version would effectively prohibit conversion away from Islam. Indeed, read in light of the Arabic version of Section 7 of the Preamble, the UIDHR embodies a commitment to converting the world's population to Islam.⁴² Hence, the UIDHR is clearly inconsistent with international standards of religious freedom.

Less than a decade later, in August 1990, the Cairo Declaration on Human Rights in Islam was adopted by the Nineteenth Islamic Conference of Foreign Ministers of the Member States of the OIC. Article 24 provides that all "rights and freedoms stipulated in [the] Declaration are subject to the Islamic Shari'ah"; similarly, Article 25 designates Islamic law as the only source of reference for the explanation or clarification of its content. Taken together, these provisions suggest that the Cairo Declaration, and hence *Shari'a*, has primacy over all other international legal instruments in the adjudication of relevant incorporated rights.⁴³ Put differently, the Cairo

40. Ibid., 161.
41. Ibid., 161. This is especially interesting in light of the Danish cartoon controversy and related conflicts concerning free speech and defamation.
42. Ibid., 162.
43. David G. Littman, "Human Rights and Human Wrongs," *National Review Online* (January 19, 2003). Littman describes a seminar (titled "Enriching the Universality of Human Rights: Islamic Perspectives on the Universal Declaration of Human Rights"), jointly hosted by the OIC and the Office of the High Commissioner for Human Rights, at the United Nations in Geneva on November 9–10, 1998. At that event, twenty Muslim experts on Islam presented papers and engaged in dialogue with each other. For the first time at a U.N. public seminar, Littman writes, no questions were allowed from the more than 250 participants representing approximately 80 states, intergovernmental and U.N. bodies, and 41 NGOs. The price tag for the event was half a million dollars, paid for by the OIC countries. See also Press Release, United Nations, High Commissioner for Human Rights Organizing Expert Seminar to Discuss Islamic Perspectives on Universal Declaration of Human Rights, U.N. Doc. HR/98/81 (Oct. 30, 1998); Press Release, United Nations, Search for Unity in Cultural Diversity is Particular Responsibility of the UN, Says UN High Commissioner, Mary Robinson, to Seminar on Islam and Universal Declaration for Human Rights, U.N. Doc. HR/98/85 (Nov. 9, 1998); Defamation of Religions, U.N. Commission on Human Rights Res. 1999/82

Declaration asserts the existence of an Islamic countermodel of human rights.[44]

Among its twenty-five Articles, there is not one that corresponds to Article 18 of the UDHR, for the Cairo Declaration does not expand the scope of religious freedom *implicit* in pre-modern times.[45] That is, on its face, the Cairo Declaration makes no guarantees at all for freedom of religion, which carries serious practical implications for non-Muslims, Muslim dissidents, and local Muslim minority sects.[46] Additionally, in favoring Islam ("the religion of unspoiled nature") above all other religious, the Declaration effectively bans other faiths from proselytizing (e.g., Article 10 prohibits "any form of compulsion on man to exploit his poverty or ignorance in order to convert him [away from Islam] to another religion or to atheism"). Likewise, as part of Article 22, free expression is permitted only insofar as it conforms with the principles of *Shari'a*—a standard of limitation that extends to advocacy, propagation, warning, and use of information.

In December 1991, the Cairo Declaration was presented for approval at the OIC Summit Meeting of Heads of State and Government held in Dakar, Senegal. Efforts to secure approval failed, in part because of a press release from the Geneva-based International Commission of Jurists (ICJ) strongly criticizing the document. Additionally, on behalf of the ICJ and the Paris-based International Federation for Human Rights, ICJ Secretary-General Adama Dieng (a Muslim Senegalese jurist) issued a joint statement to the U.N. Commission on Human Rights in which he characterized the Cairo Declaration as gravely threatening "the inter-cultural consensus on which the international human rights instruments are based," introducing "intolerable discrimination against both non-Muslims and women," and confirming under cover of Islamic law "practices . . . that attack the integrity and dignity of the human being."[47]

(Apr. 30, 1999) in *Commission on Human Rights: Report on the Fifty-Fifth Session (22 March–April 30, 1999)*, at 280, U.N. Docs E/1999/23, E/CN.4/1999/167 (1999).

44. Mayer, "Universal Versus Islamic Human Rights," 327.

45. Abdullah Saeed and Hassan Saeed, *Freedom of Religion, Apostasy and Islam* (Burlington, VT: Ashgate, 2004), 17.

46. Mayer, "Universal Versus Islamic Human Rights," 334.

47. Littman, "Human Rights and Human Wrongs;" U.N. Commission on Human Rights, 55th Session, *Written Statement dated July 4, 2003 from the Association for World Education, a Non-Governmental Organization on the Roster, to the Sub-Commission on the Promotion and Protection of Human Rights*, para.12, U.N. Doc. E/CN.4/Sub.2/2003/NGO/15 (July 14, 2003).

Scholars are divided as to whether the Cairo Declaration defines authentic Islamic teachings on religious liberty and other human rights. For example, Mashood Baderin claims that the OIC "can provide a community framework among modern Muslim states . . . as a regional mechanism for the practical realization of international human rights law in the Muslim world," even as he recognizes the absence of an interpretive or enforcement organ for adjudicating international human rights in relation to *Shari'a*.[48] In contrast, Mayer argues that the Cairo Declaration "has no serious claim to represent Islamic teachings . . . instead . . . reflect[ing] the current policies of governments like those of Iran and Saudi Arabia, which rationalize their laws and practices curbing rights by placing them under an Islamic rubric."[49]

However, as recently as 2004, the Foreign Ministers of the Islamic Conference called for following up on the Cairo Declaration by starting to craft and debate Islamic charters on human rights, with a view to making them into binding covenants. These and related actions imbue the question of what Islamic human rights declarations signify with a certain urgency.[50] If they represent more than just the strategic deployment of religious ideas and symbols for political ends, indeed, if they constitute a newly forming *as-siyar* (i.e., Islamic international law) that could succeed in commanding the loyalty of Muslim states, then the implications for international legal standards of religious liberty—and the universality to which they aspire— would be profound. This inquiry thus occupies the remainder of the chapter, beginning with an examination of contemporary Islamic international law, and then moving to a broader discussion of potential consequences of and responses to it.

III. INTERPRETING THE EMERGENCE OF CONTEMPORARY ISLAMIC INTERNATIONAL LAW

The original members of the United Nations included only six Islamic states out of total of fifty (twelve percent). By the turn of the twenty-first

48. Baderin, *International Human Rights and Islamic Law*, 226, 28.
49. Ann Elizabeth Mayer, "Book Review: International Human Rights and Islamic Law. By Mashood A. Baderin.," review of *International Human Rights and Islamic Law*, by Mashood A. Baderin, *American Journal of International Law* 99 (2005): 305.
50. On efforts by the OIC to advance laws against "defamation of religions," laws that "provide justification for governments to restrict religious freedom and free expression," see Leonard A. Leo, Felice D. Gaer, and Elizabeth K. Cassidy, "Protecting Religions from 'Defamation': A Threat to Universal Human Rights Standards," *Harvard Journal of Law and Public Policy* 34 (2011).

century, that number had grown to thirty-seven Islamic states out of a total of nearly one hundred sixty members (twenty-three percent).[51] As the participation of Islamic states in the international community has grown, so, too, has their willingness not only to voice their differences with the West, but also to act on them.[52] In so doing, these countries have drawn upon a long tradition of Islamic international law, one whose two basic principles—treaty and reciprocity—are rooted in Qur'anic commandments.[53]

As-siyar, or Islamic international law, "encompasses public and private international law including a well-defined catalogue of rights of minorities, rights to the environment, humanitarian laws, laws of armed conflict, diplomacy, and human rights. It predates contemporary international law by many centuries and has a wider remit than its comparatuer."[54] Nevertheless, there is substantial debate about the relationship of *as-siyar* to domestic law. For example, it is recognized as an integral part of Islamic law and jurisprudence, and it grew into a fully functional body of *Shari'a* several centuries before the advent of Western international law.[55] Thus, as Middle Eastern scholar Majid Khaduri clarifies, "[t]he *siyar*, if taken to mean the Islamic law of nations, is but a chapter in the Islamic *corpus juris*, binding upon all who believed in Islam as well as upon those who sought to

51. Gamal M. Badr, "A Survey of Islamic International Law," in *Religion and International Law*, ed. Mark W. Janis and Carolyn Evans (Boston: Martinus Nijhoff Publishers, 1999), 97.
52. See, e.g., Daniel Philpott, "Global Ethics and the International Law Tradition," in *The Globalization of Ethics: Religious and Secular Perspectives*, ed. William M. Sullivan and Will Kymlicka (New York: Cambridge University Press, 2007), 17–37.
53. Badr, "A Survey of Islamic International Law," 98. For example, Badr writes, the "duty of honoring a treaty with non-Muslims is even given priority over the duty of mutual help among believers where the two duties are in conflict." Badr continues by suggesting that Islamic international law could make several contributions to Western thought, including a concept of the state as subject to higher norms (i.e., not merely an instrument of political will), emphasis upon ethical considerations (e.g., the moral responsibility of individuals), and well-developed theories of diplomatic and consular inviolability and immunity. Ibid., 99–101.
54. Shaheen Sardar Ali, "The Twain Doth Meet! A Preliminary Exploration of the Theory and Practice of *as-Siyar* and International Law in the Contemporary World," in *Religion, Human Rights and International Law: A Critical Examination of Islamic State Practices*, ed. Javaid Rehman and Susan C. Breau (Boston: Martinus Nijhoff Publishers, 2007), 89. For an example of how classical models of Islamic diplomacy might be updated to accord with modern international law, see Perry S. Smith, "Of War and Peace: The Hudaibiya Model of Islamic Diplomacy," *Florida Journal of International Law* 18 (2006).
55. Ali, "The Twain Doth Meet!," 90.

protect their interests according to Islamic justice."[56] In principle, then, the prescriptions of *as-siyar* apply to Muslims without regard to nationality.

Importantly, while *as-siyar* is sourced by divine law as revealed in the Qur'an and *Sunnah*, some Islamic scholars and jurists argue that it should not be understood as precluding revision. Rather, it should be interpreted with regard to "the living and developing Islamic view of international law and relations" (Gamal Badr), upon which the "mind of the jurist" and the "human element" are pronounced (Farooq Hassan), derived additionally from sources that are "clearly devised by human knowledge and endeavour" (Shaheen Sardar Ali).[57] Theoretically, this vision of *as-siyar* is compatible with cross-cultural legal reasoning, although, recalling the tension between rationalism and ethical voluntarism, the extent of such compatibility would depend upon the underlying school of Islamic thought.[58]

Returning to the immediate debate over human rights, one way of framing the question is therefore whether the UIDHR, the Cairo Declaration, and related efforts[59] are part of a contemporary *as-siyar* (and, if so, what

56. Majid Khadduri, *The Islamic Law of Nations: Shaybanis Siyar* (Baltimore, MD: Johns Hopkins University Press, 1966), 6.

57. Ali, "The Twain Doth Meet!," 91–93. See also Badr, "A Survey of Islamic International Law."

58. For example, domestic and international laws that emerge from an orthodox jurisprudence rooted in ethical voluntarism are more likely to accord with Thomas Farr's characterization of modern Islamism: "with some important exceptions, [it] admits no legitimate distinction between the sacred and the secular. It is at base a monism that understands the ideal political order as one governed root and branch by divine (or Shari'a) law. Consequently, there is no durable moral or political concept of human freedom, and every reason for the state to employ coercion against the apostate and the infidel . . . .' Thomas F. Farr, "*Dignitatis Humanae* and Religious Freedom in American Foreign Policy: A Practitioner's Perspective," in *After Forty Years: Vatican Council II's Diverse Legacy*, ed. Kenneth D. Whitehead (South Bend, Indiana: St. Augustine's Press, 2007), 240. See also David A. Westbrook, "Islamic International Law and Public International Law: Separate Expressions of World Order," *Virginia Journal of International Law* 33 (1993).

59. For example, see the Tehran Declaration on the Role of Women in Islamic Societies and the Islamabad Declaration on the Role of Muslim Women Parliamentarians in the Promotion of Peace, Progress and Development of Islamic Societies, both of which were adopted from the platform of the OIC. Also interesting is the Arab Charter on Human Rights. Proclaimed by the Council of the League of Arab States in September 1994, the Arab Charter acknowledges *Shari'a* and purports to reaffirm the principles of the UDHR and the ICCPR, alongside those of the Cairo Declaration. Its religious liberty provisions were similarly construable as either comporting with or circumscribing international legal standards. For example, while Article 26 guaranteed freedom of belief, thought and opinion, Article 27 guaranteed free exercise to adherents of every religion without restrictions "except as provided by law." The Charter was revised in May 2004, at which time the phrase "the Islamic *Shari'a*" was replaced by "the noble Islamic religion" and, further, the UDHR and the ICCPR were distinguished from the Cairo Declaration (the principles of the former were reaffirmed, while the latter was held to be regarded).

kind), or whether they owe more to predominantly political rather than religious considerations. Parsing this question is difficult. On the one hand, Muslim nation-states have played vital roles in advocating for Islamic constitutions and international charters, and insofar as the nation-state itself is an imported Western concept, it is unclear whether its representatives have any authority to proclaim Islamic doctrine.[60] At the same time, "[w]hile the modern state technically promulgates laws based in Islam, a transnational and trans-temporal structure of legal authority underpins the application and interpretation of that law. Although his job is to apply the laws of Pakistan, a Pakistani judge may have attended seminary in Cairo ... and rely on jurisprudential texts written in 765 C.E. in what is now Iraq."[61] In light of this complex interplay between domestic, international, and transnational sources of authority, the question of what constitutes contemporary *as-siyar* is inseparable from the question of who (legitimately) speaks for Islam—the answer to which is, of course, highly contested.

Moreover, Muslim societies continue struggling to navigate two discordant currents: first, "resistance, clothed in Islamic rhetoric, against the dominant global economic and political order in order to create a separate Muslim sphere within which the Muslim polity may operate;" but also "the need to engage the broader global order, commercially and politically,

This may represent an attempt to bring the Charter in line with international human rights standards. See Mervat Rishmawi, "The Revised Arab Charter on Human Rights: A Step Forward?," *Human Rights Law Review* 5 (2005). Still, the religious liberty provisions (now consolidated in Article 30) are not unproblematic: 1) Everyone has the right to freedom of thought, conscience and religion and no restrictions may be imposed on the exercise of such freedoms except as provided for by law. 2) The freedom to manifest one's religion or beliefs or to perform religious observances, either alone or in community with others, shall be subject only to such limitations as are prescribed by law and are necessary in a tolerant society that respects human rights and freedoms for the protection of public safety, public order, public health or morals or the fundamental rights and freedoms of others. 3) Parents or guardians have the freedom to provide for the religious and moral education of their children.

60. Mayer, "Book Review," 303. In contrast, Hamid Khan identifies two important international concepts in the OIC Charter: the recognition of international boundaries (i.e., the legitimacy of nation-states as legal actors in the international arena, over and against the classical Islamic *as-siyar* doctrine of *dar al-hab, dar al-Islam* that divides the world according to the realms of belief and unbelief); and the use of nation-state concepts that closely resemble those of a Western nation-state. He interprets both concepts as indicating a willingness and capability on the part of Islamic states to participate in international affairs. Under Khan's reading, the nation-state is a vehicle of, rather than an obstacle to, Islamic legitimacy. Hamid M. Khan, "Nothing Is Written: Fundamentalism, Revivalism, Reformism and the Fate of Islamic Law," *Michigan Journal of International Law* 24 (2002): 329.

61. Naz K. Modirzadeh, "Taking Islamic Law Seriously: INGOs and the Battle for Muslim Hearts and Minds," *Harvard Human Rights Journal* 19 (2006): 202.

in order to restore some level of political and economic power to the Muslim world."[62] If, as Islamic law scholar Haider Ala Hamoudi argues it must be, the call for a return to *Shari'a* is analyzed from within this struggle,[63] then Islamic human rights declarations as *as-siyar* appear both to participate in global legal norms (through the institutional recognition of human rights[64]) and also to agitate against them (through alternate formulations of rights, including rights to religious freedom, that derive from orthodox interpretations of Islamic law and mirror restrictive provisions in the constitutions of Islamic state sponsors like Pakistan and Iran[65]).

This dual character of contemporary *as-siyar*—its inspiration in both the (geo)politics of Muslim states and the doctrines of Islam—suggests that even if "schemes like the Cairo Declaration . . . are designed to shore up the political interests of those promoting them and have only a tenuous connection to Islamic culture,"[66] religion remains highly salient to public discourse within and across Muslim states, to the perceived (il)legitimacy of international human rights norms, and to the push for and cultural resonance of Islamic alternatives. As Hefner summarizes, "it is no exaggeration to suggest that debate over human rights and democracy is today a central issue in a broader culture war now raging in Muslim-majority countries."[67] It is one which, furthermore, involves a struggle between religious and national identities in states including Iran, Turkey, and Egypt, but also in places like Europe.[68]

Thus, while certainly and strongly influenced by politics and historical situation, disparities between international legal standards of religious liberty and Islamic international law must also be understood as "a substantive conflict between formal legal rules generated by competing legal regimes."[69] While the laws and practices of many states (including Western

---

62. Haider Ala Hamoudi, "The Muezzin's Call and the Dow Jones Bell: On the Necessity of Realism in the Study of Islamic Law," *American Journal of Comparative Law* 56 (2008): 423–24.

63. Ibid., 463–70.

64. Ali, "The Twain Doth Meet!," 96–97.

65. Mashood A. Baderin, "The Role of Islam in Human Rights Development in Muslim States," in *Religion, Human Rights and International Law: A Critical Examination of Islamic State Practices*, ed. Javaid Rehman and Susan C. Breau (Boston: Martinus Nijhoff Publishers, 2007), 335–38.

66. Mayer, "Universal Versus Islamic Human Rights," 402.

67. Hefner, "Human Rights and Democracy in Islam," 40.

68. Mahmood Monshipouri, *Muslims in Global Politics: Identities, Interests, and Human Rights* (Philadelphia: University of Pennsylvania Press, 2009).

69. Modirzadeh, "Taking Islamic Law Seriously," 201. For the argument that the universality of religious liberty as a human right has suffered conceptually, in the West from relativism and in the Islamic world from failure to reexamine rigorously and

ones) conflict with human rights law, this particular conflict is unique in that it is with "a parallel and alternative legal order, [one] whose legitimacy is founded on the word of God as revealed to the Prophet Muhammad. . . . Violations arising from Islamic law . . . cannot be attributed merely to a violator state. Indeed, many of the very people suffering from the violations . . . may believe that it is their duty as Muslims to live . . . and even to go prison according to the rules of *Shari'a*."[70] Such is also another reason why modern international law (or, "Western, Christian house law") has not been universally accepted by Muslim communities, some of whom "wish to draw upon their own extensive legal heritage."[71] Some regional and strategic implications of this divergence are the subject of the final section of this chapter, to be followed in the Conclusion by its broader significance for the legal and political dilemmas of this historical moment.

IV. SOME REGIONAL AND STRATEGIC IMPLICATIONS OF THE INTERNATIONAL DEBATE

One of the great challenges in analyzing religious freedom in broad historical and comparative perspective is that its ideational and institutional history is incredibly complex. Appreciating such complexity is necessary to avoid following familiar but flawed narratives into errors of judgment and policy. For example, some activists assert global human rights norms without regard for the ways in which comparative religious context may challenge their content and enforcement. Alternatively, strong proponents of the "clash of civilizations" argument insist that religious differences are so entrenched that we must either make a separate peace or engage in semi-perpetual conflict.

But as prior literature and this book reveal, both positions are deeply problematic—the universalist thesis because it ignores religious

---

sympathetically the Islamic teachings and traditions in support of it, see David Little, Abdulaziz A. Sachedina, and John Kelsay, "Human Rights and the World's Religions: Christianity, Islam, and Religious Liberty," in *Religious Diversity and Human Rights*, ed. Irene Bloom, J. Paul Martin, and Wayne L. Proudfoot (New York: Columbia University Press, 1996), 213–39.

70. Modirzadeh, "Taking Islamic Law Seriously," 201.

71. Samuelson, "Pluralism Betrayed," 335. In contrast, Anthony Chase argues that premising human rights in Muslim-majority states on Islam "risks reifying the notion that Islam monopolizes the Muslim public sphere, rather than leaving room for normative diversity." Anthony Chase, "Liberal Islam and 'Islam and Human Rights': A Sceptic's View," *Religion and Human Rights* 1 (2006): 145.

contributions to and contestations about the form and content of human rights, and the clash thesis because it too easily conflates political and religious identity (e.g., post-colonial Middle Eastern politics and Islam), while obscuring salient differences *within* religious traditions (differences that provide an entry point for productive cross-cultural exchange). These are errors the potential consequences of which grow ever more pressing with time.

For example, the constitutional relationship between mosque and state (with corresponding implications for the provision and extent of religious liberty rights) is very much a live question in Iraq and Afghanistan.[72] The new Iraqi Constitution explicitly acknowledges the concept of human rights,[73] but it also "establishes Islam as the official religion of the State, recognizes Islam as a source of legislation, recognizes Iraq as a part of the Muslim world, guarantees the Islamic identity of its majority, allows Iraqis to choose their personal status law according to Islamic law, and requires that the Federal Supreme Court contain jurists of Islamic Law."[74] From a strictly jurisprudential vantage, it is unclear how these contradictions will (or even could) be resolved.[75]

More immediately, the constitutional commitment to human rights is sharply undermined by the state of religious freedom in the country. Seven months after the return of full sovereignty to the Iraqi people in June 2004 (U.N. Security Council Resolution 1546), elections were held and a Shi'a majority government in coalition with Kurdish political parties ascended to power. Yet despite this democratic display, successive Iraqi governments

72. For example, see Jason Lawrence Reimer, "Finding Their Own Voice? The Afghanistan Constitution: Influencing the Creation of a Theocratic Democracy," *Penn State International Law Review* 25 (2006); Stephen Townley, "Mosque and State in Iraq's New Constitution," *Denver Journal of International Law and Policy* 34 (2006). On theocratic constitutionalism in the two countries, see Larry Cata Backer, "God(s) over Constitutions: International and Religious Transnational Constitutionalism in the 21st Century," *Mississippi College Law Review* 27 (2007–2008).

73. The Constitution of Iraq, http://www.uniraq.org/documents/iraqi_constitution.pdf.

74. Mohamed Y. Mattar, "Unresolved Questions in the Bill of Rights of the New Iraqi Constitution: How Will the Clash between 'Human Rights' and 'Islamic Law' Be Reconciled in Future Legislative Enactments and Judicial Interpretations?," *Fordham International Law Journal* 30 (2006): 127.

75. For additional discussion of these and other challenges that emerged during the drafting of the Iraqi Constitution, see Shahram Akbarzadeh and Benjamin MacQueen, eds., *Islam and Human Rights in Practice: Perspectives across the Ummah* (London: Routledge, 2008). See also Ann Elizabeth Mayer, "The Respective Roles of Human Rights and Islam: An Unresolved Conundrum for Middle Eastern Constitutions," in *Constitutional Politics in the Middle East: With Special Reference to Turkey, Iraq, Iran and Afghanistan*, ed. Said Amir Arjomand (Oxford: Hart Publishing, 2008), 77–97.

have failed to halt human rights abuses that are growing in scope and severity. Instead, there was "a dramatic increase in sectarian violence between Arab Sunni and Shi'a factions, combined with religiously-motivated human rights abuses targeting non-Muslims, secular Arabs, women, homosexuals, and other vulnerable groups."[76]

Of particular concern, the U.S. Commission on International Religious Freedom notes that the Iraqi government has committed human rights violations through its state security forces (some of whose actions fail to discriminate between legitimate terrorist/insurgent targets and ordinary Sunnis marked out for their religious identity); moreover, the government has tolerated religiously motivated attacks (including abductions, beatings, executions, murder, rape, and torture) and other abuses of religious freedom carried out by armed Shi'a factions against Sunnis likewise targeted solely on the basis of religious identity.[77] Non-Muslim minority religious communities (e.g., Chaldo-Assyrian and other Christians, Sabean Mandaeans, and Yazidis) continue to confront similar violence at the hands of Sunni insurgents and foreign jihadiis, as well as "pervasive discrimination and marginalization" by the national and regional governments and by para-state militaries.[78] Even as violence between Sunni and Shi'a groups has at times abated, violent attacks against Christians have surged in recent months, leading to greater displacement of an already much persecuted community.[79]

There are problems in Afghanistan as well. The country's new constitution, adopted in January 2004, recognizes international human rights obligations (including gender equality) and provides non-Muslims with free exercise of religion.[80] Nevertheless, it fails to provide explicitly for individual rights to freedom of religion or belief, allows for the application of Hanafi jurisprudence in the absence of other applicable laws, and states that "no law can be contrary to the beliefs and provisions of the sacred

76. U.S. Commission on Religious Freedom. 2007. *Annual Report.* http://www. uscirf.gov/images/AR_2007/annualreport2007.pdf, 31. See also U.S. Commission on Religious Freedom. 2009. *Annual Report.* http://www.uscirf.gov/images/final% 20ar2009%20with%20cover.pdf, 39–56.

77. U.S. Commission on Religious Freedom. 2007. *Annual Report*, 31.

78. Ibid., 32; U.S. Commission on Religious Freedom. 2010. *Annual Report.* http:// www.uscirf.gov/images/annual%20report%202010.pdf, 67–79.

79. U.S. Commission on Religious Freedom. 2011. *Annual Report.* http://www.uscirf. gov/images/book%20with%20cover%20for%20web.pdf, 88–97.

80. The Constitution of Afghanistan, http://www.supremecourt.gov.af/PDFiles/ constitution2004_english.pdf. For additional discussion of the drafting process, see Mayer, "The Respective Roles of Human Rights and Islam."

religion of Islam."[81] Recent cases, such as that of Abdul Rahman, an Afghan citizen who in March 2006 was arrested and threatened with execution on the charge of changing his religion (formally, for "rejecting Islam"), illustrate the extent to which Muslim individuals can suffer when Islamic law is interpreted contrary to their basic (internationally) guaranteed rights.[82] To date, despite some improvements for the Hazara Shi'as, conditions for religious freedom remain "exceedingly poor" for minority religious communities (especially Christians) and for dissenting members of the Muslim majority.[83]

As one legal scholar summarizes, although Afghanistan and Iraq "are as close to democracy and respect for individual rights as they have been in many years, the elevation of Iranian-style theocrats to many of their key leadership positions remains a serious obstacle along the path to promised freedom."[84] Indeed, a core problem in these and other countries is their deep internal division. In December 2007, for instance, the Associated Press reported on a shouting match that erupted in the Iraqi Parliament when one leading Shi'ite lawmaker (Bahaa al-Araji) claimed to have evidence that a top Sunni politician (Adnan al-Dulaimi) had "branded Shiites 'heretics' and had called their murder legitimate."[85]

These foreign policy scenarios and others demonstrate that in order for Americans to better understand and act upon crucial sources of global conflict—in order for the West to participate intelligently and prudentially in debates about human rights in the Muslim world—the history, content, and role of religion must be the subject of serious inquiry. In the words of Colonel Raymond L. Bingham, Chief, House Liaison Division, U.S. House of Representatives, "we must become students of Islam."[86] Indeed, "[t]he need to understand religious culture as a key element of change in the Middle East is further evidenced by the failure of US and international efforts to effectively engage religious leaders with any measureable consistency."[87]

81. U.S. Commission on Religious Freedom. 2007. *Annual Report*, 227.

82. Ibid., 228. See also U.S. Commission on Religious Freedom. 2008. *Annual Report*. http://www.uscirf.gov/images/annual%20report%202008-final%20edition.pdf, 189–95; 2009. *Annual Report*, 144–48; 2010. *Annual Report*, 204–11.

83. U.S. Commission on Religious Freedom. 2007. *Annual Report*, 215–26.

84. Hannibal Travis, "Freedom or Theocracy?: Constitutionalism in Afghanistan and Iraq," *Northwestern University Journal of International Human Rights* 3 (2005): P121.

85. Thomas L. Friedman, "Making Peace with Pieces," *The New York Times*, December 9, 2007.

86. Raymond L. Bingham, "Bridging the Religious Divide," *Parameters* (Autumn 2006): 51.

87. Ibid., 51.

The same might be said of Europe. As career U.S. foreign service officer Timothy M. Savage observes, the Islamic challenge confronting Europe has two fronts. Internally, "Europe must integrate a ghettoized but rapidly growing Muslim minority that many Europeans view as encroaching upon the collective identity and public values of European society."[88] Externally, Europe is bordered by volatile, primarily Muslim-populated states that represent a security threat. The implications of this situation are sharply contested.

For example, international relations scholar Bassam Tibi argues that while the "Europeanization of Islam" is possible and could benefit both Europe and Islam, the "Islamization of Europe" would come at "enormous cost to both Europe and progressive elements in Islam."[89] Indeed, Tibi rejects political Islam as a transnational, universal religion that seeks to displace rather than coexist with the West.[90] In contrast, political scientist M. Hakan Yavuz challenges the "fear, supremacy, and antagonism" of European elites, claiming that this political moment represents a historic opportunity to forge a democratic pluralistic Muslim world alongside a cosmopolitan and tolerant European identity.[91]

On either view, one crucial question is how Muslims in Europe can define Muslim identity, "including the practical fulfillment of Islamic rules which are part of the *shari'a*—within the framework of European legal orders and societal needs."[92] This is especially challenging when Western European models of church-state relations, unlike Islamic ones, emphasize religious liberty rights and the neutrality of the state in religious matters.[93] Muslim reformer Tariq Ramadan insists that "you don't have to be less Muslim to be more European,"[94] although some Europeans are beginning to wonder whether they are not being asked to be less European in pursuit of

88. Timothy M. Savage, "Europe and Islam: Crescent Waxing, Cultures Clashing," *The Washington Quarterly* 27, no. 3 (Summer 2004): 25.

89. Bassam Tibi, "Europeanizing Islam or the Islamization of Europe: Political Democracy Vs. Cultural Difference," in *Religion in an Expanding Europe*, ed. Timothy A. Byrnes and Peter J. Katzenstein (New York: Cambridge University Press, 2006), 204.

90. Ibid., 205.

91. M. Hakan Yavuz, "Islam and Europeanization in Turkish-Muslim Socio-Political Movements," in *Religion in an Expanding Europe*, ed. Timothy A. Byrnes and Peter J. Katzenstein (New York: Cambridge University Press, 2006), 226.

92. Mathias Rohe, "Applications of Shari'a Rules in Europe - Scope and Limits," *Die Welt des Islams* 44, no. 3 (2004): 324.

93. W.A.R. Shadid and P.S. Van Koningsveld, eds., *Religious Freedom and the Neutrality of the State: The Position of Islam in the European Union* (Leuven, Belgium: Peeters, 2002).

94. "Who's Afraid of Tariq Ramadan?," *Foreign Policy* (November/December 2004).

coexistence with their Muslim neighbors.[95] Thus, while the immediate context is different, the situations in Afghanistan, Iraq, and Europe similarly illustrate the high stakes involved when Africa, Asia, and the Middle East meet the West.

This raises the question of practical action. For example, Middle Eastern scholar Habib C. Malik believes that in Washington, DC, and throughout the West, we should "cultivate a political culture . . . that is sensitive to matters of religious persecution, specifically to the fortunes of non-Muslim minority communities scattered through the Islamic world . . . similar to the heightened awareness that now exists regarding human rights issues."[96] This work has already begun earnestly in Washington, driven in part by the coincidence of several developments in 1997: the publication of two mass press books detailing religious persecution; a State Department report on religious freedom around the world; a private assessment of religious liberty funded by the Pew Charitable Trusts; press coverage of persecution of Christians, especially in a column by A. M. Rosenthal in the *New York Times*; a designated Day of Prayer for the Persecuted Church (November 16) joined in by Protestants and Catholics; and the introduction of the Wolf-Specter bill that would a year later become the International Religious Freedom Act.[97]

These specific acts of consciousness raising and community organizing have been crucial for generating awareness of and responses to the status

---

95. Consider, in addition to protests and death threats connected to Dutch cartoons of the Prophet Mohammad, public reaction to Anglican Archbishop Rowan Williams's statement that the integration of parts of Muslim law into U.K. law was "unavoidable." Noah Feldman, "Why Shariah?," *The New York Times Magazine*, March 16, 2008; Karla Adam, "Archbishop Defends Remarks on Islamic Law in Britain," *The Washington Post*, February 12, 2008. Additionally, when French President Nicolas Sarkozy announced a new Holocaust curriculum for France's schools, some feared that the plan would backfire, "creating resentment among France's ethnic Arab and African populations if they felt their own histories were getting short shrift." Elaine Sciolino, "By Making Holocaust Personal to Pupils, Sarkozy Stirs Anger," *The New York Times*, February 16, 2008. On the sometimes provocative intersection of multiculturalism and race in European debates, see Rachel Donadio, "Amis and Islam," *The New York Times*, March 9, 2008.

96. Habib C. Malik, "Political Islam and the Roots of Violence," in *The Influence of Faith: Religious Groups and U.S. Foreign Policy*, ed. Elliott Abrams (Lanham, MD: Rowman & Littlefield Publishers, Inc. & The Ethics and Public Policy Center, 2001), 138.

97. Samuel P. Huntington, "Religious Persecution and Religious Relevance in Today's World," in *The Influence of Faith: Religious Groups and U.S. Foreign Policy*, ed. Elliott Abrams (Lanham, MD: Rowman & Littlefield Publishers, Inc. & The Ethics and Public Policy Center, 2001), 55. See also J. Bryan Hehir, "Religious Freedom and U.S. Foreign Policy: Categories and Choices," in *The Influence of Faith: Religious Groups and U.S. Foreign Policy*, ed. Elliott Abrams (Lanham, MD: Rowman & Littlefield Publishers, Inc. & The Ethics and Public Policy Center, 2001), 35–37.

of religious freedom as a human right. However, in support of the development of a world legal tradition and in keeping with this book's emphasis upon the *religious* contribution to freedom of religion, three additional strategies merit special emphasis—religious freedom diplomacy, the witness of Western and especially American Muslims, and interfaith dialogue.

In their discussion of faith-based diplomacy, Douglas Johnston and Brian Cox delineate four factors that give religious leaders and institutions an advantage in peacemaking: 1) well-established and pervasive community influence; 2) a reputation as apolitical forces for change based on respected sets of values; 3) special leverage for reconciling conflicting parties; and 4) the capability to mobilize local, national, and global support for a peace process.[98] It is therefore not surprising that religious diplomacy can succeed where other efforts fail, while at times serving as a catalyst for an issue of pivotal importance not just to members of a particular tradition, but to the larger community as well.

For example, Thomas Farr, scholar and practitioner of the "diplomacy of religious freedom," highlights the relationship between Catholic teachings on religious liberty (e.g., *Dignitatis Humanae*) and American foreign policy.[99] He argues that the United States (whose notion of religious liberty influenced the Catholic Church in the development of its doctrine of religious freedom) can regain "its capacity to influence other nations to value religious liberty, both as an aspect of human rights and as a means of promoting justice, stability and peace within and among [the nations of the world]."[100] Additionally, some of the present deficiencies of U.S. international religious freedom policy could be addressed, Farr suggests, by "reverse pollination" from the principles of *Dignitatis Humanae*—a teaching that, moreover, could help U.S. diplomats and Muslim observers to understand how a truth-proclaiming religion might articulate and defend human freedom (even amidst religious and moral pluralism).[101]

98. Douglas Johnston and Brian Cox, "Faith-Based Diplomacy and Preventative Engagement," in *Faith-Based Diplomacy: Trumping Realpolitik*. (New York: Oxford University Press, 2003), 14. Admittedly, with regard to the second factor, religious leaders and institutions often have a decidedly political reputation. The other three factors are less subject to debate, even though they are sometimes context-dependent.
99. Farr, "*Dignitatis Humanae* and Religious Freedom in American Foreign Policy" See also Thomas F. Farr, "The Diplomacy of Religious Freedom," *First Things* (May 2006).
100. Farr, "*Dignitatis Humanae* and Religious Freedom in American Foreign Policy," 238.
101. Ibid., 238.

As presented in Chapter 3, relevant principles include the connection between the religious impulse and human dignity, the importance of and conditions for the search for truth, and the necessity of immunity for all from coercion; in short, "[t]he search for religious truth is innate and necessary to human dignity and flourishing, hence it must be protected by societies and governments."[102] It is noteworthy that Farr champions religious freedom on these grounds *and* as an issue fundamentally linked to American security.[103] His account is persuasive.

In addition to the diplomacy of religious freedom, another kind of diplomacy—the lived testimony of American Muslims—also bears strategic significance. As Farr and others including comparative historical sociologist Jose Casanova have observed, the experience of American Catholics (conveyed most profoundly by John Courtney Murray) was instrumental to the development of religious freedom doctrine in the Catholic Church.[104] Catholics in the United States were witnesses to the fact that a truth-proclaiming religion could prosper in a pluralistic society.

That said, the Second Vatican Council came at a time when intra-Christian tensions were being subsumed under the umbrella of "Judeo-Christianity" into an American civil religion (Robert Bellah), which was understood as Protestant-Catholic-Jew (Will Herberg).[105] Comparative politics scholar Thomas Banchoff invokes this historical backdrop to reveal the "distinctive contours" of today's religious pluralism—features such as the individualization of belief and the proliferation of religious identities and associations, but also "widespread public identification of Islam with terrorism, fed by fear and ignorance."[106] He notes that while the idea of a

102. Ibid., 245–47.

103. See Robert A. Seiple and Dennis Hoover, *Religion and Security: The New Nexus in International Relations* (Lanham, MD: Rowman & Littlefield, 2004); David Waters, "'God Gap' Impedes U.S. Foreign Policy, Task Force Says," *The Washington Post*, February 24, 2010. For a detailed presentation of how to engage in this type of advocacy, see H. Knox Thames, Chris Seiple, and Amy Rowe, *International Religious Freedom Advocacy: A Guide to Organizations, Law, and NGOs* (Waco, TX: Baylor University Press, 2009).

104. On a separate but related point, Casanova recalls Tocqueville: "After examining the tendency of Catholics in America to also become democratic and republican, thus belying the widespread assumption in his own France that Catholicism was a 'natural enemy of democracy,'" Tocqueville concluded that no religious doctrines in the United States were hostile to democratic and republican institutions. "The Religious Situation in the United States 175 Years after Tocqueville" (paper presented at the Working Group on Religion and Politics, Yale University, New Haven, CT, December 13, 2007), 5.

105. Ibid., 6–7.

106. Thomas Banchoff, "The New Religious Pluralism and American Democracy," *Democracy and Society* 3, no. 1 (2005): 1, 9. See also Thomas F. Banchoff, ed. *Religious Pluralism, Globalization, and World Politics* (New York: Oxford University Press, 2008).

religious and cultural heritage shared among Abrahamic faiths is a powerful one, it is also contested and will constitute a crucial and continuing issue.[107]

Insofar as they thrive here, American Muslims are thus positioned to make two fundamental contributions.[108] First, they could bear witness to the Muslim world that religious freedom is compatible with the practice of (at least certain visions of) Islam.[109] Second, they could bear witness to the West (to America *and* to Europe) that peaceful coexistence is possible.[110] These contributions are not inevitable, but they have the potential to be profound. Ramadan puts the matter more strongly:

> [Western] Muslims will get what they deserve: if, as watchful and participating citizens, they study the machinery of their society, demand their rights to equality with others, struggle against all kinds of discrimination and injustice, establish real partnerships beyond their own community and what concerns themselves alone, it will be an achievement that will make political security measures, discrimination, Islamophobic behavior, and so on drift away downstream.[111]

Further, these effects could extend beyond transatlantic borders. Islamic studies scholar John L. Esposito posits that the struggle of diaspora

107. Banchoff, "The New Religious Pluralism and American Democracy," 9.

108. For an interesting study on factors that may inhibit such flourishing, see "The Impact of 9/11 on Muslim American Young People: Forming National & Religious Identity in the Age of Terrorism and Islamophobia," (Washington, DC: Muslim Public Affairs Council, June 2007). In his new role as President Barack Obama's special envoy to the Organization of the Islamic Conference, Rashad Hussain is tasked with bolstering U.S. relations with Muslims here and abroad. Scott Wilson, "Rashad Hussain, a Muslim and New U.S. Envoy, Is Bridge between Two Worlds," *The Washington Post*, March 1, 2010.

109. Peter Berger writes in a similar spirit that " . . . it is of very great interest in the Muslim world . . . if one can show that modernity can come in both secular and religious versions." Peter L. Berger, "Religion and the West," *The National Interest* (Summer 2005): 118.

110. Co-existence in this sense implies some degree of integration. This can be challenging for Muslims who come to America fleeing violence at home, as religious identity becomes, for some, a way of calming the anxieties of dislocation by transcending time and space through the universal community of Islam. Marwa Shoeb, Harvey M. Weinstein, and Jodi Halpern, "Living in Religious Time and Space: Iraqi Refugees in Dearborn, Michigan," *Journal of Refugee Studies* 20 (2007). It can also be a struggle for those who bring tribal and cultural constraints that do not easily comport with Western-style living. Ayaan Hirsi Ali, "Blind Faiths," *The New York Times*, January 6, 2008.

111. Tariq Ramadan, *Western Muslims and the Future of Islam* (New York: Oxford University Press, 2004), 7.

communities in the West has produced a period of dynamic transformation, resulting in the evolution of Islam's development in both Western and Muslim states.[112]

For these reasons, "[i]t is critical that moderates within the American Muslim community be acknowledged and supported rather than undermined in their efforts to play a constructive role in society."[113] This is one reason why controversies such as that surrounding the so-called "Mosque at Ground Zero" are capable of doing tremendous harm to both the American Muslim community and the struggle for religious freedom worldwide.[114] Such conflicts understandably open the United States to charges of hypocrisy and the use of law as a political weapon against Islam, which undermines the ability of American Muslims (as well as Western societies and governments more generally) to argue persuasively for religious freedom and pluralism.

The quality of public debate about these issues turns in part upon the extent to which contributing parties understand the religious claims and motivations involved. Thus, a third strategy for promoting religious liberty involves cross-cultural and interfaith dialogue.[115] If, as this book maintains, differences in religious teachings and traditions are central to disagreements about the nature and scope of religious liberty rights, then the cultivation by all parties of an understanding of others' religious views is quite literally essential to mediating a solution.[116] In one formulation, this can

112. John L. Esposito, "America's Muslims: Issues of Identity, Religious Diversity, and Pluralism," in *Democracy and the New Religious Pluralism*, ed. Thomas Banchoff (New York: Oxford University Press, 2007), 148.

113. J.E. Rash, (Ahmed Abdur Rashid), "Islam at the Crossroads of Extremism and Moderation: New Science, Global Peace, and Democracy," in *Democracy and Religion: Free Exercise and Diverse Visions*, ed. David Odell-Scott (Kent, Ohio: The Kent State University Press, 2004), 151–52.

114. See also Douglas Laycock, "Conference Introduction: American Religious Liberty, French Laicite, and the Veil," *Journal of Catholic Legal Studies* 49 (2010): 41–42.

115. For an example of this from an Islamic perspective, see Tayseir Mandour, "Islam and Religious Freedom: Role of Interfaith Dialogue in Promoting Global Peace," *Brigham Young University Law Review* 2010 (2010). See also "A Common Word between Us and You," an online version of the open letter drafted by Muslim scholars, clerics, and intellectuals declaring a common ground between Christianity and Islam (2007); Benedict XVI, "Address of His Holiness Benedict XVI to Muslim Religious Leaders, Members of the Diplomatic Corps, and Rectors of Universities in Jordan" (May 9, 2009).

116. Peter Berger writes, "The boundary between belief and unbelief, between insiders and outsiders, has become porous and fragile. For the believer this means that he must constantly speak *across* this boundary, even when he speaks to those in his own community." Peter L. Berger, "Orthodoxy and the Pluralistic Challenge," *Greek Orthodox Theological Review* 48, no. 1–4 (2003): 40.

point toward Hans Küng's "global ethic" or Richard W. Bulliet's case for "Islamo-Christian civilization,"[117] though the project at hand neither embraces nor advances their views.

An alternative paradigm is put forth by theologian Chester Gillis, who defines the process of dialogue as involving the following elements: parties who come to the table with specific foundational convictions and historic commitments; determination of their similarities and genuine differences; and openness to other participants (as well as to the possibility that one's own views may evolve as the conversation unfolds).[118] Within such dialogue, religious parties can explore not only their unique beliefs and cultures, but also the content that Richard Falk suggests is common to most religions—an appreciation of suffering, civilizational resonance, an ethos of solidarity, normative horizons, the power of faith, humility and human fallibility, religious identity, and reconciliation.[119]

As Father Richard John Neuhaus eloquently observes, "[t]rue pluralism is the engagement of difference within the bond of civility."[120] It is precisely such engagement that the formation of a world legal tradition requires, if (to paraphrase Berman) the forces of world integration are to triumph over those of world disintegration, not in the spirit of pride, but guided by love of neighbor and with full respect for the diversity of its constitutive elements. That is, without doubt, an ambitious project; it is also one of the

117. See Editorial Committee of the "Council" of the Parliament of the World's Religions, "Declaration toward a Global Ethic,"(1993); Richard W. Bulliet, *The Case for Islamo-Christian Civilization* (New York: Columbia University Press, 2004); Jose Casanova, "The Sacralization of the Humanum: A Theology for a Global Age," *International Journal of Politics, Culture & Society* 13, no. 1 (1999): 21–40.

118. See Chester Gillis, *Pluralism: A New Paradigm for Theology* (Louvain, Belgium: Peeters Press, 1993); Chester Gillis, "Christian Approaches to Interreligious Dialogue," *Louvain Studies* 22 (1997): 15–38. This appears consistent with a recent agreement between the Holy See and the Arab League in favor of "'peace, security and regional and international stability' and increased attention to inter-religious dialogue." "Agreement between Vatican and Arab League," *AsiaNews.it* (April 23, 2009). For specific discussion of Catholic teachings on religious freedom in relation to Islam and inter-religious dialogue, see Gavin D'Costa, "Hermeneutics and the Second Vatican Council's Teachings: Establishing Roman Catholic Theological Grounds for Religious Freedoms in Relation to Islam. Continuity or Discontinuity in the Catholic Tradition?," *Islam and Christian-Muslim Relations* 20, no. 3 (July 2009): 277–90.

119. Richard A. Falk, *Religion and Humane Global Governance* (New York: Palgrave, 2001), 30–31.

120. Richard John Neuhaus, speech delivered to the American Jewish Committee National Convention, *Religious Liberty, Freedom of Conscience* (May 16, 1986).

most pressing legal and political imperatives of the current age. As international relations scholar Daniel Philpott concludes:

> Religious freedom embodies the moral challenge of an international system that is beginning to move past Westphalia. ... In today's world, the most difficult questions will be ones over rights and values that some argue to be universal and some argue to be the ideals of one aggrandizing civilization. . .. The heritage of the human rights tradition suggests that religious freedom is a universal right. But if it is to enjoy a popular global consensus that matches its prominence in international treaties, then such a consensus must be forged — slowly, carefully, through a process of vigorous and mutual dialogue.[121]

The philosophical and theological framework for building that consensus, and its urgency in light of threats to religious liberty not just in the Muslim world but also in the West, are explored in the Conclusion.

121. Daniel Philpott, "Diversity or Cacophony?: New Sources of Norms in International Law," *Michigan Journal of International Law* 25 (2004): 997.

CHAPTER 7

Conclusion

Toward a World Legal Tradition

Although "Islamic states from Egypt to Malaysia have endorsed rule of law," the seductive neutrality of this concept should not be employed "to hide contested normative views about human rights."[1] Indeed, insofar as Islamic international law is underwritten by a fundamentally different legal order than that of public international law,[2] and insofar as it arrives at definitions of religious freedom that diverge significantly from global human rights norms, it challenges not just the existence but the very possibility of universal human rights.

Thus, while it may be true that international human rights law provides general direction and not "a plan of implementation that can be applied mechanically, irrespective of political, economic, and cultural diversity,"[3]

---

1. Randall Peerenboom, "Human Rights and Rule of Law: What's the Relationship?," *Georgetown Journal of International Law* 36 (2005): 825, 944.
2. A fact that makes legal pluralism (e.g., formal recognition of parallel religious legal systems) more complicated than many scholars acknowledge. For an instructive overview of the literature on legal pluralism, see Paul Schiff Berman, "Towards a Jurisprudence of Hybridity," *Utah Law Review* 2010 (2010); Paul Schiff Berman, "A Pluralist Approach to International Law," *Yale Journal of International Law* 32 (2007). For an outstanding introduction to the legal, philosophical, and theological implications of Islamic law in the Western world, see Rex Ahdar and Nicholas Aroney, eds. *Shari'a in the West* (New York: Oxford University Press, 2010). Also, for an illuminating discussion of specific issues raised by Islamic law in the European context, see Jorgen S. Nielsen and Lisbet Christofferson, eds., *Shari'a as Discourse: Legal Traditions and the Encounter with Europe*, Cultural Diversity and Law (Farnham, UK: Ashgate Publishing Limited, 2010).
3. Michael J. Perry, "A Right to Religious Freedom? The Universality of Human Rights, the Relativity of Culture," *Roger Williams University Law Review* 10 (2005): 417.

it is also doubtful that the bands of diversity can stretch to accommodate, for example, "Sharia-based punishments that the international rights regime condemns as cruel and inhumane, . . . the status and treatment of women [in Islamic fundamentalism,] . . . [or] the clash between theocracy and (liberal) democracy."[4] Two distinct, but related, problems follow from this: how to manage the challenges to the universality of human rights that emerge under conditions of religious pluralism generally, and what to do in the specific case of Islam.

Because of the rising salience of religion in world affairs, religious plural-ism has been the subject of several recent commentaries. Robin Lovin, a theorist of political ethics, writes that normative religious pluralism (i.e., a condition in which "religious diversity is encouraged and protected by social practices and sometimes by law") is upheld in most modern democ-racies and tends to result from political pluralism.[5] On this view, political reforms would almost certainly be necessary before Muslim states with recent histories of authoritarianism could generate and sustain the cultural transformations that would enable more robust protections of religious freedom. Other scholars look to the European Court of Human Rights and its "margin of appreciation" for a model of how to incorporate "a jurispru-dence of diversity within universal human rights."[6] However, this margin "cannot be invoked to avoid implementation of any particular right, or even to redefine the right with a view to regional or cultural preferences . . ." —a fact to which decisions like *Leyla Şahin v. Turkey* attest.[7]

Islamic law scholar Mohammad H. Fadel appeals to John Rawls, sug-gesting that public reason could serve as a useful strategy for principled reconciliation of Islamic law and international human rights law.[8] Fadel argues, for example, "that much of the current conflict between the

4. Peerenboom, "Human Rights and Rule of Law: What's the Relationship?," 819. For a discussion of some options for dealing with *Hudad* offenses (which are subject to harsh punishments) in a modern Islamic state, see Edna Boyle-Lewicki, "Need World's Collide: The Hudad Crimes of Islamic Law and International Human Rights," *New York International Law Review* 13 (2000).

5. Robin W. Lovin, "Religion and Political Pluralism," *Mississippi College Law Review* 27 (2007–2008): 91–92.

6. Douglas Lee Donoho, "Autonomy, Self-Governance, and the Margin of Appreciation: Developing a Jurisprudence of Diversity within Universal Human Rights," *Emory International Law Review* 15 (2001).

7. Johan D. van der Vyver, "Universality and Relativity of Human Rights: American Relativism," *Buffalo Human Rights Law Review* 4 (1998): 49–50.

8. For example, see Mohammad H. Fadel, "Public Reason as a Strategy for Principled Reconciliation: The Case of Islamic Law and International Human Rights Law," *Chicago Journal of International Law* 8 (2007).

substantive norms of human rights law and Islamic law could be resolved if human rights justifications were grounded in an overlapping political consensus rather than in foundational metaphysical doctrines that are necessarily controversial."[9] This is not altogether different from international relations theorist Jack Donelly's argument that philosophical consensus on the foundation of human rights is unnecessary in view of the practical consensus that exists.[10] Similarly, legal philosopher Martha Nussbaum links Roger Williams with Rawls, asserting that equal respect as a value can only be secured by the separation of "key moral/political values from religious ideas,"[11] in pursuit of an overlapping consensus, underwritten by the fact that citizens "respect their fellow citizens as fully free and equal . . . [thus limiting] the ways in which they will seek to enact" their religious and secular comprehensive doctrines.[12]

Though well-intentioned, these analytical moves are unpersuasive for this debate precisely because Rawlsian liberalism denies the ultimacy of the very types of religious meaning and argument that animate it. International human rights treaties are one measure of this purported political or practical consensus, and insofar as those pertaining to religious liberty are continually violated by signatories with a common religious-cultural orientation, there is good reason to suspect that the absence of an underlying philosophical consensus does indeed matter and that practical consensus will not suffice. International law theorist David Bederman, comparing Berman's notion of world law with Rawls's argument in *The Law of Peoples*, rightfully notes that Berman's vision exists beyond the realm of pure theory

9. Ibid., 701.

10. Jack Donelly, *Universal Human Rights in Theory and Practice* (Ithaca, NY: Cornell University Press, 1989).

11. Steven D. Smith has recently argued that it is precisely these secular rationalist constraints that impoverish public discourse by preventing citizens from "openly presenting, examining, and debating the sources and substance of our most fundamental normative commitments." Steven D. Smith, *The Disenchantment of Secular Discourse* (Cambridge, MA: Harvard University Press, 2011), 211. See also Eduardo Mendieta and Jonathan Vanantwerpen, eds., *The Power of Religion in the Public Sphere* (New York: Columbia University Press, 2011).

12. Martha C. Nussbaum, *Liberty of Conscience: In Defense of America's Tradition of Religious Equality* (New York: Basic Books, 2008), 361–62. See also Jean Leca, "Political Philosophy in Political Sience: Sixty Years on (Part II: Current Features of Contemporary Political Philosophy)," *International Political Science Review* 32, no. 1 (2011): 95–113. To interject some realism into this debate as it concerns religious liberty, this book has documented the explicit failure of many states and citizens to treat their fellow citizens as free and equal human beings worthy of respect. Consider the situation of apostates and religious minorities.

and is supported by facts and institutions on the ground.[13] Moreover, and of particular significance for this book, Bederman observes that Berman is influenced by shared religious and moral values among peoples.[14] Conflicts and consensus in international human rights law can be neither understood nor resolved solely through present-day liberalism. Religious beliefs and practices are an essential part of the conversation.

As part of his effort to develop a theory of religious freedom in international law, Peter Danchin thus argues for value pluralism, which "holds that the freedom to manifest religion or belief does not include the right of Muslims in Europe, or any other majority or minority religious group, to elevate their faith into the established faith governing all others in a political regime," but also requires that secular Enlightenment Europeans reassess their own tendency "to treat belief as neatly separable from disciplinary practices, cultural routines, and the education of sensory experience."[15] Danchin challenges the "dogmatic assertion" that the Kantian quest for the coexistence of multiple faiths in the same public space can only be accomplished in one way (i.e., the relegation by classical liberal theory of religion to the private realm), and calls for an "*ethos* of engagement in public life among a plurality of controversial theistic and nontheistic perspectives."[16] Insofar as "value pluralism" acknowledges a role for religion in shaping public discourse about law, this is helpful, although it remains unclear how actual legal controversies would be resolved.

Somewhat similarly, law and religion scholar Mark Modak-Truran calls for "a new constructive postmodern paradigm of law and religion that embraces legal indeterminacy as a structural characteristic of law which allows for a plurality of religious convictions to implicitly legitimate the law. . . ."[17] On his account, religious pluralism renders outdated or erroneous the unitary religious (pre-modern) or secular (modern) legitimation of law; hence, law should be desecularized in a way that allows for the

---

13. David J. Bederman, "World Law Transcendent," *Emory Law Journal* 54 (2005): 72–73; John Rawls, *The Law of Peoples* (Cambridge, MA: Harvard University Press, 2001).

14. Bederman, "World Law Transcendent," 73.

15. Peter G. Danchin, "Suspect Symbols: Value Pluralism as a Theory of Religious Freedom in International Law," *Yale Journal of International Law* 33 (2008): 61; Peter G. Danchin, "Of Prophets and Proselytes: Freedom of Religion and the Conflict of Rights in International Law," *Harvard International Law Journal* 49 (2008).

16. Danchin, "Suspect Symbols: Value Pluralism as a Theory of Religious Freedom in International Law," 61.

17. Mark C. Modak-Truran, "Beyond Theocracy and Secularism (Part I): Toward a New Paradigm of Law and Religion," *Mississippi College Law Review* 27 (2007–2008): 166.

plurality of religions and comprehensive convictions in a culture.[18] Modak-Truran's analysis is especially instructive with regard to weaknesses in the legal theories of Rawls, as well as those in Weber, Habermas, and French secularism—theories that "[aspire] to make the law secular or neutral as among different religious convictions."[19] Yet here, too, there does not appear to be a means for reconciling deep conflicts over the substantive content of law: how would the law provide for and protect religious liberty rights if certain groups, religious or secular, refused to legitimate them?

In responding to these challenges of religious pluralism, others variously posit: the importance of democratic processes for legitimating international norms in domestic Arab political contexts[20]; the need to recognize that religious liberty evolved as a human right in the West over hundreds of years (that is, human rights norms are accepted and sustained only when they are enculturated over time)[21]; and that freedom of religion is merely a specific application of more general basic liberties and can thus be dispensed with as a category of separate enumeration.[22] The second of these claims may be historically accurate, but it is not very helpful for thinking about how to move forward. The third one is simply unsustainable for many reasons discussed throughout this book (e.g., the crucial link between religious freedom and the protection of other human rights). Therefore, while each of these models sheds light on different aspects of the problem, none offers sufficient means for overcoming conflicts between competing legal, moral, and political ontologies, especially at the level of international law.

Of course, another option is to deny this way of framing the debate altogether. For instance, human rights activist Audrey Guichon claims that

18. Ibid: 231.
19. Ibid: 201–22.
20. David Mednicoff, "The Importance of Being Quasi-Democratic: The Domestication of International Human Rights in American and Arab Politics," *Victoria University of Wellington Law Review* 38 (2007). The longer-term consequences of the "Arab spring" will be particularly interesting to observe in this regard.
21. Christopher Marsh and Daniel P. Payne, "The Globalization of Human Rights and the Socialization of Human Rights Norms," *Brigham Young University Law Review* 2007 (2007): 684.
22. James W. Nickel, "Who Needs Freedom of Religion?," *University of Colorado Law Review* 76 (2005). Legal philosopher Brian Leiter makes the related argument that religious conscience claims do not warrant special protection vis-à-vis claims of conscience generally. Brian Leiter, "Foundations of Religious Liberty: Toleration or Respect?," *San Diego Law Review* 47 (2010): 957–58. Andrew Koppelman summarizes Leiter's views thus: "[T]here is no good reason for law to single out religion for special treatment and religion is not an apt candidate for respect in the 'think' sense of being an object of favorable appraisal." Constitutional scholar Andrew Koppelman, "How Shall I Praise Thee? Brian Leiter on Respect for Religion," *San Diego Law Review* 47 (2010): 961–62.

because human rights offer the best protection for human dignity, the universalist project is justified: it wants only for consideration of some cultural claims, and then human rights will be understood, experienced, mainstreamed, and legitimized—in Muslim communities and elsewhere.[23] Likewise, while recognizing that some cultural traditions will clash with global human rights norms, international law scholar Susan Breau maintains that human rights can be protected in *any* cultural context.[24] This assertion is virtually irreconcilable with the empirical evidence presented throughout Chapters 5 and 6. It is unclear, for example, how the right to covert away from Islam would be protected in a culture animated by Islamic fundamentalism and the jurisprudence of apostasy.

In one sense, however, Pope John Paul II agreed with Guichon and Breau, for he insisted upon the universality of human rights. When he first addressed the U.N. in October 1979, the Pope defended basic human rights as "the moral foundation of any just polity and of any international order capable of fostering peace among nations."[25] Between then and the time of his second U.N. address in 1995, two focal events transpired. First, the Revolution of 1989 seemed to prove "the trans-cultural moral power of human rights claims and the political potency of dedicated, often religiously-motivated human rights movements."[26] Yet, as George Weigel explains, the dissolution of Communism was also accompanied by new voices challenging the universality of human rights, initially those of East Asian autocrats, who were then joined at the Vienna World Conference on Human Rights in June 1993 by militant Islamists intent on denouncing the Universal Declaration of Human Rights.[27]

Responding to the growing threat of relativism, John Paul II insisted in his 1995 U.N. address upon the global character of the human rights revolution—one that was structured internally by a common moral core "discern[able] amidst the vast diversity of the world's cultures," essential to

23. Audrey Guichon, "Some Arguments on the Universality of Human Rights in Islam," in *Religion, Human Rights and International Law: A Critical Examination of Islamic State Practices*, ed. Javaid Rehman and Susan C. Breau (Boston: Martinus Nijhoff Publishers, 2007), 193–94.

24. Susan C. Breau, "Human Rights and Cultural Relativism: The False Dichotomy," in *Religion, Human Rights and International Law: A Critical Examination of Islamic State Practices*, ed. Javaid Rehman and Susan C. Breau (Boston: Martinus Nijhoff Publishers, 2007), 163.

25. George Weigel, "Roman Catholicism in the Age of John Paul II," in *The Desecularization of the World*, ed. Peter L. Berger (Grand Rapids, MI: Ethics and Public Policy Center & William B. Eerdmans Publishing Co., 1999), 25.

26. Ibid., 25.

27. Ibid., 26.

the very possibility of international politics (provided politics is understood as "mutual deliberation about the common good"), dependent in the
first instance upon religious freedom, and capable of being engaged by all
rational persons (i.e., it was not theologically specific).[28] This last point
echoes the approach in *Dignitatis Humanae*, which, by opening with a natural law defense of religious freedom, claims a universality grounded in
reason (albeit one supplemented by revelation).[29]

Whether Islam is similarly open to arguments based on reason (rather
than divine will) has been the subject of recent controversies involving
Pope Benedict XVI.[30] Much appears to depend upon the extent to which
Muslim intellectuals (including those who draw on rationalist strains of
Islamic thought) succeed in developing cultural and political support for
their religious reformism. This bears directly on the question of Islamic
international law, for while the contemporary *as-siyar* of the UIDHR and
the Cairo Declaration are incompatible with accepted international standards of religious liberty and thereby threaten the universality of human
rights, alternate interpretations of Islamic law and thought could (at least
theoretically) generate Islamic defenses and formulations of religious
human rights.[31]

28. Ibid., 26–28.
29. Thus, while this book agrees with David Sehat's claim that "morality . . . enforced
by law must be tied to reason," the embrace of reason allows, indeed, is supported
by some types of explicitly religious arguments. David Sehat, *The Myth of American
Religious Freedom* (New York: Oxford University Press, 2011), 290.
30. Benedict XVI, "Meeting with the Representatives of Science, 'Regensburg
Lecture,'" (September 12, 2006); James V. Schall, S.J., "God as Logos, Allah as Will,"
Zenit (October 3, 2006); "Benedict on Islam," *Commonweal* (October 6, 2006); "Open
Letter to His Holiness Pope Benedict XVI by 38 Leading Muslim Scholars and Leaders,"
Islamica Magazine (October 12, 2006); Ian Fisher, "Pope Prays in Turkey with Muslim
and Orthodox Leaders," *The New York Times*, December 1, 2006; Ian Fisher, "Vatican
Security Worries over Bin Laden Tape," *The New York Times*, March 21, 2008. See also
James V. Schall, *The Regensburg Lecture* (South Bend, IN: St. Augustine's Press, 2007);
Robert Reilly, *The Closing of the Muslim Mind* (Wilmington, DE: ISI Books, 2010).
31. But see Bassam Tibi, *Islam's Predicament with Modernity: Religious Reform and
Cultural Change* (New York: Routledge, 2009). Tibi argues that contemporary *Shari'a*,
embedded in *fiqh* orthodoxy, is an invention of political Islam—one that contradicts
democratic constitutionalism and is not open to religious reform. While he does not
reject *Shari'a* altogether, he characterizes it as a morality that was "developed by Islamic
scribes into a kind of divine civil law . . . [but one that] was never a constitutional or
state law as it is now promoted by the Islamists in the context of the shari'atization
of Islam" (128). Tibi does not believe that legal reform in Islam is yet in sight, but he
salutes the "tiny minority" of Muslims within the *umma* who persevere in such efforts,
despite the often great personal cost (128–29). Elsewhere, he identifies the conflict
between Islamic law and human rights as being one of global civilization (which he
identifies as being man (reason)-centered), and pre-modern cultures grouped in
regional civilizations (which he identifies with "a cosmological theocentric view of the

At a macro-level, this might involve Islamic law scholar Abdullahi A. An-Na'im's model of "internal discourse—cross-cultural dialogue," which stresses "the importance of domestic cultural legitimacy for the successful implementation of international human rights standards primarily in areas of perceived conflict between human rights and Islam."[32] Indeed, the desire of many Muslims to tap their own cultural resources, including *Shari'a*, has kindled efforts to elaborate the Islamic foundation of human rights and the Qur'anic authorization of religious liberty.[33]

For instance, attributing the admittedly significant differences between the West and Islam on matters of religious liberty to dissimilar cultural and historical experiences, religious studies expert Abdulaziz A. Sachedina employs an exegesis of the Qur'an to argue that various theological and philosophical roots of Western principles of religious freedom have

world"). Bassam Tibi, "Islamic Law/Shari'a, Human Rights, Universal Morality and International Relations," *Human Rights Quarterly* 16 (1994): 297. Tibi's classification appears contrary to the Catholic position that faith and reason are not only compatible, but also essentially related. This position traces back in part to Thomas Aquinas, who asserted the importance of argument by reason for engaging with those who do not share a common theology (e.g., at the time of his writing, medieval Islamic philosophers). *Summa Contra Gentiles*, trans. Anton C. Pegis (Notre Dame, IN: University of Notre Dame Press, 2009).

32. For an example of this framework applied in the American context, see Elizabeth M. Bruch, "Whose Law Is It Anyway? The Cultural Legitimacy of International Human Rights in the United States," *Tennessee Law Review* 73 (2006): 677; in the Iranian context, see Anicée (Anisseh) Van Engeland, "Human Rights Strategies to Avoid Fragmentation of International Law as a Threat to Peace: The Islamic Republic of Iran as a Case Study," *Interdisciplinary Journal of Human Rights Law* 5 (2010–11): 25–47. Also, for an attempt to build upon but also modify An-Na'im's model in the Islamic context, see Jason Morgan-Foster, "A New Perspective on the Universality Debate: Reverse Moderate Relativism in the Islamic Context," *ILSA Journal of International and Comparative Law* 10 (2003). An-Na'im elaborates on this in great detail in his recent work, Abdullahi A. An-Na'im, *Muslims and Global Justice* (Philadelphia: University of Pennsylvania Press, 2011).

33. See Guichon, "Some Arguments on the Universality of Human Rights;" Noor ul-Amin Leghari, "The Concept of Justice and Human Rights in Islam," in *Justice and Human Rights in Islamic Law*, ed. Gerald E. Lampe (Washington, DC: International Law Institute, 1997); Mashood A. Baderin, "The Role of Islam in Human Rights Development in Muslim States," in *Religion, Human Rights and International Law: A Critical Examination of Islamic State Practices*, ed. Javaid Rehman and Susan C. Breau (Boston: Martinus Nijhoff Publishers, 2007), 321–58. But see Ann Elizabeth Mayer, "Current Muslim Thinking on Human Rights," in *Human Rights in Africa: Cross-Cultural Perspectives*, ed. Abdullahi A. An-Na'im and Francis M. Deng (Washington, DC: The Brookings Institution, 1990), 154. Mayer notes, "it is highly significant that Muslims are showing a growing eagerness to incorporate international human rights protections in their legal systems and that the resistance to this in the name of applying Islamic law is largely emanating from governments and ideologues of movements aspiring to governmental power."

counterparts in Qur'anic teachings.[34] Alternatively, Middle Eastern scholar Majid Khadduri, observing that "justice would be meaningless if the fundamental rights of man were to be unrecognized or ignored by society," qualifies the freedom to change one's religion in Islam: to turn one's back on Islam after adopting it is apostasy, but "in matters pertaining to human conscience, it is inconceivable that God would prescribe death, [as] the Revelation . . . clearly stated that there should be no compulsion in religion."[35]

In a creative synthesis of old and new, Islamic law and human rights scholar Khaled Abou El Fadl suggests that *Shari'a*'s historic purpose of fulfilling the welfare of the people—constituted by necessities (*daruriyyat*), needs (*hajiyyat*) and luxuries (*kamaliyyat*)—could ground a systematic theory of individual rights based on the five basic values of the *daruriyyat* (e.g., religion, life, intellect, honor, and property).[36] Under such a system, protection of the basic value of religion could be achieved by religious liberty rights. In a similar spirit, Islamic political theorist Ahmad S. Moussalli traces the classical and medieval roots of religious rights in Islam (*al-huquq al-shar'iyya*) and their incorporation into modern Islamist conceptions of human rights.[37]

Of special interest, Moussalli describes the text of a pact (*mithaq*) published and distributed by Muhammad al-Hashim al-Hamidi to other Islamists. It states, in pertinent part: "[t]he success of the Islamic movement after it takes control of government hinges on establishment of a just and democratic system in the Arab world. Lifting the community from the tyranny that it has been plunged into necessitates that any such movement establish limits and a program for justice, *shura*, and human rights."[38] Equal rights for women and minorities, as well as freedom of thought, belief,

34. David Little, John Kelsay, and Abdulaziz A. Sachedina, *Human Rights and the Conflict of Cultures: Western and Islamic Perspectives on Religious Liberty* (Columbia: University of South Carolina Press, 1988), 53–90. On natural law in the Qur'an, see Ali Bardakoglu, "The Concept of Justice in Islamic Jurisprudence," in *Justice and Human Rights in Islamic Law*, ed. Gerald E. Lampe (Washington, DC: International Law Institute, 1997), 65–78.

35. Majid Khadduri, *The Islamic Conception of Justice* (Baltimore, MD: The Johns Hopkins University Press, 1984), 239.

36. Khaled Abou El Fadl, "The Human Rights Commitment in Modern Islam," in *Human Rights and Responsibilities in the World Religions*, ed. Joseph Runzo, Nancy M. Martin, and Arvind Sharma (Oxford, UK: Oneworld Publications, 2003), 332–33.

37. Ahmad S. Moussalli, *The Islamic Quest for Democracy, Pluralism, and Human Rights* (Gainesville: University Press of Florida, 2001).

38. Ibid., 156–57.

expression, and religion are among the specific rights enumerated.[39] Such is preliminary but notable evidence that Islamic legal and political institutions may yet, over time and with support, move toward greater compliance with international legal standards of religious freedom.

This brings us to the theoretical questions with which this book opened: whether a world legal tradition has begun to, or could yet, emerge; and what role such a tradition might play in transforming the dilemma of religious freedom. Recall that, for Berman, "world law" includes public international law, as well as the contractual and customary legal norms governing cross-border relations. Human rights law is an integral part of public international law. Thus, to the extent that the Universal Islamic Declaration of Human Rights and the Cairo Declaration on Human Rights in Islam represent a countermodel of human rights (one that conflicts with global legal norms concerning religious liberty), it would be difficult to characterize contemporary *as-siyar* as part of a (new) *jus gentium*. In such a case, the dilemma of religious freedom would appear to hold: the universality of religious human rights could not be secured alongside institutional recognition of formulations based on *Shari'a*.

Yet the fundamentalist understanding of Islam embodied in these declarations is not the only one. Muslim reformers, many of whom build on centuries-old rationalist currents in Islamic thought, offer an alternative vision of *Shari'a*—one that preserves a role for religion and religious influence in legal and political institutions (and hence may be more capable than Western models of securing cultural legitimacy in Muslim states), but one that is also oriented toward just and democratic laws that accord with international standards of human rights. Under this vision, the dilemma of religious freedom might yet be transformed: the baseline scope and content of religious liberty could perhaps be universalized, even as diverse religious and philosophical principles were invoked to legitimate the resulting laws and institutions.

---

39. For a rich and wide-ranging discussion of women and Islamic law, see Lynn Welchman, *Women and Muslim Family Laws in Arab States*, ed. Annelies Moors, Mathijs Pelkmans, Abdulkader Tayob, ISIM Series on Contemporary Muslim Societies (Amsterdam: Amsterdam University Press, 2007). See also Karima Bennoune, "Secularism and Human Rights: A Contextual Analysis of Headscarves, Religious Expression, and Women's Equality under International Law," *Columbia Journal of Transnational Law* 45 (2007); Roja Fazaeli, "All in the Family? Islam, Women, and Human Rights: A Conference Report," *Religion and Human Rights* 1 (2006): 305–10; Courtney W. Howland, "The Challenge of Religious Fundamentalism to the Liberty and Equality Rights of Women: An Analysis under the United Nations Charter," *Columbia Journal of Transnational Law* 35 (1997).

This appears to be in part what Berman meant by a world legal tradition: mutual recognition of and respect for the distinct moral and historical bases of law across cultures. It is one that, moreover, embraces "common features of the various legal systems of the peoples of the world."[40] Indeed, the forging of a world legal tradition could arguably constitute a new type of foundational consensus based on respect for the religious (and not just the secular) foundations of law, thereby increasing the possibility that political consensus on religious liberty, and perhaps other human rights issues, could be achievable and lasting.

However, while the elements of a world legal tradition are to be found in the intellectual and institutional resources of the Western and Islamic worlds, the emergence of such a tradition is not inevitable. Tensions between competing factions within Muslim societies (and the opposing Islamic schools that they represent) are serious, often violent, and very much an ongoing concern. At stake are many pressing legal and political issues, not least of which are the universality of human rights, generally, and the protection of religious freedom (that "first right") in particular.

Moreover, new threats to religious freedom are emerging in Western states. While it is true that certain formulations of Islam threaten religious liberty in the Muslim world, it is also true that increasing hostility to religion in some parts of the West threatens religious liberty in the place of its birth. Such is why the debate over religious freedom must be reframed to account for comparative religious context (i.e., not just the contributions of Islamic law to Muslim states, but also Judeo-Christian contributions to the Western legal tradition[41]). Thus, to conclude, this book offers some preliminary observations regarding law and religion in the contemporary West. These ideas are related to or suggested by this project's findings, but in need of further research and development.

Three years ago, European political theorists Phillip Blond and Adrian Pabst published a piece in the *New York Times* under the headline "Integrating Islam into the West."[42] Writing shortly after Archbishop Rowan Williams made intensely controversial remarks regarding the adoption by Britain of

40. Harold J. Berman, "World Law: An Ecumenical Jurisprudence of the Holy Spirit," Emory University School of Law Public Law and Legal Theory Research Paper Series 05–4 (February 2005): 13.

41. See, for example, John Witte, Jr. and Frank S. Alexander, eds., *Christianity and Human Rights: An Introduction* (New York: Cambridge University Press, 2010). See also Zachary R. Calo, "Human Rights and Healthy Secularity," *Journal of Catholic Social Thought* 7, no. 2 (2010): 1–21.

42. Phillip Blond and Adrian Pabst, "Integrating Islam into the West," *The New York Times*, February 14, 2008.

certain aspects of *Shari'a* law (with the goal of integrating Britain's growing Muslim population), they insightfully observe that "the genuine target of the archbishop's lecture is the increasingly authoritarian and anti-religious nature of the modern liberal state." The concern over "militant secularism" and freedom of religion or belief is thus linked with broader Western fears about "the consequences of failing to integrate a growing, devout and alienated Islamic minority within a relativistic and increasingly aggressive secular culture."

Anticipating recent statements by German Chancellor Angela Merkel and British Prime Minister David Cameron denouncing state multiculturalism as a failure, Blond and Pabst note that "communities sharing the same space but leading separate lives" serves to segregate rather than integrate, while damaging "any conception of a common good binding on all citizens." Instead of Europe's problematic secular models of integration, which they argue have failed (citing Britain, the Netherlands, Germany, and France as examples), they point to the American model—one that, by allowing for public expression of religion and individual rights alongside the relative autonomy of religious communities, has substantially removed the dichotomous choice between loyalty to the state and loyalty to one's faith. Echoing Chapter 6, they suggest that this may explain why American Muslims are better integrated than their European counterparts.

Blond and Pabst conclude, provocatively, that "[o]nly a new settlement with religion can successfully incorporate the growing religious minorities in Western Europe;" moreover, this settlement can only be achieved by the recovery of Europe's Christian roots. Why? Because "[o]nly Christianity can integrate other religions into a shared European project by acknowledging what secular ideologies cannot: a transcendent objective truth that exceeds human assertion but is open to rational discernment and debate." The proper response to religious pluralism is thus the Christian accomplishment of a non-secular model of the common good that is "the only basis for the political integration of Muslims and peaceful coexistence."

A scholarly discussion and defense of several of these themes has recently been offered by British theologian John Milbank.[43] As a preliminary matter, Milbank expands the framework to include both Judaism and Christianity. His focus is on the latter, but he acknowledges that Jewish resources are available to defend religious liberty against secularist

43. John Milbank, "Shari'a and the True Basis of Group Rights: Islam, the West, and Liberalism," in *Shari'a in the West*, ed. Rex Ahdar and Nicholas Aroney (New York: Oxford University Press, 2010), 136–57.

challenges and, centrally for his argument, support a corporatist constitutionalism that is able to comprehend "the other" (thereby providing for constitutional pluralism).[44] Rabbi David Novak draws upon Jewish tradition to offer a vigorous defense of religious liberty and human rights, which, read in tandem with Milbank's piece, illuminates many theological and philosophical commonalities between the two religious traditions that are relevant to these legal-political challenges.[45]

In any event, while Milbank's essay engages several issues of profound significance for the relationship between church and state, as well as between the West and Islam (particularly Islamic law in Western states), his discussion of religious liberty is especially relevant to this book. Milbank cautions that while the European Union "still declares that religious liberty . . . has priority over all other rights," this priority is "rooted in an ultimately Christian and not secular background. . . ."[46] There is nothing to stop a secular legal order from asserting its authority over religious bodies in the event of a conflict (e.g., a dispute about whether or not women should be ordained), and Milbank warns that many legal thinkers are beginning to move in precisely this direction. Indeed, he notes that "[s]ome secular thinkers actually now wish to abolish the right to religious freedom."[47]

This, according to Milbank (and also Blond and Pabst), is Williams's real concern—the growing hostility of the secular liberal state to religion. If classical Islam subordinated the state to religion, militant secularism increasingly looks to subordinate religion to the state: neither is compatible with religious freedom. Instead, "a genuine defence of religious liberty can only be genuinely secured from a religious perspective," for "[l]iberal principles, when pressed to a logical extreme, will always ensure that the rights of the individual override those of the group . . . .. It follows that churches will not be able to fight the threat to the integrity of religious bodies in liberal, secular terms alone . . . ."[48]

Religious freedom, a crucial aspect of human dignity, is inherently worthy of protection. Moreover, its interdependence with other human rights arguably makes it the linchpin of international human rights law. Muslim reformers are working to infuse their legal, cultural, and political traditions with robust and resonant defenses of religious liberty. It is

44. Ibid., 139, 147.
45. David Novak, *In Defense of Religious Liberty* (Wilmington, DE: Intercollegiate Studies Institute, 2009).
46. Milbank, "Shari'a and the True Basis of Group Rights," 139.
47. Ibid.
48. Ibid., 139, 145.

necessary for Western intellectuals, working in part from within Jewish and Christian traditions, to do the same. If religious liberty is to be secured, if sustainable pluralism of diverse peoples is to be achieved, a theological jurisprudence rooted in love of God and love of neighbor and informed by reason will be required. This is the calling of a world legal tradition.

INDEX

Abbasids, 142–43
Abe, Masao, 82
Abou El Fadl, Khaled, 99, 176
Adams, John, 41
Afghanistan, 158–59
Ahmadi community, persecution, 134,
    136–37
al-Araji, Bahaa, 159
al-Dulaimi, Adnan, 159
al-Farabi, 143
al-Hamidi, Muhammad al-Hashim, 176
al-Husri, Sati', 108, 109
Ali, Ahaheen Sardar, 153
al-Qaysi, Habib A., 147
al-Saadawy, Nawal, 95
American Muslims, 164–65, 179
An-Na'im, Abdullahi A., 98, 175
anti-Semitism, 97, 121, 126, 132
apostasy and Islam, 93–96
Arab nationalism 106–17, 145
Arab Republic of Egypt. *See* Egypt
Arab Spring, 132
Arend, Anthony Clark, 12–14
Arslan, Alparslan, 127–28
Ashley, Lord, 52
as-siyar. *See* Islamic international law
    (as-siyar)
Atatürk, 123–24, 126
Averroës, Ibn Rushd, 143

Baderin, Mashood, 63, 140, 142, 151
Badr, Gamal, 153
Baha'i community, 119–20
Baltimore, Lord, 52
Banchoff, Thomas, 22n85, 25n89,
    163–64

Bederman, David, 170–71
Bellah, Robert, 163
Berman, Harold J., xiv–xv, 1, 14–25,
    170–71, 177–78
Bhatti, Shahbaz, 138
Bhutto, Benazir; assassination, 136
Bhutto, Zulfiqar Ali, 135
Bill of Rights, U.S., 48
Bingham, Colonel Raymond L., 159
blasphemy laws, 135–38
Blond, Phillip, 178–79
Breau, Susan, 173
Brown, Nathan, 129
Brumberg, Daniel, 110
Bulliet, Richard W., 166
Burke, Edmund, III, 117

Cairo Declaration on Human Rights in
    Islam (1990), xiv, 83, 149–51, 174
Calvin, John, xiii, 27, 32–35, 37–38, 53
Cameron, David, 179
Charter of Rhode Island and Providence
    Plantations (1663), 47
civic republicans, 41
Concessions and Agreements of West
    New Jersey (1677), 47
Constitutions of Muslim states, religious
    liberty, 114–39
    Arab Republic of Egypt, xiv, 128–34
    Islamic Republic of Iran, xiv,
        116–22
    Islamic Republic of Pakistan, xiv,
        134–39
    overview, 115–16
    Republic of Turkey, xiv, 123–28
constructivism, 9

Coptic Egyptians, 131–32
Cox, Brian, 162

Danchin, Peter, 171
Dawisha, Adeed, 107
de Tocqueville, Alexis, 101
dhimmi system, xiv, 91–93
Dieng, Adama, 150
Dignitatis Humanae, 55, 76–81
    Catholic teachings and American
        foreign policy, 162
    human dignity, as aspect of religious
        freedom, 180–81
    Pope John Paul II, 77, 79–80, 173–74
    Second Vatican Council, 78-79, 163
Donnelly, Jack, 170
Dwight, Timothy, 42

Eberle, Edward, 43
ECHR. See European Court of Human
    Rights (ECHR)
Egypt, xiv, 128–34, 146, 148
Enlightenment views, 40–41
Erbakan, Necmettin, 126
Esposito, John, 110, 164–65
Establishment Clause, xiii, 49–51
ethical voluntarism, 143–44
European Court of Human Rights
    (ECHR), 73–76, 169
European Muslims, 160–61
Evangelicals, 40

Fadel, Mohammed H., 169–70
faith-based diplomacy, 162
Falk, Richard, 166
Farr, Thomas, 162–63
fatwa, 85, 95
Feldman, Noah, 89
fiqh (jurisprudence), 89
First Amendment of U.S. Constitution,
    xiii, 26, 38–54
freedom of religion. See also Protestant
    reformation and early origins of
        freedom of religion; religious liberty
    international human rights, 56–70
    Islamic law, 90–96
freedom to change religion or belief,
    134, 137
Free Exercise Clause, xiii, 51–54
Fuda, Farag, 95
fundamentalism, 110

Gillis, Chester, 166
Glendon, Mary Ann, 60
Gorski, Philip, 32
Great Awakening, 40
Grotius, Hugo, 3, 37–38
Guichon, Audrey, 172–73
Gül, Abdullah, 128

Habermas, Jürgen, 101, 172
Haddad, Yvonne, 144–45
Hafez, Kai, 140
Hale, Mathew, 34n33
Hamilton, Marci, 32
Hamoudi, Haider Ala, 155
Hassan, Farooq, 153
headscarf ban, 75, 128, 169
Hefner, Robert, 139, 142–43, 155
Herberg, Will, 163
hijab. See Headscarf ban
hudud offenses, 93
Human Rights in Islam, 145
human rights law. See also Islam and
        human rights; Islamic human rights
        declarations, religious freedom
    generally, 55–81
    Declaration on the Right of the
        Persons Belonging to a National or
        Ethnic, Religious, and Linguistic
        Minorities, 58
    European Court of Human Rights
        (ECHR), 73–76
    International Covenant on Civil and
        Political Rights (ICCPR), 62–64
    Prague Declaration on Freedom of
        Religion or Belief (1981), 67–68
    proselytism, 69–70
    religious minorities, 68–69
    U.N. Declaration on the Elimination of
        all Forms of Intolerance and of
        Discrimination Based on Religion or
        Belief, 64–68
    UN Convention on the Rights of the
        Child (1989), 58
    Universal Declaration of Human
        Rights (UDHR), 59–62
    U.S. Commission on International
        Religious Freedom (IRFA),
        71–72
    Vienna Concluding Document (1989),
        57n8
Huntington, Samuel P., 5

ICCPR. *See* International Covenant on
    Civil and Political Rights (ICCPR)
idealism, 8
International Covenant on Civil and
    Political Rights (ICCPR), xiii, 7, 62–64
    Article 18, 62–63
International Covenant on Economic,
    Social, and Cultural Rights
    (ICESCR), 62
international law and politics,
    intersection, 8–25
International Religious Freedom Act. *See*
    U.S. Commission on International
    Religious Freedom (IRFA)
Iqbal, Muhammad, 101
Iran, xiv, 116–22, 144, 146
Iraq, 157–58
IRFA. *See* U.S. Commission on
    International Religious Freedom
    (IRFA)
Islam and human rights, 141–46
Islamic extremism, 23–24
Islamic human rights declarations,
    religious freedom, 147–51
Islamic international law (as-siyar), xiv,
    122, 140–67
Islamic jurisprudence, 129–30
Islamic law, principles, 84–89
Islamic law and international human
    rights law, 168–81
Islamic Principle, Article 4 (Iran),
    118–19
Islamic Republic of Iran. *See* Iran
Islamic Republic of Pakistan. *See*
    Pakistan

Jefferson, Thomas, 41, 53
Jinnah, Mohammed Ali, 134
Johnston, Douglas, 162
Joy, Lina, 95
Joyner, Christopher C., 8–10
Judaism, 179–80
Judeo-Christian tradition, 147, 178

Kedourie, Elie, 106n5, 109
Khadduri, Majid, 152–53, 176
Khadem, Babak Rod, 87–88
Khan, Muhammad Zafrullah, 61, 134
Khomeini, Ayatollah, 95, 100, 116–17,
    121–22
Küng, Hans, 166

laik system, 125, 128
Lapidus, Ira M., 111, 117
legal pluralism, 127, 168n2
Leland, John, 40
Lerner, Natan, 63
Lewis, Bernard, 82, 107
Leyla Sahin v. Turkey, 75, 169
limited sovereignty doctrine, 38
Locke, John, xiii, 27, 42–46, 52, 54
Lombardi, Clark, 129
Lovin, Robin, 169
Luther, Martin, xiii, 27–31, 37–38,
    53, 99

Madison, James, xiii, 27, 41, 46–47, 54
Mahfouz, Nagib, 95
Malik, Charles, 60
Malik, Habib C., 92, 161
Mansour, Ahmed Subhy, 95
Maritain, Jacques, 6, 76
Martinez, Roman, 89
Maryland Act Concerning Religion
    (1649), 47
Mawdudi, Abu'l A'la, 145–46
Mayer, Ann Elizabeth, 142n10, 143,
    149, 151
McConnell, Michael W., 51
McNeill, John T., 33
Merkel, Angela, 179
Milbank, John, 179–80
militant secularism, 179
Mitchell, Joshua, 29
Modak-Truran, Mark, 171–72
More, Sir Thomas, 78
"Mosque at Ground Zero," 165
Moussalli, Ahmad S., 176
Mubarak, Hosni, 133
Muhammad. *See* Prophet Muhammad
multiculturalism, 179
Murray, John Courtney, 78–79
Muslim Brotherhood, 128–29, 133
Muslim World League, 148
Mu'tazila, 143

Nasser, Gamal Adbel, 109
neo-liberalism, 9
Neuhaus, Father Richard John, 166
New Haven School of Jurisprudence,
    10–12
Niebuhr, Reinhold, 36
1979 Islamic Revolution, 116–18, 145

Novak, Rabbi David, 27n3, 180
Nussbaum, Martha, 170

OIC. *See* Organization of the Islamic
    Conference (OIC)
Organization of the Islamic Conference
    (OIC), 83, 147
Oslo Declaration (1998), 74
Ozbilgin, Mustafa Yucel; assassination, 127

Pabst, Adrian, 178–79
Pakistan, xiv, 134–39
Peace of Augsburg (1955), 36
"People of the Book," 64, 91
Philpott, Daniel, 5, 167
political Islam, 109, 146
Pope John Paul II. *See* Dignitatis
    Humanae
Prague Declaration on Freedom of
    Religion or Belief (1981), 67–68
Prophet Muhammad, 86, 90, 101, 108,
    135, 149, 156
proselytism, 69–70
Protestant reformation and early origins
    of freedom of religion, xiii, 27–39
Puritans, 39–40

Rafi'al-Tahtawi, Rifa'ah, 144
Rahman, Abdul, 96, 159
Rajaie-Khorassani, Said, 6
Ramadan, Tariq, 97, 160
Rauf, Imam, 86, 88
Rawls, John, 169–70, 172
realism, 8–9
Refah Partisi (Welfare or Prosperity
    Party), 75, 126–27
relativism, threat of, 22–23, 45, 173
religious liberty. *See also* freedom of
    religion; freedom to change religion
    or belief
    absence of philosophical consensus
        on foundation of human rights,
        6, 7n26
    abuses, 119–21
    dilemma of religious freedom, 8
    Islamic reformation, 96–101
    religious freedom of groups
        distinguished from that of
        individuals, 88–89
    violations, 131–32
    Western and Islamic law, 6–8

religious minorities, 68–69
    dhimmi system, 91–93
    discriminatory legislation, 137
    Egypt, 131–34
    Iran, 119–21
    Pakistan, 134, 136–37
    "People of the Book," 64, 91
    Shari'a, 91–93
    Turkey, 125–26
religious pluralism, 4, 35–36, 41, 169,
    171–72, 179
Republic of Turkey. *See* Turkey
Roosevelt, Eleanor, 59
Rosenstock-Huessy, Eugene, 19
Rosenthal, A.M., 161
Rumi, Jalal al-Din, 101
Rushdie, Salman, 95

Sachedina, Abdulaziz A., 175
Sadat, Anwar, 129
Salafist groups, 133
Sap, John, 33–34
Saudi Arabia, 148
Savage, Timothy M., 160
Second Vatican Council. *See* Dignitatis
    Humanae
Secularism, 3, 107, 123–26, 180
separation of church and state. *See*
    Luther, Martin
separation of mosque and state, 86–87,
    103, 123, 157
Shari'a, xiv, 82–101, 129, 135–36,
    142–43, 176
Six-Day War, 109
Sodano, Cardinal Angelo, 120
Soroush, Abdolkarim, 99–101
Stilt, Kristen, 130
Sullivan, Donna, 67
Sunnis (Ash'arites), 143

Tabandeh, Sultanhussein, 95, 145
Taseer, Salman, 138
Tibi, Bassam, 160
Treaty of Westphalia (1648),
    35–36
Truett, George W., 26
Turkey, xiv, 75, 123–28
Twelver Ja'fari school, 119–20, 144

UDHR. *See* Universal Declaration of
    Human Rights (UDHR)

UIDHR. *See* Universal Islamic Declaration of Human Rights (UIDHR)
Ul-Haq, General Zia, 135
Umayyad dynasty, 142
UN Convention on the Rights of the Child (1989), 58n9
UN Declaration on the Elimination of all Forms of Intolerance and of Discrimination Based on Religion or Belief (1981), xiii, 64–68, 147
  Prague Declaration on Freedom of Religion or Belief (1981), 67–68
Universal Declaration of Human Rights (UDHR), xiii, 6, 59–62, 73, 82–83, 95, 145–46
Universal Islamic Declaration of Human Rights (UIDHR), xiv, 83, 147–48
UN membership, Islamic states, 151–52
U.S. Commission on International Religious Freedom (IRFA), 71–72, 131–32, 137
U.S. Constitution, First Amendment. *See* First Amendment of U.S. Constitution

value pluralism, 171
van der Vyver, Johan, 2
Vatican II. *See* Dignitatis Humanae
Velayati, Ali Akbar, 120
Vienna Concluding Document (1989), 57n8
Vienna World Conference on Human Rights, 173
Voll, John, 110

Wagner, William, 20–21
Washington, George, 41
Weigel, George, 80, 173
Westphalia Treaty (1648), 35–36
Williams, Archbishop Rowan, 178, 180
Williams, Roger, xiii, 27, 42-44, 53, 170
Witte, John, Jr., 30, 36, 38–39
Wolf-Specter Bill, 161
world legal tradition, 14–25, 168–81
Wright, Robin, 99–100

Yavuz, M. Hakan, 160

Zaid, Nasr Hamid Abu, 95